A GUIDE TO CHINESE AFFAIRS

A GUIDE TO CHINESE AFFAIRS

Robert M. Liu

Writers Club Press
San Jose New York Lincoln Shanghai

A Guide to Chinese Affairs

Writers Club Press
an imprint of iUniverse.com, Inc.

For information address:
iUniverse.com, Inc.
620 North 48th Street, Suite 201
Lincoln, NE 68504-3467
www.iuniverse.com

ISBN: 0-595-13906-X

Printed in the United States of America

Contents

1

"Talk Politics"—What the Heck Does That Mean?

One of the best ways to understand China is to live under its communist system for a period of time, picking up the language of the land and watching the way local people live day in day out. Since 1979 when China opened its door to the outside world, many Western reporters have done just that and their numerous reports about China have certainly helped people in the West understand the most populous country in the world. There are also books and articles written by Chinese persons after long years of sufferings under the rule of the late Chairman Mao Zedong. You bet there isn't a single word of praise for Mao in such books and articles, as the authors tend to believe that because of what they learned firsthand about the so-called Mao Zedong era they are definitely entitled to vent some of their bitterness against one of the greatest tyrants of the twentieth century.

On the other hand, those who have spent the terror-ridden years under Mao as well as the relatively relaxed years after Mao (e.g. the first few years after the Cultural Revolution when the Chinese people were filled with hope for Deng Xiaoping's reforms, thinking that they were going to have their first taste of freedom in decades) may provide more balanced views on China's political and economic systems, since they are looking at the picture from their vantage point of comparison and may in some degree be devoid of both excessive bitterness over the old system and excessive optimism about China's ongoing reforms.

Talking of the language of the land, even a good knowledge of the Chinese language may not be enough to help one understand what a Chinese person really means, which fact makes understanding China even more difficult than one can imagine. The following anecdote indicates how even people born in a Chinese-language environment might also get confused in the Chinese language.

In autumn of 1996 when I was still living in Hong Kong, a friend of mine came from Shanghai to see me. We were both born in Shanghai and went to the same high school at a time when China was suffering from severe food shortages after the late Chairman Mao Zedong plunged the country into his People's Commune and Great Leap Forward drive in the late 1950s. We were speaking the language of our home town Shanghai—Shanghai dialect, which is different from both Mandarin (the official Chinese language) and Cantonese (the language of southern China and Hong Kong). And as an experienced translator, I had always flattered myself that I had a perfect knowledge of the Chinese language. I was wrong.

I had not been back to Shanghai for many years but had kept up-to-date on Chinese affairs by reading the English and Chinese newspapers and magazines available in Hong Kong. In one of the Chinese-language magazines, I had come across a short phrase that I had difficulty grasping the meaning of. That phrase was "talk politics". With much humiliation, I admitted to my friend I had a comprehension problem and asked him what it meant, adding that it was China's President and Secretary General Jiang Zemin who had used the phrase in his speech.

Then I said, "These days, it's money people want to talk, not politics. Everybody's busy looking to make a quick buck. You know that. Besides, for years, those who talked politics got into trouble. Why urge them to talk politics now?"

Apparently, my question betrayed an ignorance of the phraseology currently in use in China, which amused my friend. With a smile, he pointed out that "talk politics" was not a call to discuss political issues at all but was a request from Secretary General Jiang Zemin that the cadres (communist party officials) in the provinces and the various sections of the government obey the orders of the Party Central. He explained that Jiang Zemin was worried by the laxity of discipline in the Communist Party that made it difficult to ensure execution of his orders.

"The cadres don't carry out orders, so Jiang wants them to 'talk politics'. 'Talk politics' means 'please obey orders'," said my friend.

It took me quite a while to figure out how "talk politics", which normally means "discuss political issues", had ended up meaning "please obey orders". At first, I didn't have a clue, but then a Mao-era slogan came back to my mind and helped me out.

Again, it was in those hectic days under the late Chairman Mao Zedong that I first heard the slogan: "Politics in command". I was a teenager struggling with the various subjects in my curriculum and the great amount of homework I had to handle in order to pass school tests. Never did I ask myself what that slogan meant. It was not until later when Mao had launched his Cultural Revolution (1966—1976) that I started to catch on to the significance of "politics in command", because by then an extra word had been added—"Proletarian politics in command"—and almost every middle-class household in Shanghai had been ransacked by the Red Guards, the storm troopers of the Cultural Revolution. I noticed that nobody discussed political issues in public if their views were different from those printed in the state-controlled newspapers.

In retrospect, I would guess that in China "politics" simply means "the interests of the communist authorities" and that "politics in command" in the Mao era must have meant: "Mao's political beliefs in command."

That explains why those who didn't share Mao's views were in trouble during his reign.

Now after twenty years of economic reforms and openness to the outside world initiated by the late paramount leader Deng Xiaoping, the present-day China under President Jiang Zemin, who is also Secretary General of the Communist Party, is different from Mao's China. Slogans of the bad old days like "proletarian politics in command" have faded out of memory. State controls have been relaxed and economic freedoms allowed to blossom to a quite extensive degree.

Understandably, the new freedoms have created an environment where provincial cadres (and party officials in various sections of the government) would rather look after their own interests than those of the Party Central. To them, the temptation to ignore Beijing's orders by way of protecting their own interests has become strong. They may not openly disobey orders, but there are ways to find excuses for not carrying out orders.

One of the easiest ways to offer such excuses is to "talk difficulties", that is, to stress or exaggerate the difficulties the provinces (or specific sections of the government) might face in executing the Party Central's orders. As a result of cadres talking "difficulties", orders from the top may remain ignored for months in a row. Such delaying tactics certainly weaken the authority of the Party Central. If this worries President Jiang Zemin, it's not surprising at all. In fact, there are signs that the problem of cadres disobeying the Party Central's orders may be more serious than is known to the general public. The following stories should shed some light on the seriousness of the problem.

In a speech made on July 13th, 1998, President Jiang Zemin expressed his concern about the rampant smuggling activities that had taken a heavy toll on China's customs tax revenues, promising to take effective measures to curb smuggling. Why had smuggling become such a big problem? Because the military was involved.

So, on July 21st, 1998, the four general departments of China's People's Liberation Army convened a meeting to explain the spirit of President Jiang's July 13th speech to military personnel. But shortly afterwards, on July 26th, 1998, a sea battle broke out and lasted for more than fifty minutes between the navy and China's coastal police acting in conjunction with customs anti-smuggling personnel. During this sea battle, four patrol boats under the command of the coastal police and the customs personnel were seriously damaged, two of which sank at last. Casualties on the part of the coastal police and the customs personnel were heavy with thirteen dead and scores of others wounded.

On August 21st, 1998, China's State Council and the Communist Party's Central Military Commission issued a joint investigation report, saying that the July 26th smuggling incident had caused serious consequences. According to the document, several business organizations controlled by the navy, the Regional Military Command of Shandong Province, and the Economic and Trade Department of Shandong Province chartered four oil tankers to smuggle nearly seventy thousand tons of refined oil (purchased in North Europe) to China.

When the four oil tankers approached Chinese waters, the navy dispatched four gunboats, two submarines and one transport vessel to escort the oil tankers to a military port in Yantai, Shandong Province, where the refined oil would have been transported to Hebei Province and Henan Province for sale as planned. Estimated profits: Renminbi 28 million yuan plus (about US$3.30 million). But the plan fell through, as the Ministry of Public Security and the Customs House General had deployed twelve patrol boats to intercept the oil tankers on information supplied by informants. On July 26th, 1998, when the patrol boats tried to stop the oil tankers, the navy's transport vessel and gunboats turned around and crashed into the patrol boats. One of the navy's gunboats opened fire, killing three and wounding five on the police command boat.

In mid October of 1998, the officers of China's South Sea Fleet at Beihai Naval Base and Zhanjiang Naval Base as well as the officers of Guangxi Autonomous Region Military Command authorized a China-controlled company in Hong Kong to charter three transport vessels from South Korea to smuggle two hundred fifty luxury sedans into the country. The luxury automobiles were being unloaded at Beihai Military Port when anti-smuggling personnel and customs officers arrived, announcing a central government directive to stop the unloading and seal the cargo. In the meantime, the customs officers started to speak on the microphones of their vehicles, trying to convince the military officers to stop unloading the luxury cars. But they were pulled out of their vehicles by soldiers and detained till all the luxury sedans had been unloaded and carried away.

Also in mid October of 1998, the officers of South Sea Fleet at Shantou Naval Base, Shantou Garrison and Shantou Military Police authorized a China-controlled company in Hong Kong to charter five transport vessels from Dalian Ocean Transportation Company and a South Korean company to smuggle nearly three hundred vehicles including sedans and vans from Japan and South Korea into China. On the morning of October 17th, 1998, the military smugglers' transport vessels entered Chinese waters off the shore of Shantou. When discovered by customs personnel on patrol boats, the smugglers' vessels didn't stop. Instead, the transport vessels speeded up and crashed into the patrol boats, two of which sank. As a result of the incident, two customs officers were missing. In the meantime, the military personnel at Shantou Naval Base opened fire on anti-smuggling personnel's vehicles that had moved into the base, wounding two anti-smuggling officers.

The incidences mentioned above certainly caused serious concern among Chinese leaders. According to sources in Beijing, in October 1998, as a measure to enhance its supervision over the military, the Central Committee of the Communist Party decided to appoint Premier Zhu Rongji to the Central Military Commission, thereby giving him the authority to preside over the affairs of the Central Military Commission if and when President Jiang Zemin had to leave Beijing on inspection tours around the country or for overseas trips. Shortly after his appointment, Premier Zhu Rongji flew to Beihai, Guangxi Province, on October 21st, 1998 in a military plane together with Deputy Chief of General Staff Qian Shugen. The following day, October 22nd, Zhu Rongji arrived in Shantou, Guangdong Province. Obviously, he was looking into the military's involvement in smuggling activities.

Some media reports have described President Jiang as a party moderate, because he appears to be eager to establish a moderate image for himself. His way of convincing provincial cadres (and party officials in various sections of the government) is to have his request couched in tactful terms, which are hardly free of the traditional rhetoric of the Communist Party, though. For instance, at a meeting on the work of the Central Commission of the Communist Party held in August 1998 at Beidaihe, a special summer resort for Chinese leaders, Jiang called on the high-ranking officials of the Communist Party "to study Deng Xiaoping Theories, to 'talk politics', and to nurture noble ideals." Then he said that the officials of the Communist Party had an obligation to conscientiously study, understand, implement and advocate the theories, guidelines and policies of the Central Committee of the Communist Party but absolutely had no right to refuse to implement party policies or alter party policies at their pleasure.

The term "talk" seems to mean "respect" or "stress" rather than "discuss", while "politics" definitely refers to the supreme interests of the Communist Party. And if party officials in the provinces and various sections of the government are to respect or stress the supreme interests of the Communist Party, they, of course, must obey the orders of Secretary General Jiang Zemin and the Central Committee of the Communist Party. Hence, now "talk politics" means "obey the Party Central."

Times have changed and so have many aspects of Chinese life, but China remains a communist country not only in name but also in essence, and the rhetoric of communism lives on, though I am aware that some business people don't really see China as a communist country—they see China as a market with great potentials. Those who find themselves intrigued by Chinese affairs may need a good knowledge of China's communist rhetoric and phraseology to guide them away from misunderstandings. In other words, a knowledge of Orwellian doublespeak could be very helpful to students of Chinese affairs.

By the way, in summer of 1997, Mr. Mark Mobius of Templeton Investments, who has spent much of his time visiting emerging markets around the world to look for new investment opportunities for his clients, was quoted as saying that he didn't believe China was a communist country.

I'm afraid China's political dissidents like Mr. Wei Jing Sheng, who spent eighteen years in prison, may not agree with Mr. Mobius, because the dissidents look at China from a political perspective while Mr. Mobius looks at China from a business perspective. Besides, Mr. Mobius hasn't had an opportunity to see firsthand the steely workings of China's communist state apparatus as Mr. Wei Jing Sheng must have.

But it is true that the market-oriented reforms have brought capitalist characteristics to the everyday life of the Chinese people to the point where China no longer meets the standards of classic Stalinist communism. It's a mixed bag in which capitalism and communism manage to live an uncomfortable coexistence for now. And smart business people like Mr. Mobius must have seen some kind of a bright spot in China—though, personally, I can hardly agree with him that China is not a communist country.

Over the past 50 years, the Communist Party has always been the ruling party. Today, it continues to insist on one-party dictatorship and continues to control the most important sectors of the economy. If it is not communist, why does it call itself communist? Because the Chinese people are in love with communism? Because the Chinese people are idiots who love communist control? No. China remains communist, because the left-wing conservative faction of the Communist Party is much stronger than the party's moderate faction, whereas the party's liberal-minded politicians are just too weak to assert themselves.

Still, any person who thinks that the rhetoric and phraseology of the Communist Party are nothing but lip service could be quite wrong, because rhetoric serves practical purposes in China. For example, China's so-called democratic parties which have been under the control of the Communist Party for half a century now appear to be discontented with the pathetic role the Communist Party intends them to play in Chinese politics and, in order to seek a bigger say, some members of the so-called democratic parties have started to criticize the officials of the Communist Party, whereas, hoping to maintain the status quo, the officials of the Communist Party tend to resort to the rhetoric and phraseology of the Communist Party.

In March 1998 when China's "Political Consultative Conference" was convened in Beijing, some Shanghai-originated committee members of "the Political Consultative Conference" (usually members of the so-called democratic parties) criticized Shanghai's communist party officials for receiving special benefits through their privileges and said that such privileges had caused grievances among ordinary people as joblessness grew.

Three months later, in late June 1998, the standing committee of Shanghai Political Consultative Conference held a symposium and Shanghai's communist party boss, Secretary Huang Ju, came. Guess what? He said that the democratic parties should "talk politics", voluntarily accept the leadership of the Communist Party and overcome the influences of (bourgeois) liberalization. He said that the democratic parties must keep in line with the policies and guidelines of the Communist Party and that any intention to step out of line politically could be very dangerous. "Talk politics"—what the heck does that mean? I believe by now I've perfectly grasped its meaning. It means you'd better respect the interests of the Communist Party and obey the Communist Party. It means "behave yourself or else".

Apparently, to respect the wishes of the Communist Party is not what some people would like to do. In early 1998, a man in Beijing by the name of Fang Jue issued a statement entitled "China Needs New Changes— Platform of the Democratic Faction". In the beginning, except for a police house surveillance that lasted for twenty-four hours after the issuance of the statement, nothing much happened to Mr. Fang Jue. He was able to continue to run a private business of his own. Later, he even joined a non-governmental organization called "China Development Union", which held periodic discussions on current Chinese affairs. The participants in the discussions often raised politically sensitive issues and even made bold demands for the nationalization of the military (meaning the military should be controlled by a national government rather than by the Communist Party), the transformation of China's political structure, the implementation of a federal system and a pluralistic party system in China, and the direct election of the president of the country. China's military is controlled by the Communist Party through its Central Military Commission, and under China's Marxist constitution, the president of the country has to be the leader of the Communist Party or somebody appointed by the Communist Party. If the demands of "China Development Union" were accommodated, communism in China would come to an instant end. Unfortunately, things didn't work out that way. In the summer of 1998, Mr. Fang Jue disappeared. A reporter trying to contact Fang discovered that Fang's home telephone had been cut off and that Fang's business office was sealed and guarded by police.

There is reason to suspect that the Communist Party and President Jiang Zemin are worried that the number of people unwilling to "talk politics", that is, to obey the Communist Party and behave themselves, is growing. In late August 1998, the Central Committee of the Communist Party, the State Council and the Central Military Commission issued a joint directive to China's various provincial party committees, urging provincial party officials to strengthen social stability and political stability at the grassroots level in cities, villages, schools, workplaces and neighborhoods. The directive described the maintenance of social stability and political stability as a difficult, long-tern, strategic task and requested communist party committees and relevant government authorities at various levels to eliminate potential causes of instability, unrest or disturbances. The document admitted that most of the problems had been caused or exacerbated by the work styles and conduct of the officials of the Communist Party and that derelict party officials had to be disciplined or removed and incompetent party committees and government sections restructured.

The communist leadership's sense of crisis is evident. The problem is that in order to maintain the "stability" of the communist dictatorship, the leaders continue to practice Marxism for all the evidence that its efficacy as a ruling philosophy is declining by the day as the world moves into the next millennium.

2

The Tiananmen Square Military Crackdown of June 4th 1989

Anyone who has ever flown from North America to Shanghai or Beijing or Hong Kong should have a strong feeling that we live in a very small world—so small that we can reach the other side of the world in a twinkling, that we now call our world the global village, that the giants in the village like the United States and China cannot afford to have serious misunderstandings between them. Therefore, understanding China and its intentions has become extremely important. Likewise, it is important for China to understand the United States and its intentions. According to press reports, President Jiang Zemin's staff includes people holding Ph.D.'s earned in the U.S. If it is true, it's a blessing. But no matter how hard we try to understand China, some of the questions about the behavior of the Chinese leadership will remain unanswered.

For instance, few people in the West would believe that the People's Liberation Army killed nobody at Tiananmen Square in the military crackdown of June 4th 1989, because CNN broadcasted numerous scenes of gore and dead bodies that day. Yet, during his visit to the United States, China's Minister of Defense Chi Haotian told Congress that no students had been killed INSIDE Tiananmen Square on June 4th 1989, adding, "I assume responsibility for my words."

One would ask: Who are the guys he thinks he's kidding? We all know a lot of people were killed or wounded on June 4th 1989 at Beijing's Tiananmen Square—that is, in the vicinity of Tiananmen Square. It makes no difference whether the killings took place inside or outside the Square. Then, why did Mr. Chi Haotian make a point of being specific as to where casualties had not been caused? Did he mean to say: "I assure you we don't kill people INSIDE Tiananmen Square because that's where we welcome visiting Western leaders"? Was he trying to tell President Bill Clinton: "Don't worry about stepping on blood INSIDE Tiananmen Square when you visit Beijing because the killings took place only OUTSIDE Tiananmen Square"? This is just one of those puzzles that baffle one's mind when one tries to understand China.

However, if we presume that Mr. Chi was visiting the United States with the intention of improving the relations between the United States and China, we may view his statement that no students were killed INSIDE Tiananmen Square on June 4th 1989 as an attempt to repair the image of his country. And if Mr. Chi and other Chinese leaders attach importance to the image of their country, it is a good sign. It is in the interest of China and the Chinese people as well as in the interest of the West, if Chinese leaders are concerned about China's international image—which by any standards leaves very much to be desired. One would feel more comfortable dealing with people who are rational enough to see the need to repair their image. Only, it doesn't work if the method of image-repairing is by trying to cover up facts that are already well known to the world. China's communist state apparatus is a monster—that image is hard to eliminate because it is the reflection of its true nature.

*   *   *   *   *   *

The following is part of an eyewitness account of what happened in June of 1989 at a spot called Muxidi, three or four kilometers west of Tiananmen Square:

"In fact, Muxidi, three or four kilometers west of Tiananmen Square, was a flashpoint where many earthshattering events took place. For instance, it was at Muxidi that the army started to fire on the people, so Muxidi was one of the spots where people suffered heavy casualties. It was also at Muxidi that a helicopter carrying high-ranking officials of the Central Military Commission of the Communist Party hovered over the advancing troops to issue orders to fire on the people....The troops fired at the Minister Buildings (where many party and government officials lived) at Muxidi causing casualties....On June 4th, 5th and 6th 1989, armored military vehicles moved down Muxidi and repeatedly fired on those hiding at roadsides and at the buildings nearby causing casualties. Under these circumstances, the railway general controller on duty was killed by a bullet that flew into his office.

"After the troops made an attempt to break through the crowds of protesters in order to enter Tiananmen Square early on the morning of June 3rd 1989—though without success, the entire city of Beijing was shrouded in an atmosphere of extreme tension. At midday June 3rd, for the first time, the troops used tear-gas on the crowds of people around Liubukou (a spot in Beijing). On the afternoon of June 3rd, when I got back home from work, the Beijing Martial Law Command had already begun to repeatedly broadcast its public announcement on TV. It was a curfew prohibiting people from turning out into the streets in the evening. Many people including myself sensed an imminent storm since it was clear that the troops were about to take harsh measures to deal with the crowds at Tiananmen Square.

"After supper, out of extreme curiosity, I came down to Fuwai Avenue (a street in the Muxidi area). I wanted to know whether anybody was still out in the street, whether people were all staying indoors. To my surprise, the street which had a width of about eight vehicle lanes was crowded with people talking about the events that had taken place on the previous night and earlier that day. They had all ignored the curfew imposed by the Martial Law Command. Many people in the crowd were very concerned about the fate of the students at Tiananmen Square....Some people moved the solid cement cones separating the vehicle and the bicycle lanes to the middle of the road. Others pushed the cars parked at roadsides and the buses parked at the nearby bus terminal as well as some trolley buses to the middle of the road, hoping these could stop vehicles carrying military troops.

"In order to have a more clear view, I entered a residential high-rise on the street and climbed to its tenth floor, where I could see everything down in the street. I estimated the width of the street at 20 to 30 meters, and as far as I could see, it was almost completely covered with people....More to my astonishment, thousands of bicycles were piled on the roadsides—an indication that many of the people down there had come from other districts of the city by bicycle to witness any event that might happen here because they knew Fuwai Avenue was the only thoroughfare from Beijing's western suburb to Tiananmen Square. Looking at the thousands of people—I guess there were about one million people out in Beijing's main streets at the time, I thought that they like myself must be very sure that the People's Liberation Army would absolutely not fire upon unarmed people....

"At about 6:00 p.m., several military helicopters flew westwards along Chang An Street. Then after hovering at low altitudes over Muxidi for a while, they flew toward the west. I believe that some high-ranking military officers were on board the helicopters observing and analyzing the situation in preparation for a report to the Central Military Commission. The appearance of the helicopters immediately intensified the tautness of the atmosphere, as the people in the crowds realized that the military was ready to take action....A group of several hundred people shoved five or six trolley buses up the Muxidi Bridge, blocking all the vehicle lanes. By then, the crowds at Muxidi had already been thrown into great suspense.

"Shortly after 9:00 p.m., from where I stood in the high-rise, I could hear crowds of people far to the west shouting as the sound-waves surged toward me like tides at sea. It was dark. Despite the light from the road-lamps, I couldn't see what was happening in the distance. But judging from the noise of the crowds, I could tell the troops had already advanced to somewhere not far from Muxidi. Soon I noticed wounded people being continuously carried into the Fu Xing Hospital located at Muxidi. So, I ran downstairs. In the street, I saw a young man running toward the Fu Xing Hospital, his hand covering his bleeding head. "They really started to attack, bastards, fascists!" he scolded. Wanting to know more about the clash between the troops and the protesting crowds, I walked across the Muxidi Bridge stepping through its sidewalk and arrived at the area near the west end of the bridge.

"What I saw astonished me. Tens of thousands of people huddled together in the road (about several tens of meters wide) forming a human wall (about 200-300 meters thick) confronting the troops, who were about 300 meters away from the bridge. Nobody could squeeze through this human wall, which moved forward and backward now and then, uttering the deafening noise of slogan shouting. I turned to the left and walked across to the southern side of the street. Then I sidled westward along the northern wall of the building that housed the Central Liaison Department of the Communist Party and made my way through the crowds to the front gate of the Beijing Railway Administration, where I found myself standing to the right of the troops and watching them advancing with my own eyes. In the forefront of the troops were a group of about one hundred anti-riot soldiers who moved slowly forward with shields and heavy clubs in their hands. Right behind them were tanks and truckloads of soldiers and armored vehicles.

"While lots of spectators stood on either side of the road—with a few among them also shouting slogans though without trying to cause a conflict with the troops, those who were determined to stop the advance of the troops crowded in the middle of the road. Students including quite a few girls were in the forefront of this crowd. Hand in hand, they formed a human wall about thirty meters away from the troops....The students were pretty calm, knowing that the soldiers were only acting on orders and that any conflict with the soldiers could only make things worse and give the authorities an excuse to crack down. They still cherished the illusion that somehow they could exercise an influence on the soldiers with peaceful dialogue and convince the soldiers to turn back. But all this attempt was futile. The troops were not at all affected by any dialogue, any shouting or even weeping—they moved forward regardless....

"Soon I noticed that angered by the anti-riot soldiers' attack, some people in the crowd started to throw stones at the soldiers. But the anti-riot soldiers wore helmets and wielded shields, so throwing stones at them wouldn't hurt them. Picking up the stones, the soldiers threw them back at the crowd, wounding many people's heads....Attempting to stop the violence, the students yelled at those behind them but failed to produce any effect. In this state of chaos, they appeared completely helpless. They could neither prevent the troops from advancing nor stop the people behind them from throwing stones. They were caught in the middle of a violent event—like a lonely boat on a stormy sea. While I admired the students' bravery and great composure, their helplessness induced a sadness in me. Turning my eyes off, I walked away and returned to the residential high-rise.

"By about 10:00 p.m., the troops had advanced to the west end of the Muxidi Bridge, but the barricade set up on the bridge earlier by the protesters stopped them. Part of the protesting students and citizens had walked down the bridge sidewalks and joined the crowds near the east end of the bridge. The barricade separating the protesters and the advancing troops was made up of two or three layers of vehicles, buses and trolley buses, which were too heavy for the anti-riot soldiers to remove. Besides, without the support of the tanks and armored vehicles close behind, the anti-riot soldiers did not dare to walk through the bridge sidewalks and advance any further. So they moved behind the tanks, one of which ran up the bridge at full speed in an attempt to break through the barricade. At the same time, on the other side of the barricade, a group of several thousand protesters, shouting "one, two, three", rushed toward the barricade as in a tidal wave and threw themselves onto it. Under the great impact from both sides, this barricade of vehicles, buses and trolley buses uttered a thundering noise but didn't budge from the middle of the bridge. The impact of the tank had been somehow offset by the weight of the protesters' bodies. A roar of cheers erupted among the large crowds of protesters and spectators. After a few more unsuccessful attempts to break through the barricade, the tank retreated amid the protesters' cheers....

"Greatly moved by the protesters' determination, I realized it was a demonstration of the people's strength. But now after the tank's attempts to break through the barricade had failed, the troops started to fire canisters of teargas, which flew over the barricade and fell among the crowds. As the smoke of the teargas spread, the crowds were forced to scatter. At that moment, a tank sped up the bridge and crashed into the barricade with a loud noise, causing two trolley buses in the barricade to budge off, leaving a two-meter gap. But when the tank backed off in order to make another thrust against the barricade, thousands of students and other protesters rushed over and pushed the two trolley buses back into position to eliminate the gap. What's more, they again threw themselves onto the barricade to offset the impact of the tank from the other side. Thus, the stalemate between the protesters and the troops entered a more intense stage, where thousands of protesters scattered with the explosions of teargas canisters but gathered again to block the tank's advance as the smoke of teargas dissipated. I had never seen such a shocking and moving scene in any film....

"All of a sudden, the tank's engine stopped. Scarcely had the protesters figured out what this unexpected quietness meant, when the sharp cracks of gun shots cut across the night air. I saw people running away from the bridge. Within ten seconds or so, I could see no one on the bridge or in any of the nearby streets. The protesters and spectators had all hidden themselves behind the trees and buildings on either side of the road. About one hundred soldiers wearing helmets and carrying assault rifles crossed the bridge, stepping through its sidewalks. At the east end of the bridge, they fanned out and started to fire aimlessly into whatever was in front of them. Then two tanks ran up the bridge side by side, bumping into the barricade of vehicles and buses. After three to five impacts from the tanks, the barricade gave way to the troops.

"Now, the first echelon of the 38th Army began to cross the bridge and advance toward the center of the city like a fierce beast. In the forefront were assault-rifle-wielding soldiers, who, while marching forward, fired horizontally toward the front as well as at either side of the road to clear the way for the troops. Close behind were a large body of troops complete with tanks, armored vehicles and trucks—with foot soldiers safeguarding both flanks, who sporadically fired their assault rifles at either side of the road. The soldiers on top of the tanks and armored vehicles who also carried assault rifles kept looking around and occasionally fired at what they believed to be suspect targets. Coming through the night air, loud and clear, the reports of the assault rifles were as frequent as the noises of crackers set off by people in celebration on Chinese new year's eve. Nobody dared to attempt to stop the troops any more. Some of the people hiding at the roadsides might have already been shot.

"Knowing that the troops were after first blood, those hiding in the dark at the roadsides kept shouting, "Fascists! Fascists!" But at the time, like all the other people watching from the residential high-rise, I thought the troops were firing rubber bullets only to scare off the crowds....Since the people watching from the high-rise where I was situated and those watching from other buildings didn't believe the soldiers were firing real bullets, they didn't hide inside in spite of the sounds of gun shots. I noticed that the several tens of large public balconies of the Minister Buildings (facing north) were jammed with several hundred people in pale-colored shirts standing against a background of light from their rooms.

"As the reports of gun shots grew more and more frequent, the emotion of the tens of thousands of protesters down in the streets intensified. They kept shouting, "Down with fascists!", while the soldiers turned to fire toward where the slogan-shouting came from. Several soldiers stepped off the road and ran toward a group of young people shouting slogans in front of the Fu Xing Hospital, firing their assault rifles....It was really a scary scene. Suddenly, somebody in the high-rise I was in shouted a slogan, only to cause the soldiers to immediately raise their rifles and fire on the building. First, some trolley-bus electric cables snapped with sparks, then bullets hit the cement wall somewhere above my head. Sparks bounced off the wall as pieces of cement fell. It was only then that the people watching from the high-rise awoke to the fact that the troops were firing real bullets. Like all the other people watching from the building, I cowered with fear. When I raised my head again to look outside, a more horrible scene caught my eye. The soldiers were firing at the Minister Buildings as the hundreds of terrified people out on the balconies rushed inside for cover. Soon all the lights went out and the entire Muxidi area was plunged into great terror....

"By midnight, half of the troops had already passed the Muxidi Bridge. A military jeep abruptly pulled up between Building No. 25 and Building No. 22 (one of the Minister Buildings). Three officers jumped off the jeep. Hiding behind it, they started to fire frantically at Building No. 25 for no apparent reason, as if they were not at all concerned about any serious consequences of shooting at residential buildings. Some soldiers not only fired their guns, but also set fire to vehicles. One of the buses which had been used to form the barricade now lay by roadside in front of Building

No. 20 after it was knocked off by the tanks. As the troops passed by, I saw several soldiers walk near the bus and set fire to it, creating false evidence that a riot had taken place.

"By 1:00 a.m. or so, the troops had all passed the Muxidi area. The sounds of frequent gun shots now came from the eastern part of the city. Up to this point, I had no idea how many people had been wounded or killed, as I didn't see any corpse in the street. Many people had been hiding behind the trees at the roadsides where there were no lights. From where I was in the residential high-rise, I couldn't see anything down there. But then I saw people come out of hiding as they were aware that the troops had passed. What I saw petrified me: From all directions, about one thousand people were carrying the dead and the wounded or helping the wounded toward the Fu Xing Hospital. Some of the dead and the wounded were carried on three-wheeled carts or bicycles. Others were carried by those who had not been wounded. Some of the wounded were walking toward the hospital with the assistance of other people....

"All the dead and the wounded had been shot while hiding at the roadsides. Seeing this misery, I went downstairs and ran to the Fu Xing Hospital. Though I wanted to walk in to have a look, I stopped at the entrance, as I saw wounded people all around, blood and gore all around, faces twisted with anger and fear all around. People all around were yelling and crying, whereas the wounded were groaning in great agony. Filled with anger and grief, I was shivering all over at the sight. Turning off my eyes, I was about to walk away, when several middle-aged men who earlier had carried wounded people into the hospital came out and told me that the hospital was full of corpses and wounded people and that the floor of the Emergency Room was covered with blood. They said to me, "It's too horrible to look at. Better not go in." ..... I returned home, feeling very tired....But I couldn't sleep with the scenes of soldiers firing guns and the scenes of dead bodies being carried off repeatedly flashing across my mind....

"At 6:00 a.m., June 4th 1989, I picked up my camera and walked out toward the Fu Xing Hospital. While passing Building No. 22 and Building No. 24, I noticed that some people were talking about the killings which had happened in the Minister Buildings the night before. As it turned out, two people had been killed and several others had been wounded by the soldiers when they fired at the Minister Buildings on the night of June 3rd 1989.

"One of the dead was the son-in-law of Mr. Guan Shanfu, deputy chief procurator of the Supreme People's Procuratorate. On the night in question, the man entered his kitchen (8th Floor, Building No. 24) to drink water, but when he switched on the light with his back to the window, a bullet came in and hit his head from behind. He was killed right on the spot. The other person killed that night was the maid working for Mr. Li Chuli, elderly retired deputy director of the Central Liaison Department of the Communist Party, living on the 13th Floor of Building No. 22. At the time, Mr. Li wanted to see how the troops would march into the city of Beijing, so he asked his maid (age: 65) (who had been looking after him for more than twenty years) to help him into his balcony. Mr. Li was seated in a chair with the maid standing by his side, when a bullet hit her abdomen. She died of excessive loss of blood....

"I was told that the Fu Xing Hospital's mortuary was filled to capacity and that many dead bodies had to be left out in the bicycle booth. Upon hearing this information, I turned quickly and walked toward the hospital.

"There were two notices at the gate of the hospital, one of which must have been posted the night before when wounded people were carried in for emergency surgery. It said the hospital was unable to take in people with brain wounds because it had no brain surgeons and recommended that people with such wounds should be sent to the nearby Railway Hospital or the Navy Hospital. The other notice, which might have been posted earlier that morning, included a list of dead people with indications of their sex and an announcement that because there was no space in the hospital to keep all the corpses and no way to preserve them in the hot weather, the hospital was going to send them to a crematorium within a few days. The notice requested the families of the dead to come to the hospital and identify the victims as soon as possible. Many of the dead on the list didn't even have a name: x x x male; x x x female; and so on and so forth. Most probably, they had been dead when they were carried into the hospital by people who didn't know their names at all.

"I counted up the number of dead people on the list—43 in all with females accounting for one fourth of the total. A young man told me that the hospital had received orders from the authorities not to allow anyone in to gather information. Seeing that I was carrying a camera, he knew I wanted to take photographs, so he said that there were a lot of corpses in the bicycle booth outside the hospital building. I came to the bicycle booth and saw a man standing at the door. He allowed only those who had come to identify corpses to enter. But I could look inside through the door. I saw more than ten corpses lying on the ground all covered with white cloths. Several people looking for missing relatives were inside the bicycle booth examining the corpses.

"Aware that I was taking pictures, a woman doctor came over. She neither intended to stop me, nor wanted to know what my occupation was. Apparently, she could tell that I had sympathies for the victims and wanted me to know how she felt about the tragedy. She told me a lot about how emergency treatment had been given to the wounded the night before. She said that no one in the hospital could have expected the troops to perpetrate such atrocities. So, as usual, there had been only one doctor on duty at each clinic. "Only a small number of doctors and nurses were in the hospital—inadequate to deal with the large number of wounded people carried in," she said.

"According to her, there had been more than 380 seriously wounded people carried into the hospital the night before—more than ten times the number of doctors and nurses present at the time. All of the hospital's operating-tables had been used to give emergency treatment to the wounded. She said that there had been a lack of plasma because the blood bank's truck couldn't come through with soldiers all over the place shooting at moving vehicles. She said that the doctors and nurses had been crying while giving emergency treatment as many of the wounded young people died on the operating-tables for lack of plasma. She said that she had never seen such a horrible event in her long career as a doctor. According to her, those who had been carried into the Fu Xing Hospital accounted for only the people wounded east of the Muxidi Bridge. Those wounded west of the bridge had been carried to the Railway Hospital....She said that dead and wounded people had been carried into more than forty hospitals in the city of Beijing.

"Later, I got more information about the tragedy from people working at other hospitals. A head nurse working at the Children's Hospital told me that she had been on duty that night when she heard the reports of guns. Looking outside, she noticed that while crossing the Fu Xing Men Bridge from west to east, the troops were firing downward at the people hiding at either side of Er Huan Road. Soon the Children's Hospital was full of wounded people with the floor of the emergency room covered with blood....In a street section no more than 400 meters long extending from the Fu Xing Men Bridge to Lishi Road, the soldiers had wounded more than 200 people and killed more than 20. A doctor working at the Beijing University Hospital told me that the ambulances and the doctors and nurses of the Beijing University Hospital and the Xiehe Hospital had been actively involved in rescuing the wounded from Tiananmen Square after the troops opened fire, because the two hospitals were near Tiananmen Square. In the beginning, the ambulances would carry away both the dead and the wounded. But later, the wounded were so many that the dead had to be left behind. She (the doctor) mentioned several spots inside Tiananmen Square where dead bodies had been left behind: the area in front of the Golden Water

Bridge; the area around the Flag Mast; and the area in front of the History Museum....

"She told me that of all the hospitals giving emergency treatment, the Xiehe Hospital had taken in the most dead bodies—more than one hundred. Most of these people had been killed in a street section that extended from Tiananmen Square to the Wangfujing shopping center—less than one thousand meters. According to other sources, because the troops fired wantonly as they moved into Tiananmen Square, they killed and wounded many spectators, as well as some hospital personnel ministering to the wounded and some plainclothesmen dispatched by the police and the military to mix with the spectators...."

*   *   *   *   *   *

But, well, according to General Chi Haotian, no students were killed inside Tiananmen Square in June of 1989. It's up to the reader to decide whether to believe him or not. As to me, I do believe that the general wishes that no one had been killed at Tiananmen Square. As the old saying goes, the wish is the father to the thought. The general may now truly think that no one was killed inside Tiananmen Square on that tragic night in 1989.

Looking at the military crackdown from a political scientist's perspective, one would basically see the tragedy as a display of the nature of China's communist state apparatus and the inevitable consequence of transplanting the Soviet political model in China. Once such a Stalinist monster has been established, no one is able to transform it overnight. With the benefit of hindsight, it is now easy to say that the students of Beijing may have been driven by frustration to the point of desperation in deciding not to leave Tiananmen Square before the massacre began. Had they left the Square at the urging of the then Secretary General Zhao Ziyang, the students would have strengthened the hand of the liberal-minded Mr. Zhao in his efforts to convince the conservative forces of the Communist Party that to use peaceful means to resolve the dispute between the government and the students was in the best interest of the country.

China's paramount leader Deng Xiaoping couldn't have transformed the country's communist political model into a pluralist democratic mechanism even if he had wanted to, because the communist state apparatus during the Deng era was never a one-man's show capable of being maneuvered singlehandedly. Some of Deng's long-time colleagues were critical of the capitalist characteristics of his economic reforms. After the student demonstrations gathered momentum at Tiananmen Square, Deng's conservative colleagues blamed the unrest on Deng's reforms, claiming the reforms had added fuel to "bourgeois liberalization"—a communist buzzword for people's demand for freedom of speech, expression and thought. Deng had to listen to those critical voices and make concessions.

At his time of life, Mr. Deng couldn't afford to be seen by his long-time comrades as being ready to bury communism in China, because what was considered to be the Devil by the Free World remained—and still remains—a sacred cow in China. In June of 1989, the Communist Party as a whole—not Deng Xiaoping alone—was confronted with a painful choice: either to end one-party dictatorship as China's liberal intellectuals hoped or to crack down with force. The Communist Party chose the latter to preserve one-party dictatorship, though some individual party members with liberal inclinations expressed their reservations. Unfortunately, the strength of such liberal-minded party members as the then Secretary General Zhao Ziyang was outweighed by the conservative forces of the Communist Party.

Apparently, the left-wing conservative forces of the Communist Party were wary of the possibility that the liberal-minded members of the Communist Party and the liberal-democratic forces of the Chinese society represented by some of the Tiananmen Square protestors like Mr. Wang Juntao (a well-educated young man who was later arrested and imprisoned for a long time, before the Chinese government eventually released and exiled him to the U.S. under international pressures) might form an unholy alliance against the old system, since that would threaten the conservatives' grip on power. At this critical juncture of history in the spring of 1989, Mr. Deng Xiaoping sided with the conservatives in suppressing the demands for political change from both the party liberals and the protestors, because he felt that his regime was threatened by the liberal forces and that he had to turn to the conservatives for support.

In the 1980s, there was a well-known party liberal in Shanghai by the name of Qin Benli. Mr. Qin Benli was editor-in-chief of Shanghai's popular financial newspaper, The World Economic Herald, which kept calling for political reform until the peak of the student demonstrations when the then Shanghai party secretary Jiang Zemin ordered the paper shut down—probably on instructions from Beijing after Mr. Zhao Ziyang was put under house arrest. It was alleged that Mr. Qin Benli's newspaper had a close relationship with Mr. Zhao Ziyang's think tank, whose members were basically well-educated party liberals. After the military crackdown, two well-known members of Mr. Zhao's think tank, Mr. Chen Yizi and Mr. Yan Jiaqi went into hiding to escape arrest and then fled the country. Eventually, they arrived in the United States to live in exile. Mr. Qin Benli was not arrested. Nor was he expelled from the Communist Party. But he died of cancer in 1991. He was a chain-smoker. China's conservative forces were very strong in the 1980s—they still are today. The liberals tried their best to introduce political change but failed. Hopefully, future historians will say that the liberals failed but failed heroically.

Now the Chinese government says that the military crackdown of June 4th 1989 was necessary and justifiable in the sense that it restored "stability". The truth is that the crackdown restored stability under one-party dictatorship, not stability under democracy, and so is hard to justify from a historical perspective. Had the Communist Party chosen to eventually end one-party dictatorship and promised democratic political reforms in June of 1989, the students would have left Tiananmen Square peacefully and no one would have been killed. Alas, to the Communist Party, the term "stability" only means stability under one-party dictatorship or simply the survival of the communist regime.

Still, the tragedy of June 4th 1989 may have accelerated the wheel of history, since it demonstrated clearly to the moderate faction of the Chinese leadership that the old system transplanted from the Soviet Union had many disadvantages, that the Chinese people would not tolerate the old system forever, and that further reforms were necessary if the regime was to survive. But in the first few months after the military crackdown there were signs that the left-wing conservative faction of the Communist Party wanted to rolled back some of the reforms introduced since 1979, questioning the wisdom of the reforms because the reforms appeared to have weakened the state's control over people's lives. Then shortly afterwards, the Berlin Wall collapsed and all the communist regimes in East Europe came tumbling down like sand castles. Finally, the Soviet Union, the place of origin of communism, fell apart in autumn of 1991. Nothing could have demonstrated more clearly that state controls upon which all communist regimes rely could not last forever.

In early 1992, Deng Xiaoping visited the southern border town Shenzhen to launch his second round of market-oriented economic reforms that included the opening of stock markets in major Chinese cities like Shanghai and Shenzhen. Since then, capitalist economic methods have become increasingly accepted and may have even taken root in China.

While commenting on the Sino-British Joint Declaration by which Hong Kong's capitalist ways of life would be allowed to continue for fifty years as from July 1st 1997, former British Prime Minister Margaret Thatcher once said that Deng Xiaoping was a wise man and that perhaps Deng knew communism didn't work. Apparently, Mrs.

Thatcher was trying to explain why Deng had agreed to give Hong Kong another fifty years of capitalism and why she believed the Sino-British Joint Declaration was a good document.

True it was Deng who ordered troops to crack down on the demonstrators at Tiananmen Square on June 4th 1989 to preserve his authoritarian regime. But it may also be true that Deng was a wise man as pointed out by Mrs. Thatcher, that he was a pragmatic "capitalist-roader", which title was bestowed on him by the late Chairman Mao Zedong and his shrewish wife Jiang Qing at the peak of the Cultural Revolution (1966-1976). In China, names and titles are important. Whatever one does, one has to give it a good name. Unfortunately for Deng, "capitalist-roader" was not a good title in the leftist Mao era—even today few Chinese officials would like to assume the title "capitalist-roader". "Socialist" continues to be the correct term to use in contemporary China. But unknown to Mao and Jiang Qing was the fact that many people in China based their hopes on Deng Xiaoping during the nightmarish leftist upheavals of the Cultural Revolution because they believed Deng was a true capitalist-roader and would deliver someday. Indeed, after he was reinstated in office in 1977, Deng first maneuvered himself into a dominant position and then in 1979 started to deliver on his promises, that is, to initiate his market-oriented reforms allowing people to have more economic freedoms—though always in the name of socialism.

China is a country with a long history of civilization where wise men have been born. More than two thousand years ago—that is, long before Jesus Christ was born—China's best-known scholar and wise man Confucius (551-479 B.C.) said: "Those who work with their brains rule and those who work with their brawn are ruled." China is not a country where stupid people who can't work with their brains can rule for long. To introduce capitalist economic methods in the name of socialism may have been a wise move by Deng to shield himself from the criticisms by his conservative colleagues.

Another positive outgrowth of the tragedy of June 4th 1989 was the intense attention that the massacre caused the international community to pay to China's human rights record. Thanks to CNN's in-depth coverage, the monstrous nature of the communist state apparatus was exposed in the international media spotlight, resulting in strong international pressures for Chinese leaders to improve their human rights record—at least to the extent acceptable to themselves.

People who have lived under the late Chairman Mao Zedong, the late strongman Deng Xiaoping and China's current top leader President Jiang Zemin may tell the world that things are far better today than when Mao was calling the shots. But Mao's China was hermetically sealed to the outside world. Although thousands and thousands of tragedies took place during Mao's reign, few were reported by Western media because the full detail of totalitarian atrocities under Mao was hidden behind the iron curtain. Whereas China's current open-door policy certainly makes it difficult for Chinese officials to cover up infamous incidences involving the detention of dissidents and the poor treatment and poor medical care received by political prisoners. Oftentimes, bad news travels quickly and crosses the border overnight, sparking off uproar in the international media followed by further demands from the international community that the Chinese government live up to international human rights norms.

The current Chinese leadership is a group of technocrats educated in either Moscow or China's best universities. They definitely know the importance of image and want to be respected by the international community. Chinese culture sets great store by education and respect, fostering an environment where young people receive education not necessarily because they want to use their education in the future to make money, but because their parents keep telling them that educated people are respected. That is a typical Confucianist view of life. Although Confucianism was severely condemned by the leftist radicals during the Cultural Revolution, Confucian theories have been treated with much more respect in China in recent years. Not a bad thing at all, because Confucianism will cause China's technocratic leaders to realize that it is in their interest to improve China's human rights record in exchange for international respect, as long as human rights improvements do not jeopardize the survival of their regime.

From the 19th century till 1945 when World War II ended, China suffered invasions by foreign powers including Great Britain and Japan and was treated by Western powers like a second-rate country despite China's long history of civilization, which fact has had a negative impact on the psychology of the Chinese people, inducing a national inferiority complex. All of modern China's national leaders ranging from Dr. Sun Yat-sen and Generalissimo Chiang Kai-shek of the Nationalist Party to Mao Zedong, Deng Xiaoping and President Jiang Zemin of the Communist Party have wanted one thing in common: to be treated as an equal by Western powers. Today, this has become a reality because China is just too important to world peace and stability not to be treated as an equal, though the residue of the national inferiority complex may have been carried over from the past. The problem is that to be treated as an equal, one has to act as an equal and to act as an equal, one has to observe certain universal rules—such as those set out in the United Nations International Covenant on Civil and Political Rights.

China's technocratic leaders now frequently meet Western leaders on an equal footing. Consequently, each time some Western leader frowns upon China's human rights record, the Chinese leadership is likely to feel embarrassed by the loss of face they suffer, no matter how small that Western leader's country may be. It is possible that someday at one of those Politburo meetings in Beijing, President Jiang Zemin or some party moderate might have to single out human rights as an issue that needs to be addressed, since it is getting more and more clear that being one of the most important countries in the world, China can't do without the respect of the international community. After all, respect is a commodity that we human beings all crave for, and people holding university degrees and rubbing shoulders with Western leaders must be among those who crave respect more than anything else, especially if there was some respected scholar like Confucius among their ancestors.

There is a Chinese saying about "face", which goes: "Man needs face as a tree needs its skin." It means that every man wants to be respected, even though he may not deserve it. Chinese leaders have to ask themselves what they must do to deserve the respect of the international community. Perhaps, they can find the answer by reading Confucius, not Karl Marx or Lenin, because one would wonder: Why must the sophisticated leaders of today's China cling to the unworkable creeds of foreign ideologues like Marx and Lenin, when China itself has a great treasure of proven cultural values and traditions?

But Confucianism aside, as of this moment, the Communist Party has no intention of allowing the Chinese people to speak freely about what they really think of Marxism and communism. The Communist Party doesn't see the freedom to speak one's mind as a basic human right. Rather, under China's communist constitution, to express anti-communist views is a "counter-revolutionary crime". No matter how many international human rights treaties the Chinese government may sign, it would be naive to think the communist regime would be serious about honoring them. As far as the communist regime is concerned, signing international human rights treaties is nothing but an attempt to save face or to improve its international image. As for the implementation of the international human rights treaties signed by the communist regime, it could be a completely different kettle of fish, because to allow the Chinese people the freedom to criticize the old system would mean the beginning of the end of communism in China.

And without the communist system, what could so many communist party officials do for a living? Do they have the ability to make a living in a real free market with a real fair level ground? Whatever the brand name, communism or socialism, politics is business—it is about the control of resources. In order to control the country's resources, the Communist Party has to prevent people from criticizing the old system, though it keeps saying that the Party is fighting "for the great ideals of communism." How? By killing unarmed demonstrators at Tiananmen Square?

3

Western Influences in Modern China

Marxist ideology and totalitarianism aside, however, it might be useful to know that certain strange phenomena or paradoxes have existed in the history of modern China, one of which has been the strong pro-western attitude held either consciously or subconsciously by a certain number of Chinese people despite the humiliation China suffered at the hands of Western powers in the 19th century and the conflicts and disputes that have existed between China and the United States ever since the 1949 communist revolution.

The derogatory term used of Westerners "yang-gui-zi" (foreign ghosts), which came into use in the 19th century when China was invaded by Western powers, is no longer used in China except jocosely. In 1995, when I crossed the border from Hong Kong into Shenzhen (one of China's major special economic zones) to act as an interpreter for a meeting between an American company and a group of Chinese officials, I was surprised to hear the Chinese officials use a totally different term: "our American friends".

In the 1950s—that is, not very long ago, in historical terms—China billed America its Number One enemy and U.S. imperialism a paper tiger. Then in the 1960s, America was downgraded on China's scale of enemies from Number One to Number Two and for the first time in years didn't have to bear the flak alone, because the Soviet Union which had been communist China's best friend plus Big Brother in the 1950s turned out to be China's Number One enemy due to ideological differences. By the 1990s, Americans had somehow become "our American friends" to Chinese officials. There appear to be certain forces within the Chinese bureaucracy (especially the well-educated) that have genuine friendly feelings toward the United States.

As to ordinary Chinese citizens, the question is whether they know that each year, America buys billions of dollars' worth of goods from Chinese firms, enabling them to operate with a profit and keep millions of workers on payrolls. Probably not, since the state-controlled press may not want to publicize the extent to which the country relies on its overseas markets, even as its best foreign customer, the United States, buys one third of Chinese exports, accounting for 6.9% of China's GDP.

Basically speaking, it is not far-fetched to say that modern China has a strong tradition of Western influences. Modern China's founder and first revolutionary leader, Dr. Sun Yat-sen was educated in Honolulu, U.S.A. and his wish was for China to rank among the big powers of the world (i.e. the Western powers). Generalissimo Chiang Kai-shek's wife was educated in America and Chiang's country, The Republic of China, was one of America's closest allies in modern history.

Mao Zedong's 1949 communist revolution interrupted this tradition of Western influences and his anti-U.S. rhetoric in public was horrendous, but in private he was trying to learn English with the help of his personal doctor Li Zhi-sui and admired the United States more than any other country in the world. He kept China's door closed to the West for more than twenty years but finally welcomed President Nixon to Beijing in early 1972 and met Nixon again in 1975 even though Mr. Nixon had already resigned his presidency because of the Watergate bugging scandal. I am not saying that Mao was pro-Western, but I do believe that the positive influences from the Western world remained in China even during the leftist Mao era and that people both in and outside the Communist Party have accepted that the West is way ahead in almost every area.

As to China's late paramount leader Deng Xiaoping who died in February of 1997, according to a Newsweek Magazine article published right after his death, from the 1960s U.S. politicians had regarded Deng Xiaoping as the most pro-American leader in the Chinese government. Deng sent his son Deng Zhifang to America to earn a Ph.D. in the 1980s. According to media reports, Deng Xiaoping's grandchildren are currently in the U.S. attending one of America's best schools. Deng visited the United States in 1979 and opened China's door to American businesses shortly afterwards, though it is important to note that Deng's move didn't turn the country into a real open free market.

Right after he took control of the Chinese government in the late 1970s, Deng Xiaoping decided that China had to improve its relations with the United States to resist the expansionist pressures from the former Soviet Union, because China shared a several-thousand-mile-long border with the Soviet Union and had historically suffered in conflicts with Russia. Deng Xiaoping believed that there should be no major conflicts between the United States and China since there was no common border between the two countries. Instead, he believed that in order to accomplish modernization, China must develop a friendly relationship with the richest and most advanced country in the world, the United States. But apparently, the conservative left-wing of the Communist Party has had strong reservations about the moderates' efforts to pursue Mr. Deng's policy toward the United States, especially when U.S. politicians criticized China's human rights record. The left-wing hardliners have regarded such criticisms as an attack on China's communist system.

There was a minor episode during Deng's visit to the United States which received no attention from the media at all. 1979 was the year when America's ally, the Shah of Iran, was in serious trouble amid popular uprisings instigated by Iran's religious leader Khomeini. The Voice of America interviewed Mr. Deng Xiaoping in the U.S. and broadcasted the interview worldwide. Deng was speaking in Mandarin but with his strong Sichuan (Province) accent and there was a translator beside him. The interviewing Voice-of-America correspondent asked Mr. Deng's opinion on the Iranian situation. Mr. Deng answered, "I hope the United States will do more work on Iran." The translator translated Deng's answer for the Voice-of-America correspondent, but the correspondent didn't seem to understand, so he asked again hoping to get a clearer idea of what Deng really meant. Mr. Deng repeated, "I hope the United States will do more work on Iran."

Anyone with a good knowledge of the Chinese language should have taken Mr. Deng's comment as an indication that the elderly Chinese statesman would like to see the United States help the Shah of Iran to stay in power by all means. In the Chinese language and especially in the parlance of the Communist Party, "do work" means to exercise influence. Mr. Deng wanted the United States to exercise more influence on the Iranian situation, because he knew without U.S. intervention, the Shah of Iran would fall. It could have been interpreted as a call for the United States to intervene in Iran. Since the Shah was a close ally to the United States and the United States had vital interests in Iran (a major oil-producing country in Southwest Asia), Mr. Deng's pro-Shah stance should have been regarded as very pro-American indeed, because it suggested that Deng saw Iran as America's sphere of influence and recognized America's right to intervene in Iran if the Shah so requested. Had the United States intervened to keep the Shah in power, history might have taken a different course in Iran.

In the aftermath of the military crackdown of June 4th 1989, President George Bush told reporters that he had tried to contact Deng Xiaoping by telephone but there was nobody in Deng's office to answer the call. President Bush appeared perplexed when expressing his disappointment to the press. Why? Perhaps because he didn't believe the pro-American Mr. Deng had ordered the military crackdown. Perhaps because he was wondering whether Deng had been put under house arrest by the leftist faction of the Communist Party as the media suspected at the time.

Later, when it became known that it was Deng who had made the decision to crack down on the demonstrators and that Deng continued to be in control of the situation, President Bush sent his National Security Adviser General Scowcroft to Beijing to meet Deng Xiaoping. To be sure, it was as much an attempt to find out China's intentions with regard to the course of its future political and economic developments as it was an effort to eliminate misunderstandings if any between the United States and China. President Bush definitely made the right move, as General Scowcroft successfully convinced China to keep its door open to the outside world, though, during the 1992 presidential campaign, the general's mission was unjustly labeled as "coddling dictatorship" by the then Democratic presidential candidate Bill Clinton.

According to reports in Hong Kong's Chinese media published after the meeting between Deng Xiaoping and General Scowcroft, Deng sounded hurt amid criticisms of the military crackdown from the entire Western world, saying, "It is us who have suffered damage." By whom? While Deng didn't point out categorically, the Chinese authorities claimed that the Central Intelligence Agency (the CIA) had involved itself in instigating the students of Beijing to demonstrate. If Deng had believed that the claim was true, he should have felt hurt and betrayed.

There is a Chinese saying which goes: "When in difficulties one knows who one's true friends are." The meaning of this Chinese saying is similar to that of the English proverb: "A friend in need is a friend indeed." If U.S. politicians' judgment about Deng Xiaoping was correct, i.e. he was pro-American, then Deng Xiaoping might have taken people like President Bush, President Nixon and Dr. Kissinger as his American friends and might even have expected America and his American friends to help him out when he was in difficulties. Strange to say, in some sense, these American statesmen were really Mr. Deng Xiaoping's true friends! How? Remember those difficult days during the Cultural Revolution (1966—1976) when Deng Xiaoping was condemned as China's number two capitalist-roader by the leftist radicals? Who were Deng's friends? Who were wishing that Capitalist-Roader Deng Xiaoping could stage a comeback in Chinese politics? You bet most American politicians were!

But in 1989, it was a different situation where Deng Xiaoping was in power and his regime was under pressure from the liberals to make political reforms. His aides sent him reports to the effect that the CIA had involved itself in helping the student demonstrators to topple his government. If it was a misunderstanding, it must have been one of the most dangerous misunderstandings in the history of Sino-U.S. relations. No U.S. president could afford to sit around doing nothing about a misunderstanding of such magnitude, especially if corporate America had billions of dollars worth of investments in China.

While the United States does have a legitimate interest in finding out what is going on in Communist China through the CIA at all times, it would make no sense, however, for the CIA to involve itself in toppling any Chinese politician considered to be pro-American like Mr. Deng Xiaoping. Rather, the entire Free World would like to see moderate (hopefully pro-American) Chinese politicians continue to exert their positive influences in Chinese politics. Fortunately, despite the Chinese authorities' claim that the CIA had involved itself in the student movement, Mr. Deng Xiaoping continued to stress the importance of a good relationship between the United States and China till the end of his life.

Among China's well-educated, pro-Western views and opinions frequently emerge, indicating the country's intellectuals strongly hope that the government will learn from the United States, not only on the economic level, but also on the political level, though they all stop short at calling communism erroneous because Chinese law doesn't tolerate criticism of Marxist ideology. While pro-western views do not always get published in China, the communist-controlled Xinhua News Agency gathers intellectuals' opinions and prints the same in its Materials For Internal Reference, which is only released to the high-ranking officials of the Communist Party. The following is some of the liberal views printed in Materials For Internal Reference (August 1998):

"Some of the scholars at Shanghai Academy of Social Sciences pointed out that the exposure of Clinton scandals and the investigations conducted by the judicial branch indicate that the United States has a sound social system and that U.S. citizens have the right to supervise and prosecute government officials including the president."

"One of the officers of the September 3rd Society noted that to a rather extensive degree, the judicial system of the United States ensures that every U.S. citizen has equal rights and obligations. Although President Clinton holds significant powers, the exercise of his powers and his personal behavior are both under the supervision of the people. This provides a solid basis for America's political stability and continuity.....The judicial system of the United States is built on the basis of the country's social system."

"A Beijing scientist said that the judicial system of the United States as part of its social system is worthy of research and emulation by China. In the 1950s, Liu Shaoqi, Deng Xiaoping and Chen Yun (three late leaders of the Communist Party) all mentioned with emphasis the advantages of America's judicial system lie in the fact that the public can exercise the right to supervise and superintend the government and the president. It's nearly fifty years since the founding of the People's Republic (of China), yet we still don't have an effective mechanism of supervision. Such a state of affairs should cause the Communist Party, the government and the Standing Committee of The National People's Congress to do soul-searching. Currently, our country faces numerous evils on the social-political level, the economic level and the moral level. Needless to say, this is a problem resulting from our legal system. It involves such major issues as the role of the Communist Party, its power, the legal system, and the proper place that law should hold."

"Some teachers and (communist) party committee cadres at the University of Beijing, the Chinese People's University, the Nankai University, the Fudan University and the University of Nanjing have written to express their views: The exposure of President Clinton's scandals and the investigations by the judicial branch reflect the role of the existing system of supervision in the United States. The social system of Singapore and the social system of the United States are not exactly the same, but both countries have sound judicial systems and sound mechanisms of supervision. Yet, judging from the way the existing judicial system of our country operates, it still has a strong tinge of feudalism. Basically speaking, the rule of man or the rule of bureaucrat manipulates the fairness of justice and the equality of citizens before law. This is the root cause of the corruption among party officials, the revulsion of the people against the status quo and the instability of our society."

Given that part of China's well-educated are now bold enough to express such pro-American opinions as recorded above, it is logical to believe that the country's liberal forces are growing as the ongoing reform and open-door policies lead people to compare China's communist system with the system of the United States and the systems of other Western countries. It is also logical to presume that liberal forces exist not only outside the Communist Party, but also inside the Communist Party. Liberal-minded party members and party officials are certainly asking themselves what to do with the old system, though they can not afford to openly voice their misgivings about Marxism and communism.

Perhaps, a large proportion of China's intellectuals hold pro-Western views and are eager to learn from the West. The question is: What should the United States and other Western countries do to help China come to the fold of the Free World? Since China is a country with a tradition of strong Western influences as well as a large number of people eager to learn from the West, the least the West should do is to promote trade ties as well as cultural ties with China, provided that a proper and sustainable trade balance can be maintained. That means that as cheap Chinese products continue to pour into the U.S. and other Western countries, efforts to open the China market should intensify. Always remember that the Chinese people as a whole hold very friendly feelings toward the Western world. Thus, Western products and services are sure to go down very well with Chinese consumers. Theoretically speaking, the long-term potential of the China market is unlimited, should the ruling party there decide to bury communism in the future—a very remote possibility, though.

In the cultural arena, Hollywood movies could easily rule the Chinese movie theater industry if it were not for the numerous restrictions imposed by the communist bureaucracy. Yet, Chinese entrepreneurs (or wheeler-dealers) and consumers have a way to get around bureaucratic restrictions. For instance, although government regulations only allow a very small number of foreign films—probably as few as 10 per year—to be shown in Shanghai's movie theaters, the residents in that city are now able to watch as many Hollywood movies as they like at home, because these days, video compact disks (VCD's) are available and they come cheap in pirated editions, thanks to the booming black market. To give the reader an idea of just how cheap these VCD's are, here's an example: Price tag on VCD "Eye Wide Shut" with Chinese subtitles: RMB 11.00 yuan each (about US$1.32). One Shanghai movie fan told me that he has a collection of about 500 video compact disks of Hollywood films including "The Rock" and "Entrapment" both starring Sean Connery and that he hopes the affordable pirated editions will remain available. Intellectual property rights infringements aside, I am happy for Shanghai's residents. At least, they now have access to Hollywood's great productions.

Few things in this world can remain unchanged forever. In fact, almost everything is changing, and so is communist China. During the leftist Mao era which ended in 1976 when Mao died, nobody in Shanghai had ever seen Sean Connery's performance in any of his "007—James Bond" movies. Now, many people there must have "007" in their VCD collections. Freedom works, and trade and cultural ties with China will certainly promote changes for the better, though this does not mean that the nature of the communist state apparatus will change soon. On the contrary, in my judgement, the nature of the communist state apparatus is one of the few things that will remain unchanged till communism is buried in China.

However, there might be ways to convince China's leaders that it would be in their interest and certainly in the interest of their country and their people, if they could find a way to phase out communism by degrees and eventually implement democratization as defined by the international community. Here, definition is important. For the communist regime in Beijing defines its one-party dictatorship as "People's Democracy". To be sure, that is not how the international community defines "democracy". The Communist Party's definition of the term can only fool idiots brainwashed by the regime over the years, since the prerequisite for true democracy is the freedom of expression, which continues to be lacking today in China despite its economic reforms.

On the other hand, "to phase out communism" does not mean that China's leaders have to end their one-party dictatorship overnight. Rather, it is understandable that the leaders of the ruling party may have to consider the vested interests of its various factions. Politics is business and business bargaining always takes time. Yet, at the end of the day, the various factions of the ruling Communist Party need to negotiate a solution to the fundamental problem of communism, that is, in the final analysis, it doesn't work anyway with or without reform. Sooner or later, either they the leaders themselves or their successors or their children and grandchildren will have to bring communism to a natural end, so as to enable their country to fall in line with the rules of the international community. China's current top leader President Jiang Zemin appears to have a strong interest in things Western. Although he does not have a reputation for being a party liberal, he shouldn't be regarded as a communist hardliner either. He appears to be pragmatic, hoping to maintain stability under a system which, he himself probably knows, is an anachronism.

When Mr. George Bush was in the White House, he never ceased his efforts to engage China, and he certainly did the right thing when he sent General Scowcroft to Beijing after the June 1989 Tiananmen Square military crackdown to keep China's door open and America's trade ties with China intact. But then in 1992, he was enigmatically accused of "coddling dictatorship" by Democratic presidential candidate Bill Clinton.

Now, President Bill Clinton claims that "constructive engagement" is his policy toward communist China. Though he seems to be ready to make far more concessions to the Chinese communists, he never calls his own China policy one of "coddling dictatorship". For instance, the Clinton administration opposes "The Taiwan Security Enhancement Act" adopted by the International Relations Committee of the U.S. Congress, because it believes that to enhance Taiwan's ballistic missile defenses "would fuel an arms race and could shatter efforts to get Beijing to reduce missile stocks" or "would send Beijing ballistic" in the words of Vice President Al Gore.

The truth is that Beijing is already very ballistic with its ICBM rockets, some of which were paraded through Tiananmen Square on October 1st 1999 in celebration of the 50th anniversary of the founding of the People's Republic. It does not need to be "sent ballistic". The Clinton administration acts as if it has never read a tidbit of history, as if it does not know that the Beijing regime is a one-party dictatorship. However, if the officials of the Clinton administration have indeed read history, they should know that appeasement has never helped to get any dictatorship "to reduce arms stocks". Did British prime minister Arthur Neville Chamberlain manage to get Adolf Hitler "to reduce arms stocks" in the late 1930s with his policy of appeasement toward Nazi Germany? Could anyone convince Saddam Hussein of Iraq "to reduce arms stocks" in 1990 before his troops invaded Kuwait? Nobody could have! All dictatorships are alike. They understand only one language—the language of strength. Appeasement does not work.

According to the state budget published by the Chinese government, since 1989, China's military spending has been increasing by a double-digit percentage each year, from RMB 24.60 billion yuan (about US$3.20 billion) in 1989 to RMB 104.60 billion yuan (about US$12.60 billion) in 1999. These officially published figures do not include China's invisible special expenditures on its military research and development projects and its heavy purchases of weaponry and military equipment from Russia. So, China's military spending growth far exceeds its economic growth.

Apparently, the Clinton administration either is afraid to displease the Chinese communists or is willing to make concessions in order to please them. No wonder, critics say the Clinton administration has been pursuing a wrong-headed and dangerous policy of appeasement toward Beijing. In the light of media reports that Johnny Chong and Charlie Trie (two probable communist agents) funneled large amounts of money originated from communist China's intelligence establishment into the Democratic Party's campaign coffers to ensure Bill Clinton's re-election in 1996, it is very much in evidence that the Communists like Clinton's China policy because it plays into their hands.

That said, engagement with communist China continues to be absolutely necessary for the United States, no matter who is in the White House. The challenge is how to engage China without making undue and unprincipled concessions, because it is important to remember all the time that the Beijing regime is a communist dictatorship whose principles are in direct conflict with the beliefs and values of the Free World, for all the smiles and relatively moderate images from some of China's top leaders. If the Clinton administration's policy of "constructive engagement" toward China is designed as an excuse for granting the Communists what they want, then, let's be honest and call a spade a spade.

History has repeatedly demonstrated that undue and unprincipled concessions to any dictatorship based on a policy of appeasement could lead to endless trouble, because such concessions would be interpreted as signs of weakness and only serve to strengthen the hand of the hardliners in the adversary's camp, inviting them to ask for more. The problem is that there is no way to please them (the hardliners) enough. If they prepare to start a war, no one is able to get them "to reduce arms stocks". Before taking action, they tend to whip up irrational "nationalism" or "patriotism" to justify their war preparations. When they are ready and believe they can win, their war machine strikes out like a bolt from the blue. Those who express their concerns because they see signs of danger more clearly than others do are often dismissed as being "paranoid", until war breaks out to surprise the "non-paranoid" majority.

No one could have convinced Adolf Hitler "to reduce arms stocks" before Nazi German troops invaded and occupied Poland in 1939. No one could have convinced North Korea "to reduce arms stocks" before it invaded and occupied much of South Korea in 1950. No one could have convinced Saddam Hussein of Iraq "to reduce arms stocks" before his troops invaded and occupied Kuwait in 1990. So, if the hardliners in the People's Liberation Army and the Communist Party plan to "liberate Taiwan" as they have repeated said they will, no one can "get Beijing to reduce missile stocks", because their war preparations will continue according to plan anyway. The Clinton administration is either smoking pop or trying to fool the ladies and gentlemen in Congress, assuming they all have low I.Q's.

4

The Communist State Apparatus— a Real Monster

President Jiang Zemin is not a Deng-type strongman because he does not have the kind of power base that the late Deng Xiaoping had in the military. Although the Communist Party claims that the military is under the leadership of the Party, the history of power struggle between the various factions of the Communist Party has painted a different picture where the man calling the shots has always been the one in control of the military. The late Great Dictator Mao Zedong, who assumed full control of the Communist Party's military forces at its historic meeting in Zunyi, Guizhou Province in 1935, launched his Cultural Revolution to purge his political rivals in 1966. The late strongman Deng Xiaoping, who assumed control of the military after Mao died, ousted the liberal-minded party secretary general Zhao Ziyang and called out his troops to crack down on the Tiananmen Square democracy movement in June 1989. Now, President Jiang Zemin holds the title of Chairman of the Central Military Commission of the Communist Party, but whether he is really in control remains to be seen. The hardliners in the military could force his hand.

President Jiang Zemin has the appearance of toeing a thin line between the reformers and the Communist Party's conservative left wing, frequently looking over his shoulder to make sure that whatever he says does not offend either faction to any extreme degree. He certainly needs the support of both camps to keep the boat steady.

President Jiang sent his son, Jiang Mianheng, to Drexel University, Philadelphia, U.S.A. to earn a Ph.D. in the 1980s. After working briefly in the U.S., Dr. Jiang Mianheng returned to China in 1992. It is difficult to portray President Jiang Zemin as a strong anti-U.S. Communist Party hardliner, because one would ask: What anti-U.S. politician in China would send his son to America to earn a Ph.D. and then wait for his boy to return home only to tell him that American capitalism works far more efficiently than the Soviet model transplanted in China? Yet, at the same time, President Jiang Zemin certainly does not want to be seen as "China's Gorbachev" by the conservative left wing of the Communist Party. In fact, he is definitely not "China's Gorbachev". Having failed to carry out any meaningful political reform since February of 1997 when Mr. Deng Xiaoping died, President Jiang Zemin proves to be a mere reflection of China's political reality. Why?

First of all, President Jiang Zemin is unlikely to forget what happened to the reformist leader of the former Soviet Union, Mr. Gorbachev, who was hailed by the Western world because of his political reforms but then became a nobody overnight when he and his family were put under house arrest during a 1991 putsch launched by the conservative left wing of the Soviet Communist Party. Secondly, President Jiang is unlikely to forget what has happened to the relatively liberal-minded leaders of the Chinese Communist Party in recent history, such as Hu Yaobang and Zhao Ziyang (two previous party secretaries general). And thirdly, the military may not be completely under President Jiang's control, whereas the moderate and liberal factions are not strong enough to counterbalance the conservative left-wing forces of the Communist Party.

Former U.S. President Ronald Reagan called the Soviet Union the Evil Empire. Even after Mr. Gorbachev had become the leader of the Soviet Union and had started his glasnost reforms, President Reagan continued to regard the Soviet Union as the Evil Empire. As we now realize, he did so correctly, because the Soviet communist state apparatus was a monster which even Mr. Gorbachev, the head of the Soviet Communist Party, could not control. As we now understand, Mr. Gorbachev was not a monster though he was the leader of the Soviet Union. Rather, he was "a man we can do business with" as Mrs. Thatcher put it. Yet, for all the glasnost reforms pursued by Mr. Gorbachev, the Soviet communist state apparatus remained intact and continued to be a monster till its last day in existence.

So, those who watch the situation in contemporary China may need to remind themselves frequently of the history of the former Soviet Union, because after the 1949 communist takeover, the Soviet political model (the monstrous Stalinist communist state apparatus) was transplanted in China by the late Chairman Mao Zedong, who like Stalin was a great dictator.

The communist state apparatus in China has an official name: "Proletarian Dictatorship". To fool the Chinese people, the late Chairman Mao Zedong said that his regime was a "People's Democratic Dictatorship" which would grant "democracy" to "the people" but would at the same time deal out harsh dictatorship to his enemies. The history of Mao's Cultural Revolution indicates that under Mao's "People's Democratic Dictatorship", those who allowed themselves to be enslaved by the communist state apparatus without protest survived while those who expressed their misgivings about the system in any form got crushed. During the leftist Mao era, "the people" definitely referred to the former, not the latter.

Even today, after two decades of reforms and openness to the outside world, the Communist Party's definition of "the people" remains problematic, because as we can see, "the people" certainly does not include those who speak out against communism and the Communist Party. Those who do so are either jailed or exiled by the communist authorities as "the enemies of the people". In China's rubber-stamp parliament, The National People's Congress, there isn't a single voice speaking out against communism and the Communist Party, because those opposed to communism and the Communist Party are regarded as "the enemies of the people" and so are not represented in the "People's Congress".

The Communist Party always claims to represent the interests of the people of the entire country. While it is true that the Communist Party has indeed introduced economic reforms in the interest of the people since 1979 resulting in far more economic freedoms for the people than ever before, it also has a history of committing serious mistakes (and crimes) against the interests of the people:

For starters, it was the Communist Party that transplanted the model of central planning from the Soviet Union only to cause economic stagnation. Whether the ongoing economic reforms will successfully get rid of the Soviet model remains to be seen. Chances are they won't, because the Communist Party continues to uphold the Marxist principle of "socialist state ownership" of the means of production. To put it simply, the Communist Party still wants to control the economy and the marketplace.

Secondly, it was the Communist Party that transplanted the Stalinist political model of one-party dictatorship from the Soviet Union only to enable Mao Zedong to launch the Cultural Revolution and plunge the country into a disaster. Then the Communist Party allowed the Cultural Revolution to continue for ten long and dark years until Mao died because the Party had no mechanism to keep its leader, Mao, in check as long as he was alive.

The Communist Party now admits that the Cultural Revolution was a disastrous mistake but blames the disaster on Mao's close ally Lin Biao and Mao's wife Jiang Qing, not on the Communist Party itself and its leader Mao Zedong. So, it seems that although the Communist Party claims to represent the interests of the people, its leaders do not believe that the Party has to take responsibility for its actions and mistakes. What they do is to blame the defeated faction in power struggle and claim the Party is capable of correcting its own mistakes. As to the late leader of the Communist Party, Mao Zedong, though it is well-known that Mao Zedong launched the Cultural Revolution that bankrupted the Chinese economy and caused the deaths of countless innocent people, thereby perpetrating a high crime, the Communist Party refuses to condemn Mao Zedong as a criminal and expects the people to believe that Mao was a great man. Yet, the fact that Mao Zedong had his long-time colleague State President Liu Shaoqi persecuted and tortured to death belies any claim that Mao was a virtuous man.

Furthermore, the Communist Party chose to call in troops to crack down on unarmed protestors at Tiananmen Square in June of 1989 rather than to promise democratic political reforms. And, now, it maintains that the military crackdown was a correct course of action, not a mistake at all.

The Chinese people didn't give the Communist Party any authorization to lead the economy into a blind alley called "central-planning", or to continue the Cultural Revolution for ten years, or to impose one-party dictatorship forever. It is the Communist Party that made these choices on behalf of the country and claimed they were in the best interest of the Chinese people. History has proven the Communist Party wrong. There is no proof whatsoever anywhere in the world that one-party dictatorship serves the people's best interests, now that all the one-party dictatorships in Eastern Europe have been discarded by the people there, whereas the people of communist North Korea are literally starving under one-party dictatorship, though, to be fair, I must hasten to point out that the ongoing market-oriented economic reforms started by the late paramount leader Deng Xiaoping have made China's one-party rule more bearable than before.

"Proletarian Dictatorship" and "People's Democratic Dictatorship" both sound scary because they suggest clearly that the functions of the communist state apparatus are poised to serve the purposes of dictators, not reformers, and the history of the Communist Party certainly bears out this pessimistic view of mine.

Even a casual look at the stories of some ordinary Chinese citizens is likely to reveal a lot about the nature of China's communist state apparatus. One story goes: Mr. Li Zhiyou (born in 1970) scrawled some words on the walls of certain department store toilets as well as on a few public notice boards. He soon got into serious trouble, because the authorities didn't like what he had written in the toilets: "There's no human rights under the leadership of the Communist Party"; "The police are bandits" etc. These words may be quite true or only partially true or completely or partially untrue. They just reflect what Mr. Li thought of the leadership of the Communist Party. The problem was he chose to express his views in the form of public toilet graffiti. If China's communist state apparatus respected such human rights as freedom of expression, nothing would have happened to Mr. Li. Unfortunately, expression of anti-communist views and sentiments is a felony in communist China and so Mr. Li was arrested in December of 1998 and sentenced to three years' imprisonment in May of 1999.

Another story: Mr. Lin Hai (born in 1968), a Shanghai software company executive, was arrested in March of 1998. His crime? Mr. Lin had exchanged E-mail addresses with overseas Internet publishers. Unfortunately for him, one of the publishers held strong anti-communist views and sent its anti-communist content to the addresses provided by Lin. To punish Mr. Lin for exchanging E-mail addresses with that overseas Internet publisher, a Shanghai "People's Court" handed down a two-year jail sentence. Nothing could be more absurd than such punishment.

Mr. Lin's wife said her husband was an apolitical guy who was only interested in exchanging E-mail addresses with overseas Internet pals.

But being apolitical may have put Mr. Lin at a disadvantage, because his lack of interest in political issues led to his ignorance of the nature of the communist state apparatus, and that was his undoing. Apparently, he had little knowledge of how the communist state apparatus operated and so got involved in things that apolitical guys like himself shouldn't get involved in under communist China's political realities. But, here is the question: Is China's communist state apparatus a monster?

I prefer to call China's communist state apparatus Stalinist because the term serves as a good reminder of its nature to Western readers. After all, the communist system was transplanted by China's late Great Dictator Mao Zedong from the Soviet Union after the 1949 revolution. Besides, the official name of the communist state "The People's Republic of China" is alleged to have been granted by none other than Joseph Stalin himself as he considered communist China to be just another satellite state under the leadership of the Soviet Union like "The People's Republic of Mongolia", "The People's Republic of Poland", "The People's Democratic Republic of Korea" etc.

However, some experts in Chinese affairs have dug deep into history and come up with findings that may shed new light on the nature of China's communist state apparatus. According to these findings, Mao Zedong added a few feudalistic touches to his state control machine. Being a diligent student of Chinese history, Mao had a perfect knowledge of the various methods employed by ancient Chinese emperors to control state power. His focus was on the spy control system established by the first emperor of the Ming Dynasty, Zhu Yuan Zhang, which consisted of three divisions: (1) "Dong Chang"; (2) "Xi Chang"; and (3) "Jin Yi Wei". "Dong Chang" was an office for eunuchs appointed by the emperor to monitor the people's activities. "Xi Chang" was another office for eunuchs but its function was to monitor the internal affairs of the emperor's court. "Jin Yi Wei" was the palace guard. The three divisions of the spy control system all had unquestionable allegiance to the emperor himself and were well organized and highly effective in gathering the kind of information that the emperor needed. The feudalistic period in Chinese history lasted for more than two thousand years, but the Ming Dynasty (1368—1644) was the real heyday of ancient Chinese spies. No wonder, Mao had a special interest in the history of the Ming Dynasty.

After he gained absolute power to control the Communist Party, Mao Zedong established a three-division spy control system just as Emperor Zhu Yuan Zhang did. He appointed one close confidant Xie Fuzhi as head of the Central Political Security Department and another close confidant Kang Sheng as head of the Central Political and Legal Commission. In addition, he established the third division of his control system in the military—the Third Branch of the General Staff under the Communist Party's Central Military Commission.

Mao's spy infiltration mechanism was far more effective than Emperor Zhu Yuan Zhang's spy system. Working for Mao's intelligence gathering operation were two types of spies: the grassroots spies and the senior-level spies. The grassroots spies' task was to monitor the activities of ordinary people and lower-level party and government officials. The senior-level spies had a far more important role to play—they had to monitor the activities of senior party and government officials including the members of the Central Committee of the Communist Party and the ministers of the central government as well as the senior officials of the party, the government and the military working in the provinces.

During the leftist Mao era, "Accusation/Exposure Boxes" were installed all over the country. In shape, they looked like ordinary letter boxes. In nature, they were anything but ordinary. An informant could put any anonymous material into an Accusation/Exposure Box, accusing anybody of any crime without incurring any liability. If the authorities knew the identity of the informant, the strict rules of confidentiality would prevent the name of the informant from being disclosed to the accused. If the authorities suspected a man of involvement in seditious activity, they would first of all contact his friends, colleagues and even relatives to get information that could be used against him.

After the 1949 communist revolution, Mao Zedong forbade the members of the Communist Party's central leadership to have private bodyguards. Their bodyguards had to be appointed and therefore controlled by the Central Security Guard Bureau and had to be rotated periodically. The Central Security Guard Bureau did everything possible to ensure that these bodyguards had unquestionable allegiance to the chairman of the party's Central Committee, Mao Zedong, because they had to play a double role in their relations with the senior officials, that is, to ensure the physical safety of the senior officials as well as to monitor their activities. If a senior official's speech or conduct suggested he was opposed to Mao Zedong's position on any issue, his bodyguard (plus informant) would report to the Central Security Guard Bureau. Then, if Mao decided to put him under arrest, the Central Security Guard Bureau would dispatch its personnel to carry out the arrest.

During the Cultural Revolution (1966—1976), Mao's political rival, State President Liu Shaoqi, was kept under house arrest by his own bodyguards, who scolded and tortured Mr. Liu for nearly three years, breaking his legs and ribs. They gave Mr. Liu only one meal every three days and forced him to eat on the floor just like a dog. They didn't allow Mr. Liu to wash his face, to take a bath, or to have his hair cut. Sometimes, they tied his limbs to his bed to prevent him from moving. By the time he died, his hair and beard had grown several feet long. Apparently, Mao had given instructions to the bodyguards to the effect that Liu Shaoqi had to be eliminated, but it was up to the bodyguards to decide how to carry out Mao's instructions.

The appointments of senior party and government officials' secretaries were also controlled by Mao Zedong. During the Mao era, each senior party or government official had several secretaries. His security secretary would be appointed by the Central Security Guard Bureau, while his confidential secretary would be appointed by the Central Confidentiality Bureau. In addition, the Secretary Bureau of the Office of the Central Committee would appoint a political secretary, a language secretary and an everyday-life secretary for him. Like the bodyguards, these secretaries had unquestionable allegiance to the supreme leader of the Communist Party, Mao Zedong. In case a senior official's speech or conduct suggested he was opposed to Mao's position on any issue, his secretaries would instantly become informants and report to their respective controllers according to "the principles of organization" of the Communist Party. If his speech or conduct was regarded as seriously in breach of the party line, some spy master would report his case directly to the Great Leader Chairman Mao. Then it was up to Mao to decide his fate. As indicated by the tragic death of State President Liu Shaoqi, the Great Leader was not a generous man.

What about the senior officials' service personnel such as domestic servants, cooks, janitors, medics, and chauffeurs? They were all appointed and controlled by the Service Bureau under the Office of the Central Committee of the Chinese Communist Party. Before they could enter the houses of the senior officials, the Service Bureau would stringently screen their backgrounds and gave them vocational training. Apart from providing services to meet the various everyday life needs of the senior officials and their families, the service personnel had a secret "political task", that is, to report to their respective controllers about the activities of the senior officials on a regular basis.

Throughout his life, the Great Leader, Mao Zedong, maintained a horrible secret "special-case" investigation system, under which Mao could appoint a "special-case team" at any time to investigate any senior official he suspected of disloyalty. Once such an investigation began, the "special-case team" would immediately detain the senior official in question and keep him incommunicado. There was no regulation to oblige the "special-case team" to announce the arrest. Thus, there was no need to start public legal proceedings, and the public would never know the details of the case.

A "special-case team" normally consisted of five to seven members plus some personnel appointed by the Central Security Guard Bureau or the Public Security Ministry, who were all loyal to the Great Leader and ready to use intimidation, coercion and torture to make the senior official under investigation confess to all the crimes allegedly committed by him. Quite a few senior officials committed suicide or were tortured to death while being investigated by "special-case teams" during the leftist Mao era.

In recent Chinese history, all the well-known reformers have suffered miserably. During the Cultural Revolution (1966—1976), Deng Xiaoping, who was Secretary General of the Communist Party at the time, was severely criticized for his reformist economic theories, condemned as a "capitalist-roader" and then put under house arrest. Deng's like-minded colleague, State President Liu Shaoqi, was arrested and tortured and then died under the dubious circumstances of Chairman Mao's "People's Democratic Dictatorship".

After Deng was reinstated in office in 1977, he made his close ally Hu Yaobang (another well-known reformer) Secretary General of the Chinese Communist Party. Hu Yaobang was out-spoken, sincere and very popular in the reformist camp. But these qualities of his made him intolerable to the conservative left-wing forces, who staged a coup, so to speak, and ousted Hu Yaobang in early 1987. According to some reports in Hong Kong's Chinese press, after he was removed from office, Mr. Hu Yaobang was virtually under house arrest until his death in spring of 1989, which sparked off the historic student demonstrations at Tiananmen Square.

After the ouster of Hu Yaobang, Deng Xiaoping made Zhao Ziyang (another of his allies) Secretary General of the Chinese Communist Party. Zhao Ziyang was a well-known and successful economic reformer who had earlier made China's agriculture more productive by allowing Chinese farmers to run their own business on a household contractual basis, but his style in addressing China's political issues such as ideological liberalization were absolutely unacceptable to the conservative left wing of the Communist Party. When the students of Beijing staged their demonstrations after Hu Yaobang's death in spring of 1989, Zhao Ziyang appeared sympathetic toward the students. He tried to persuade the students to leave Tiananmen Square but all to no avail. Later, he was also ousted and was condemned as being supportive of the student demonstrations and the civil unrest.

According to reports in Hong Kong's Chinese press, Mr. Zhao Ziyang remains under house arrest to this day, his every move subject to the approval of the Politburo of the Communist Party. Whatever the truth, one thing is for sure: It is a dicey business to make reforms in China, especially if reforms expand into such uncharted territories as political liberalization, freedom of expression, freedom of the press, political pluralism and so on, since they continue to be the Communist Party's forbidden areas.

While touring southern China in early 1992, Deng Xiaoping said that historically, leftist influences in China had been strong and scary. These very words from the mouth of the late paramount leader of communist China should serve to convince us that China's communist state apparatus with its strong, traditional leftist influences is a monster which not only intimidates ordinary people, but scares China's reformers as well. If Deng regarded leftist influences as scary, who else would have the courage and strength to tackle leftist influences and reform the monstrous communist state apparatus?

Will President Jiang Zemin take up this role? By all appearances, Mr. Jiang is either unable or unwilling (or probably unable and therefore unwilling) to make the necessary political changes to tame the monster, given the risks described above. This does not mean that Mr. Jiang Zemin is a monster. But it is important to remember that the communist state apparatus of which Jiang is the leader remains a monster and that Jiang would have to act in accordance with the wishes of the monstrous communist state apparatus when necessary.

China's dissidents accuse President Jiang Zemin of wanting to become a dictator. President Jiang says that's not true. He says those who know him well should understand that he has no intention of becoming a dictator. While there is no hard evidence that personally, President Jiang wants to become a Mao-type great dictator, the communist state apparatus may give him little choice. First of all, as mentioned above, the official name of the communist state apparatus is "Proletarian Dictatorship", so the group of senior communist party officials who constitute China's leadership is a dictatorship with absolute power. There are no checks and balances between separate branches of government, since all political entities in communist China are under the leadership of the Communist Party. Balance of power, if any, under the current system might exist between the moderates and the conservative hardliners. The liberals who have serious doubts about Marxism-Leninism are not strong enough to show their true colors.

Secondly, even if personally, President Jiang chooses not to act like a dictator, the communist state apparatus would expect China's leadership to act like a dictatorship. The conservative leftist forces of the Communist Party would expect President Jiang to act like a communist dictator. If President Jiang acts like a liberal, he could put his own safety and the safety of his family in jeopardy, because no one can guarantee that the conservative hardliners of the Communist Party will not conspire against any liberal-minded party leader. In fact, China's conservative leftist forces have never hesitated to plot against those who intended to pull China out of its Marxist-Leninist quagmire. China's constitution, which was formulated by the late Chairman Mao Zedong to guarantee that his dictatorship would last forever, stipulates that the country must remain under the leadership and therefore the control of the Communist Party in accordance with the principles of Marxism-Leninism. The hardliners can always use the constitution to crush any attempt by the liberals to liberalize the old system, whereas any Chinese citizen who dares to openly question the legitimacy of the Chinese constitution would certainly end up in jail.

The hardliners have a strong weapon in their hands, that is, Marxism-Leninism. Whereas the man in the street may snigger at Marxism-Leninism as being irrelevant to his life, the Communist Party continues to hold Marxism-Leninism as its totem, and the basic Marxist principles of state ownership of the means of production and one-party rule are creeds that the Communist Party does not allow its members to break.

One of the Communist Party's late senior leaders, Mr. Chen Yun—a true believer in Marxist economics—said in life that China's socialist planned economy, otherwise known as command economy, was and should remain a "bird cage economy". He compared China's centrally planned economy to a bird and the principles of Marxism to a bird cage and cautioned China's reformers against allowing the bird to fly out of the cage. If the reformers abide by Mr. Chen's instructions, allowing the bird to fly only within the boundaries of Marxism, very little can be achieved in the way of economic reforms.

Likewise, China's political reform could be compared to a bird and the principles of Marxism to a bird cage. The liberals may want to pave the way for real political reform and democratization, but the conservative left wing keeps reminding the reformers that they must cling to Marxist creeds and must not allow political reform to go beyond the principles of Marxism-Leninism. That is as good as to say, "You can make political changes but must not change the Communist Party's one-party rule. You can make economic reforms but must maintain the Communist Party's control of the economy."

Thus, as we can see, the reformers' hands are tied by the principles of the Communist Party's ruling philosophy, Marxism-Leninism. In order to get round the ideological barriers set up by the left-wing hardliners, the reformers have to claim that their reformist measures are in line with socialist principles. For instance, while the hardliners condemn market economics as capitalist-oriented, the reformers insist that China's socialist economy should also respect the rules of the market-place, thereby becoming a "socialist market economy". Eager to help the reformers, China's well-known liberal economist Hu Jinlian has worked hard toward providing a theoretical basis for China's economic reforms. For instance, he claims that China's socialist economy also has a mar-ketplace to deal with.

Such silly debate is just an indication of the difficult situation con-fronting China's reformers. The following anecdote will illustrate how the hardliners could influence the behavior of any party secretary gen-eral in China:

As mentioned above, Mr. Hu Yaobang was a popular, liberal-minded secretary general of the Communist Party during the 1980s. But under the pressures of the communist party apparatus, even Mr. Hu, the party secretary general, had to act out of character and speak like a left-wing hardliner on certain occasions. For instance, in summer of 1981, a meeting in memory of one of China's best-known pre-revolution authors, Lu Xun, was held in Beijing's People's Hall. At the meeting, Mr. Hu Yaobang delivered a speech. To the astonishment of the liberal-minded intellectuals present, he suddenly started to accuse certain authors of being once again involved in "anti-communist party activ-ity". Saying that some authors intended "to stab our party in the back," he threatened punishment. Yet, on the afternoon of the same day, he convened an emergency meeting to explain to the senior members of China's literary community that the written version of his morning speech had been altered beyond recognition by some party heavy-weights and that he had had no alternative but to read accordingly.

Many people in the West may consider China's communist system to be an enigmatic operation run by unfathomable officials of the Communist Party, so they tend to do simple deduction and ask such questions as: "Since communism is such a bad system, why don't they scrap it?" "Who are they?" "Are they bad guys or what?" Undoubtedly, "they" refers to the officials of the Communist Party, and the questions are as straight-forward as the ones that kids tend to ask when watching a Hollywood action movie: "Is he the bad guy?" "Is he the good guy?" But the reality in China is far more complicated than Hollywood fiction. As mentioned above, once the Stalinist political model is set up, it is hard to transform and even harder to scrap. It takes more than just "the good guys" to change the horrendous system. In many cases, "the good guys" don't have the upper hand. So, while communism is definitely a bad system originated from the former Soviet Union, to label all communist party officials as "bad guys" may be coming it a bit strong.

Take Mr. Hu Yaobang as an example. Mr. Hu joined the communist revolution as a teenager, naively believing that the revolution would save China from corruption and injustice since in his view, there could be no corruption and injustice under communism. After the 1949 revolution, he was appointed to take charge of the Communist Youth League and became a protégé of the then Secretary General Deng Xiaoping. During the Cultural Revolution, he was persecuted by the leftist radicals. After Mao Zedong died in September 1976, Mr. Hu became Deng Xiaoping's right-hand man and started to rehabilitate a large number of people who had been persecuted during the Mao era. Soon it became known to the country that Mr. Hu Yaobang was a man of character and integrity who helped the helpless. In other words, Mr. Hu was definitely a good guy. But in early 1987, because of his liberal inclinations, he was severely condemned by the conservative forces of the Communist Party, ousted and put under house arrest until he died of broken heart in spring of 1989. No injustice under communism?

Many true believers in Marxist ideologies have suffered horrendous misery or even died tragic deaths under communism, because at least in the beginning they were too naive to know what communism was all about—in short, communism denies the individual what he is entitled to and gives the leader excessive power to control the individual in the name of collective interest, thereby restricting individual innovation to a minimum. Some of the true believers never managed to figure it out. Some of them did, but by the time they did figure it out, it was too late—they had gotten so deep in the game that everything about their lives was already controlled by the Communist Party—everything ranging from their livelihood to their access to information. An irony of life? A practical joke by Fate? Or, rather, the inevitable consequence of misguided faith?

Now, back to the sad story of Secretary General Hu Yaobang: Though sympathetic toward Hu Yaobang, under the communist system, the Chinese people didn't have a say as to who should be their leader. In the meantime, the leadership of the Communist Party apparently didn't believe that ordinary Chinese people's kind feelings toward Mr. Hu Yaobang deserved its attention at all when it decided to remove Mr. Hu unceremoniously. Yet, Mr. Hu's death grieved and angered the students of Beijing to such an extent that they took to the streets and placed countless wreaths in memory of Mr. Hu at the People's Heros Monument in Tiananmen Square. This was their way of saying to the arrogant Communist Party hierarchy that the injustice of the communist system was unacceptable to them. The strong emotion and sorrow they expressed over Mr. Hu's death seemed to indicate that they suspected that the injustice of the Party's decision to oust Hu Yaobang had killed him. Later, as the citizens of Beijing joined the students, the scale of the protests grew beyond control and frightened the Communist Party so much that it called out troops to crack down on the protesters, sparking off the historic event now known as the June 4th 1989 Tiananmen Square Massacre.

While the story of Mr. Hu Yaobang is indeed a tragedy, it is also proof that the officials of the Communist Party are not all "bad guys". The truth is that "the good guys" in the Communist Party often suffer if they fail to toe the party line strictly. It would be prudent to presume that "the good guys" are still there but that they may need time to find ways to introduce the necessary changes without causing too much of a shock to the country. Yes, the old system is a monster, but to kill the old system abruptly might cause instant chaos and anarchy among a population of ONE BILLION AND THREE HUNDRED MILLION, even if there were some kind of a Hercules capable of killing the monster. The mere statistics on China's population growth are scary. First of all, this figure (1.30 billion) accounts for 22% of the world population. In the 21st century, China's population will snowball to more alarming proportions and could reach one billion and six hundred million by 2050. China's arable land, which accounts for only 7% of the world's arable land at present, continues to shrink by more than five million mu (about 333,500 hectares) per annum. Unable to find livelihood in their native villages, large crowds of peasants are leaving for the cities to find work, whereas the already overcrowded cities are experiencing difficulties in handling the serious issue of unemployment. By rough estimates, China's urban jobless population exceeds 25 million.

Stability is really important to China, because it provides a basis for economic development, which in turn creates business opportunities for the rest of the world, whereas any unrest in China could cause shock waves through global financial markets, given the high exposure that U.S. and European multinational corporations have in Asia. Hopefully, China's leaders will come to conclude that democratization will enhance stability and prosperity if properly implemented. The communist party machine should at least allow the various factions of the Party the freedom to express their different views and opinions at internal meetings as a step toward the internal democratization of the Communist Party itself—probably with President Jiang Zemin as the mediator.

But it seems that the Communist Party is worried that democratization will cause instability and chaos. Basically speaking, that is a symptom of paranoia. First, for all the complaints and grievances China's liberal-minded intellectuals might have against the old system, they are not at all radicals bent on overthrowing the current leadership. Secondly, they certainly don't have the capability to do so. Besides, the growing private sector of the economy offers them numerous opportunities to become financially successful. They may continue to complain but are not likely to go to extremes. In the 1980s, China's liberal-minded intellectuals never demanded the removal of Secretary General Hu Yaobang or Secretary General Zhao Ziyang. On the contrary, they appeared to be pleased with the two party leaders' moderate images. It was the left wing of the Communist Party that caused the downfall of both Hu Yaobang and Zhao Ziyang. So, the left wing of the Communist Party could very well be a source of instability. After all, who plunged China into the abyss of political disaster called "The Great Proletarian Cultural Revolution" in the 1960s? It was the left wing of the Communist Party. The moderates were too weak to restrain Mao Zedong and his leftist allies.

Today, there is no evidence that China's liberal-minded intellectuals would like to see the removal of President Jiang Zemin or Premier Zhu Rongji. Chinese are very pragmatic human beings—they want prosperity and stability, meaning they want to make money under stable conditions. Their logic is simple: If the two men, Jiang and Zhu, can keep things going, why bother? Also, they know to run the country and its economy is a tough job. It requires expertise and experience. Ironically, no matter how much liberal-minded intellectuals may dislike the status quo, the reality is that after more than half a century of one-party rule, nearly all those with expertise and experience in government work are now inside the Communist Party. Although people complain about the old system, they still hope the leaders will reform the Communist Party and introduce something new. They would like to have prosperity and stability under democracy. That, if achieved, would be something new in China.

As an episode that took place in Buyun Township in early 1999 indicates, political democratization could help the ruling party, rather than destabilize the situation. Buyun is a very poor rural township with no highway passing by. It is more than 50 kilometers away from Suining Municipality, Sichuan Province. The only access to the township is an earthen road that becomes muddy whenever rain pours. Over the years, the only way of financial survival for the people of the township has been to leave home and find work elsewhere. Originally, there was a small registered population of about 16,000 people. Now, more than 4,000 of that population have already left. Many families live on small remittances from relatives working out of town. Life is definitely not easy for the locals. The pressures of poverty have led to many grievances among those still living in the township. At the end of 1998 when the tenure of the township chief was about to expire, the township's peasants strongly demanded that they hold direct elections to produce a good township chief to lead them out of poverty.

The communist party committee of the township referred the matter to the party committee of Suining Municipality. Worried that the peasants' grievances could lead to unrest and street demonstrations, the communist party committee of the municipality decided to let the peasants elect a "good township chief" to take charge of the township's economic development. In the final round of elections, there were three candidates, of whom, two were peasants. The third candidate was a communist party official by the name of Tan Xiaoqiu, who eventually won the election, because most voters decided that it would be in their interest to elect somebody with experience in township government work to handle the township's economic affairs. Buyun's direct elections created no chaos. Instead, this small step toward democratization enhanced stability and may have even given the ruling party some kind of an aura of legitimacy.

One option available to the Communist Party is to allow the communist state apparatus to become less severe, so that some kind of a compromise arrangement acceptable to both the Communist Party and China's liberal intellectual community could emerge. Yet, until a really democratic and pluralistic mechanism is eventually born in China, even party liberals may have to continue to mimic the Marxist rhetoric of the Communist Party, because they, too, have to submit to party discipline in order to survive under the system. So, it is difficult to tell who "the good guys" are, because in public, both "the good guys" (the party liberals) and "the bad guys" (the leftist conservatives) claim to uphold "the banner of Marxism". No matter how ridiculous "the banner of Marxism" may appear in the eyes of the rest of the world, that is the brand name under which the Communist Party runs its business. Whoever confesses that he has recanted Marxism-Leninism gets kicked out of the ruling party. If all "the good guys" confess they no longer believe in Marxism-Leninism, they are all out. Then, who's going to mitigate the excesses of the old system? Remember that the moderates (and liberals) are in a position to mitigate the unbearable, only if they stay in the Communist Party. To a great extent, whether China will have a really democratic political system depends on the wisdom of the moderates and liberals. They will have to decide when to do the right thing. After all, it is their lives which are being affected by the system.

It doesn't take a genius to see that there has always been a tacit alliance between "the good guys" (the party liberals) and China's liberal intellectuals, because while the party liberals need the support of the liberal intellectual community to push the reforms, both economic and political, the liberal intellectuals look to the party liberals to give them the green light to aspire for more freedom of expression. Besides, since the party liberals cannot openly voice their misgivings about Marxism-Leninism, they would like to see such basic Marxist concepts as state ownership of enterprises and one-party dictatorship challenged by liberal intellectuals.

As a rule, party liberals are fond of phrases like "emancipation of thought" and "break through forbidden areas". For instance, in early 1998, China's well-known party liberal and elderly statesman Wan Li again called for "emancipation of thought" in four areas: (1) reform; (2)

economic development; (3) the existing political system and legal system; (4) Marxist theories.

What does that mean? It seems that the well-known party liberal was telling people that something was seriously wrong with China's communist system and the Marxist principles of the Communist Party because the old system and the principles of Marxism were blocking China's economic reform and economic development. Mr. Wan Li is a highly respected figure in China with an impeccable record of contributions to the country, which fact may have emboldened him to signal his displeasure with the status quo, though he didn't openly challenge Marxism. But if the Communist Party is really going to "emancipate thought" on Marxism, the only possible result would be for the Party to dump this whimsical Utopian ideology from the 19th century on the ashes of history. Thus, shortly after Mr. Wan Li spoke on "emancipation of thought", the Secretariat of the Central Committee of the Communist Party issued a directive to the effect that some of Comrade Wan Li's opinions deviated from the party line and therefore shouldn't be publicized. Apparently, the Communist Party didn't want China's liberal intellectuals to take advantage of Mr. Wan Li's views on "emancipation of thought" in advancing their cause for further liberalization.

The leftist conservatives of the Communist Party hate this tacit alliance between the liberal intellectuals and the party liberals. If they see evidence that a certain liberal-minded party official is closely associated with the liberal intellectuals, they'll go after the liberal-minded party official. For instance, former Secretary General Hu Yaobang appeared to be very friendly toward some liberal intellectuals. Were the hardliners watching him? Maybe. Anyway, the hardliners started to accuse Mr. Hu Yaobang of instigating "bourgeois liberalization" in the mid 1980s and eventually ousted him in early 1987. The tragedy of Mr. Hu Yaobang suggests that party officials need to keep their distance from the liberal intellectuals, because the hardliners would suspect them of conspiring with the liberal intellectuals to instigate "bourgeois liberalization" if they appeared to be too close to the intellectuals.

Presumably, President Jiang Zemin is in a more tenable position today than Mr. Hu Yaobang was, since most of the members of the Old Guard—the senior leaders of the communist revolution—are now dead. But by all appearances, Jiang Zemin is a cautious man who needs the cooperation of the conservative hardliners and so certainly does not want to displease them.

In spring of 1998, a book entitled "Cross Swords" was published in China under the auspices of a member of President Jiang's think tank, Mr. Liu Ji. The book discusses the status of "emancipation of thought" in China. An apparent production by the liberals designed to give China's reforms a boost, "Cross Swords" praises the late paramount leader Deng Xiaoping and his reforms as well as President Jiang Zemin. Understandably, soon after the book's release, the left-wing conservatives started to attack the book and Mr. Liu Ji.

At last, President Jiang Zemin found it necessary to make his comments known to the public. To observers' surprise, President Jiang didn't criticize the conservatives. Instead, he criticized the book compiled by his own man, Mr. Liu Ji. He said the book contained too much criticism of leftist tendencies and too little criticism of rightist tendencies. In Chinese politics, the liberals are regarded as leaning toward the right, while the conservatives are regarded as leaning toward the left. In order to avoid being regarded as leaning toward the right by the conservatives, President Jiang chose to criticize the liberal intellectuals. Obviously, he was anxious to distance himself from the liberals. Given the political reality in China, President Jiang may have done the right thing to keep himself out of trouble, though it may not have been the right thing to keep reforms out of trouble. The story shows that though the liberals are now able to make limited inroads in the ideological arena, the left-wing conservative forces are still very strong. Whoever thinks democracy is dawning in China must be out of touch with reality, because the rules of the game in Chinese politics remain the same as in the 1980s. Namely, in order to survive under the system, a communist party official has to uphold Marxism-Leninism on all public occasions. He must not act like a liberal. He must make it clear that he is not leaning toward the right.

In all probability, President Jiang Zemin does not have the stamina to transform the monstrous communist state apparatus even if he wants to. He knows the communist state apparatus could jump out of control and devour him as it did the previous secretaries general of the Communist Party if he is not careful. The current situation in China does not project a stable picture where President Jiang Zemin could issue an order to scrap the communist system and then sit back, waiting for his order to be executed (even if that were his intention). To think that President Jiang Zemin has absolute control of China's communist state apparatus and so is able to make major changes singlehandedly is to have a delusion.

As mentioned above, even the late paramount leader Deng Xiaoping had to listen to voices critical of his market-oriented economic reforms and make concessions to his conservative colleagues. It is inconceivable that a technocrat like Jiang Zemin with no experience in the military could command absolute control and power to introduce fundamental changes to the communist state apparatus in the near future, though rumors have it that at one time, Jiang instructed his aides to explore various possibilities for political reform, that Jiang's aides compiled a manual on democracy for high-ranking officials to read, that Jiang showed some interest in other countries' presidential systems and appointed Mr. Chang Baigang (deputy director of Political Research Institute of the Academy of Social Sciences) to prepare a report on the various presidential systems around the world, and that Jiang was quite impressed with what he saw in the United States during his 1997 visit there, especially America's political system.

The question is what kind of political change the Communist Party is willing to accept. In China, names are often deceptive. For example,

"People's Democracy" sounds good but is not democracy at all in the true sense of the term. Likewise, "possibilities for political reform" sounds good but may not forebode full-scale democratization. To be sure, it won't. Pessimism notwithstanding, President Jiang Zemin seems to have taken a small step in allowing China's numerous rural villages to hold elections at the grassroots level. Whether the demands of China's enormous rural population will be truthfully voiced in the National People's Congress remains to be seen, because the Communist Party's track record shows it has a strong penchant for manipulation in order to ensure the results of elections serve its interests. That is to say, whatever plans may be in the making to mollify the people, the Communist Party will not allow changes to destabilize its control over power. The officials of the Communist Party are a privileged group, whereas political reforms would certainly restrict or damage their privileges. That's why only a small number of liberal-minded party officials would accept political reform and democratization. The majority of party officials are likely to oppose political reform. Much of the talk about "socialist democracy" is just lip service to fool the people. Only an idiot brainwashed by the Communist Party would believe in "socialist democracy" under a communism dictatorship!

The above-mentioned rumors about political reform may indicate the likelihood of limited relaxation, since they seem to have originated from people close to President Jiang Zemin's staff. But in China, rumors are often used as trial balloons to serve political purposes. First, the rumors are signaling to China's liberal-minded intellectuals that President Jiang Zemin intends to do something about political reform, thereby taking the wind out of the intellectuals' sails or even winning some support from them. Secondly, the trial balloons will help President Jiang Zemin's aides to gauge the extent of support or opposition to political reform among party officials as well as ordinary people.

In addition, those rumors about possible political reform in China could be an indication of differences of opinion between the leftist conservatives and the moderates and liberals in the Communist Party on whether and how political changes should be made to alleviate the problems confronting the communist regime.

The risk is that the rumors may have raised people's expectations for political reform beyond what the Communist Party is prepared to deliver. In the past, talk about political reform used to emerge before a major event erupted. For instance, there was persistent talk about political reform in the few years preceding the Tiananmen Square student protests in spring of 1989. But at last, as we know, the Communist Party decided to carry on with one-party dictatorship and suppressed the protests by force. To put it bluntly, as long as the Communist Party is reluctant to bury communism, political reform in China is likely to become a wild-goose chase.

5

Permission to Found Political Organizations?

In early September 1998, China's State Council issued a directive allowing Chinese citizens to apply for permission to form political organizations. But the same directive provided that the political platforms and charters of all political organizations had to be examined and their principal members investigated by government authorities before permission was granted or denied, that seditious political activities by those seeking to form political organizations would be punished, and that political activities by those who applied to form political organizations with the intention of overthrowing the government with the help of foreign anti-communist forces would be dealt with according to the law.

As we can see, the draconian restrictions specified in the State Council directive turned the so-called "permission for Chinese citizens to form political organizations" into a joke. But soon after the issuance of the State Council directive, a certain number of people in Zhejiang Province, Shandong Province, Hunan Province, Hubei Province, Liaoning Province, Jilin Province, Heilongjiang Province, Jiangsu Province, Beijing and Shanghai submitted applications to local government authorities for permission to form a political party by the name of

"The Chinese Democratic Party". In Nanjing (Jiangsu Province), Xuzhou (Shandong Province) and Hefei (Anhui Province), some intellectuals (including five committee members of provincial Political Consultative Conferences) submitted applications to form "The Socialist Party of China".

What happened to these applicants? According to media reports, shortly after the United Nations High Commissioner for Human Rights, Mrs. Robinson, concluded her visit to China in September 1998, the Chinese authorities outlawed The Chinese Democratic Party and the Public Security Bureaus (i.e. the police) around the country started surveillance over those involved in founding The Chinese Democratic Party and then arrested them. Later, some of them were released with a warning, but eventually, on December 22nd 1998, the founding members of The Chinese Democratic Party, including dissident Xu Wenli, were sentenced to outrageously long prison sentences ranging from eleven to thirteen years.

Yet earlier in the same year, the Chinese government had signed the U.N. International Covenant on Civil and Political Rights, an international treaty that safeguards the freedom of speech and the freedom of assembly, as well as other liberties. Obviously, when it comes to choosing between honoring international treaties and preserving its monopoly on political power, China's monstrous communist state apparatus stands ready to breach its international pledges without hesitation.

The above-mentioned crackdown on political dissidents illustrates clearly that it is hard to trust the communist regime to honor international treaties, because in its glossary, every term is defined according to its needs, one of which is to maintain absolute control over political power. Thus, the Western World is inevitably in dispute with Beijing on human rights issues as Beijing interprets international treaties in its own way. For instance, in China, "the freedom of speech" certainly means the freedom to say what is permissible under the communist system. Speech not permissible under the system is considered to be "counter-revolutionary" or "subversive" according to the country's communist constitution and is punishable by prison sentences ranging from three to thirteen years. It is true that President Jiang Zemin is eager to improve China's international image, so he smiles cordially whenever he meets a Western leader. But the smiles on his face won't change the monstrous nature of China's communist state apparatus.

Bill Clinton visited China in June of 1998, hoping he could help improve human rights there. He didn't for all his good intentions. He couldn't outsmart the Chinese communists. Instead, he gave communist China what it wanted: America's promise not to help and support Taiwan. The consequences of his China policy may have been an encouragement to the hardliners in the communist regime. Shortly after Bill Clinton's China visit, Beijing started to rattle its sabers, threatening to take over Taiwan by military force.

Chances are that in the Communist Party, the liberals and the hardliners are moving in opposite directions: The liberals want to introduce more political relaxation to improve China's international image, while the hardliners want to keep the situation strictly under control. Consequently, although Chinese citizens are said to have the right to form political organizations according to the State Council directive, the security forces of the communist state apparatus are poised to jail those who apply to form political organizations. In the end, the status quo—the old system—prevails, leaving the moderates to play a central role. But there must be some forces out there that caused the communist regime to issue the said State Council directive in the first place. Still, the question remains: What is the intention of the communist regime? To me, its intention is clear: It wants the rest of the world to believe that Chinese citizens are "free" to form political organizations whereas in reality they are not free to do so. It is nothing but a shameless game that the regime is frequently up to.

Even as those seeking legal permission to form political organizations ran into trouble with the authorities, some Chinese citizens appear to have formed secret organizations. At least, one such organization accused the Communist Party of having degenerated into a privileged bureaucratic class. In early September of 1998, the Communist Party Committee of Shanghai Municipality, the Government of Shanghai, the Standing Committee of the People's Congress of Shanghai, the Communist Party Group of the Political Consultative Conference of Shanghai, the Communist Party School of Shanghai, the Garrison of Shanghai, and the Armed Police Headquarters of Shanghai received copies of a document entitled "Letter To People From All Walks of Shanghai" from a secret organization called "The Socialists' Union of Shanghai".

The document, which contained more than three thousand Chinese characters, claimed that the ruling Communist Party had degenerated into a privileged bureaucratic class bent on exploiting and oppressing the people with the power in its hands. It called on communist party officials "who really love the motherland, believe in socialism and uphold the charter of the Communist Party to do soul-searching, serve the people and become true servants of the people." It said, "The officials of the Communist Party must face up to the realities of society and the demands of the people and make revisions and reforms, if they are to avoid political unrest and social retrogression." It also called on "people from all walks to launch a lawful, reasonable and rational struggle to safeguard the rights and obligations granted to the people by the Constitution." In addition, the document listed a number of examples of how party and government organizations and the leading officials of such organizations had exploited and oppressed the people both on the political level and on the economic level.

Apparently, the Communist Party is under enormous pressure to make changes amid signs that the government's efforts to reform the state-owned enterprises are facing unsurmountable difficulties, even as unemployment spirals upward and grievances against bureaucratic corruption increase. In the meantime, the collapses of various dictatorships around the world toward the end of the 20th century such as those in Eastern Europe and the Suharto regime in Indonesia which fell during the 1997-1998 Asian financial crisis must have served as a warning to President Jiang Zemin.

On November 16th, 1998, the office of China's State Council released a research report entitled "The Impact on China of the Political Situations in Indonesia and Malaysia". The document pointed out that the public had strong grievances against corruption among communist party officials and their privileges, since such corruption and privileges had led to an unfair distribution of wealth. The document warned that public grievances in China could trigger political disturbance at any time and cause the situation to deteriorate to a far more serious extent than in Indonesia. In addition, the document admitted that some college teachers and students in Beijing, Shanghai and southern China had opined that China's college teachers and students had less political rights than the teachers and students in Indonesia.

To see things in perspective, one would have to conclude that after more than twenty years of economic reform and relative openness to the outside world, today's Chinese society is quite different from what it was during the leftist Mao era when equalitarianism was the order of the day and ignorance the rule rather than the exception. So, theoretically speaking, the great changes which have taken place in China's economic and social structures since 1979 have already turned its existing political system into an awkward anachronism. Well, this is a reality that the Communist Party has to live with and adapt to.

China's perennial economic problems have worsened due to the irrationality of its political system, causing the various factions of the ruling Communist Party to propose different solutions. While the dislocations and the improper allocations of resources in the economic arena are apparent to experts, the differences of opinion between the factions as to how to resolve these problems may lead to a crisis of regime going forward.

Furthermore, apart from the party liberals and the liberal intellectuals, the number of people looking for political change has increased. Even senior party officials and members of President Jiang's think tank admit that China has to seek political reform and democratization as a way out. But it is only reasonable to presume that before taking any major step, President Jiang will have to consult the generals of the People's Liberation Army and the various factions of the Communist Party to reach some kind of a consensus. Some of the senior PLA generals were loyal followers of the late paramount leader Deng Xiaoping and have pledged allegiance to President Jiang Zemin on condition that Jiang upholds Deng's basic principles, which boil down to economic liberalization under one-party rule. It would be naive to think that all the PLA generals and all the factions of the Communist Party are in favor of political reform. Those opposed would make their displeasure known, which President Jiang would have to take into consideration in the decision-making process.

Whereas the late Chairman Mao Zedong could suppress dissent within the Communist Party by accusing his rivals of engaging in "anti-party activity", President Jiang couldn't possibly use sheer intimidation against either the conservative faction or the liberal faction. As a cautious man, he is sure to weigh the pros and the cons in the best interest of the communist regime, while listening to the opinions of the various factions of the Communist Party: the mainstream moderate faction to which Jiang himself belongs; the leftist conservative faction; and the liberal faction. Besides, since he is the president of the country, it would be rational to presume that he might have to consider the interests of hundreds of millions of ordinary Chinese citizens as well. So, the burden of responsibility that rests on his shoulder must be quite formidable.

Yet rumor has it that despite his moderate image, President Jiang Zemin does not have a high prestige with ordinary Chinese citizens. According to some analysts, President Jiang may not have a high prestige with communist party members either. That could pose a problem for him, since in order to keep the situation under control and get things done, he needs a high prestige. Oftentimes, he acts as a mediator between the various factions, pursuing a middle course. He can certainly continue in this way for a while, but not forever. Eventually, he will have to join forces with either the conservative hardliners or the liberals. To President Jiang Zemin, neither choice is palatable, since to join forces with the conservative faction would mean the end of China's economic revitalization program, while to side with the liberal faction, which is weak at least on the surface, would likely incur serious risks for himself. The cautious President Jiang Zemin is neither a Mao-type hardliner nor a Gorbachev-type liberal. While some people think Jiang is leaning toward the left, others think he is just too timid to carry through the reforms. Maybe, he is sitting on the fence, waiting to see which way the wind blows. Maybe, that is exactly why he is neither walking in dangerous territory nor enjoying great prestige with his people. But under the circumstances, what else can he do?

In order not to rock the boat, President Jiang Zemin has to keep the economic reforms on track, whereas, on the political front, some cosmetic changes to the old system might be as much as he is able or willing to do. In the meantime, although the Communist Party refuses to admit that Marxism as a political-economic philosophy is preposterous, China's economic reforms are beginning to assume quite a few capitalist characteristics—an indication of China's willingness to learn from the West at least in the economic arena. For instance, when Chinese officials send their children abroad to study, the usual destination of choice is America—not Moscow any more, certainly not communist North Korea or Cuba—because they know where their children can get the kind of education and knowledge that will be useful in business.

On the ideological front, it is getting more and more difficult for the Communist Party to control people's thinking as books and magazines deviating from orthodox Marxism (though not openly condemning Marxism) are being published. In fact, many magazine articles in China are calling for political reform and democratization. Chinese intellectuals are discussing political and economic issues, including the problems created by China's state ownership system. Some intellectuals even call for the Communist Party to change its name.

At a meeting convened in June of 1998 by the Chinese Academy of Social Sciences in celebration of the 77th anniversary of the founding of the Communist Party, the Communist Party committee of the Academy disclosed that some intellectuals in the Communist Party had proposed that the Communist Party should rename itself "The Republican Party" or "The People's Party" if it was to restore its prestige and ability to rally the people around itself. Under such circumstances, the conservatives are sure to continue to pressure President Jiang Zemin to restrict "bourgeois liberalism" or "bourgeois liberalization", even as party liberals and liberal intellectuals look to President Jiang to flash the green light for "emancipation of thought". As for the mainstream moderates like President Jiang himself, to maintain stability at all costs is probably their top priority since they fear that any dramatic move could tip the situation beyond control.

In 1998 as the Chinese government attempted to improve its relations with the United States, a limited degree of tolerance for unorthodox ideologies lasted for a short period. Perhaps, at the time, the Chinese leadership wanted the rest of the world to believe that it was trying to improve its human rights record. As mentioned in the first chapter, there was a non-governmental organization called "China Development Union" in Beijing. Periodically, it would hold discussions on sensitive political issues. Under the scrutiny of the communist authorities, "China Development Union" continued to exist till November of 1998. On October 5th 1998, the authorities even allowed the organization to hold its first National Representatives Congress, prompting Beijing intellectuals to wonder about the authorities' motive behind their permission for this political forum to exist and launch its activities.

"China Development Union" said that it intended to promote structural political reform, constitutional democracy and human rights improvement in China. But none of such goals could possibly be tolerated by any totalitarian regime for long. At one time, the organization had nearly four thousand members including a well-known dissident by the name of Xu Wenli. It even claimed to have a plan for expanding its membership to one million within three years among China's intellectual community. "China Development Union" had its own publication which printed a periodic report entitled "Green Paper On Chinese Issues".

The founder of the organization, Mr. Peng Ming, believed that a reunified China in the future including both the mainland and Taiwan should be renamed "The Federal Republic of China". (Apparently, the existing official name of the country "The People's Republic of China" sounds communist.) "China Development Union" had a human rights committee, an anti-corruption committee and a rural work committee. Mr. Peng Ming believes that China's current state land ownership system is counter-productive to the development of the country's agriculture. He says China needs some degree of private land ownership. The communist authorities tolerated the "heresies"of "China Development Union" till November of 1998, when they searched the office of the organization and confiscated Mr. Peng Ming's passport. Later, he was arrested.

If Mr. Peng Ming thought that twenty years of economic reform and relative openness to the outside world might have changed the nature of the communist state apparatus, he was completely wrong. The Beijing regime's brand name "Communist" hasn't changed. The brand name of any business reflects its nature. If the brand name remains the same, the nature of the business remains the same as well. Sooner or later, its true colors will be hoisted.

On November 16th 1998, China's State Council issued a document entitled "Notice of Decision to Resolutely Attack and Punish the

Subversive and Sabotage Activities of Hostile Forces and Elements". Obviously, the term "hostile forces" refers to China's political dissidents. The document, which was released to the police and security forces of the provincial governments, was a clear indication that after a period of debate, the conservative hardliners in the Politburo of the Communist Party once again had the upper hand. So, organizations with strong political affinities like "China Development Union" would not be tolerated.

Shortly after the release of the November 16th 1998 document, Chairman of the Standing Committee of the National People's Congress Li Peng, universally viewed as a conservative hardliner due to his role in the 1989 Tiananmen Square crackdown, said that the government would not allow Chinese citizens to practice political pluralism and that the Chinese Constitution stipulated that the Chinese Communist Party must act as the "leading force". But who wrote the constitution and had it passed in the communist-controlled People's Congress in the first place? The Communist Party. So, in the very beginning, the Communist Party manipulated everything to ensure its monopoly of political power and to enable people like Mr. Li Peng to cite the constitution as a legal basis for communist dictatorship.

Mr. Li Peng also said there were eight "democratic parties" in China, which, though not acting as opposition parties, could "participate in Chinese politics". The question is: How? Since the "democratic parties" are not allowed to oppose the decisions of the Communist Party, what else is left for them to do? The history of the People's Republic shows that the only choice for the "democratic parties" is to behave as the Communist Party expect them to. Rule Number One: Cooperation. Rule Number Two: No opposition. Rule Number Three: Willingness to be controlled by the Communist Party.

Apparently, Mr. Li Peng's statement was an attempt to close the door on political reform. Although the Communist Party may want to call some of its cosmetic changes "political reform", no fair-minded person would take it seriously. Outside China, the term "political reform" is defined as pluralist multi-party democratization, so anything short of political pluralism can hardly be accepted as true political reform by the international community.

So far, the actions of the communist state apparatus have demonstrated to the world that it will never tolerate pluralist multi-party democratization. In December of 1998, while discussing what the Chinese government would do in 1999, President Jiang Zemin again stressed the importance of "stability" under the rule of the Communist Party. In a clear reference to China's political dissidents, he said that any destabilizing factors should be "nipped in the bud". More than 60 years earlier, in the 1930s, Generalissimo Chiang Kai-shek of the Nationalist government in Nanjing also stressed "stability" under the rule of the Nationalist Party, trying everything possible to nip China's communist movement in the bud. In the end, he failed. Isn't there anything better than one-party dictatorship to maintain stability?

Among the ancestors of the Chinese, there were quite a few well-known sages like Confucius, Mencius, and the Mohist scholars, to name just a few, who based their life philosophies and political philosophies on sheer common sense and whose theories have helped ancient dynasties to maintain stability over the centuries. Today, however, it appears that the Chinese leaders believe that they cannot maintain stability unless they jail those who think independently and speak their minds. Shouldn't they spend time reading Confucius rather than Marx to find a better way of maintaining stability? After all, Confucianism reflects common sense with "Chinese characteristics"; Marxism doesn't.

6

President Jiang Zemin— China's Political Barometer

While visiting the United States in autumn of 1997, President Jiang Zemin took time to drop by the New York Stock Exchange, the very heart of American capitalism. At the close of the session, he struck the NYSE gavel. In doing so, President Jiang made what could be seen as a pro-American gesture. It might have suggested that he had already consolidated his position at home to the point where he was at least comfortable showing his appreciation of American capitalism. It might also have suggested that he was able to continue market-oriented economic reforms without compromising his authority. At the 15th Congress of the Communist Party held in 1997, he gave permission to privatize small and medium-sized state-owned enterprises but called for the large state-owned enterprises to form into leviathan-like conglomerates similar to South Korea's ailing chaebols. To be sure, the Communist Party still wants to control China's major industries.

Yet despite his intention to preserve the Communist Party's grip on the large state-owned enterprises, I would like to presume that President Jiang Zemin is a moderate or a conservative moderate, not a hardliner. According to Hong Kong's Chinese media reports, Mr. Jiang Zemin used to be a protégé of former Shanghai Mayor Wang Daohan, a university professor-turned-politician and a well-known member of the Communist Party's moderate faction. The reports said that Mr. Wang Daohan had groomed Jiang Zemin for years before finally recommending Jiang to the late paramount leader Deng Xiaoping.

After the military crackdown of June 4th 1989, Deng Xiaoping had to find somebody to replace the liberal-minded Zhao Ziyang as secretary general of the Communist Party. Mr. Deng could have chosen the then premier Li Peng, a well-known party conservative, for the job, but he didn't. Instead, he handpicked Jiang Zemin, a technocrat from Shanghai—a coastal city with a history of strong Western influences—to maintain the balance of power between the various factions of the Communist Party, because Mr. Jiang Zemin appeared to be acceptable to all the factions at the time. So, by simple (but hopefully not naive) deduction, I tend to assume that Mr. Deng would not have chosen Jiang Zemin as his successor if he had not been certain that Mr. Jiang was a moderate like himself.

In recent Chinese history, the moderates of the Communist Party including Deng Xiaoping and Jiang Zemin have all shown a strong desire to improve China's relations with the Western world. While I am not sure if I should call this desire of theirs a pro-western tendency, I do believe they must have learned that if China is to become a really modernized country, it must sell goods to and get the knowhow from the West. President Jiang Zemin certainly knows that good relations with the United States are in the best interest of the moderate faction.

Yet the hardliners in the Communist Party and the military will not allow President Jiang to make the necessary concessions on such issues as human rights, Taiwan, Tibet and America's growing trade deficit with China to achieve the goal of better relations with the U.S. Instead, they, the hardliners, want President (and party secretary general) Jiang Zemin to coax as many concessions as possible from the United States. So, there's the rub. On the one hand, the moderates and of course the liberals are eager to improve relations with the U.S. On the other hand, there is a very strong hardline conservative faction in the regime that sees the United States as its Number One enemy. Going forward, the situation depends very much on the status of the hardliners' influences. If their influences remain strong, it would be difficult for the relations between the two countries to improve.

On March 22nd and March 24th 1999, several meetings regarding the situation in Yugoslavia were held at China's five military academies (The University of Defense, The Academy of Military Commanders, The Air Force Academy, The Naval Academy and The Academy of Artillery). Present at these meetings were General Zhang Wannian and General Chi Haotian, the two vice chairmen of the Communist Party's Central Military Commission. The generals saw NATO's bombing of Serbian military targets as "U.S. hegemonist military aggression against Yugoslavia", rather than the consequence of President Milosevic's policy of ethnic cleansing against the Kosovo Albanians.

In his speech at The University of Defense, General Zhang Wannian said: "Fifty years of experience by the People's Republic of China since its founding have demonstrated to us that the global strategy of U.S. hegemonists is to establish a global hegemony that dictates to the nations of the world. At one time, we had to face the political isolation, military containment and threat and economic blockade imposed on us by U.S. hegemonists. But we didn't collapse. Nor did we compromise. Instead, we have stood proudly in the east of the earth, upholding our unequivocal principles and solid actions against U.S. hegemonism."

General Chi Haotian, who told Congress during his visit to the U.S. that nobody was killed inside Tiananmen Square in the June 4th 1989 military crackdown, even believes that China has to prepare for war against the United States. At a gathering in The Academy of Military Commanders, he boasted: "Our military forces have developed state-of-the-art weaponry and possess a certain number of nuclear arms. On an international level, we are in the forefront of laser and neutron weapon research and development. Our most fundamental policy is to confront U.S. hegemonism, power politics, military blackmail and military intervention, so as to safeguard the independence, sovereignty and dignity of our motherland. In case U.S. hegemonism launches military intervention and aggression against our country or manipulates some military bloc to launch military aggression against us, we will certainly make a counterattack. Once war breaks out, the land of the United States, i.e. the land of the aggressor, will suffer a fatal blow.....The United States has aircraft carriers and the so-called most advanced B-1 stealth bomber. We don't have such weapons. But we have sophisticated, state-of-the-art weaponry that we can use to inflict a fatal blow."

Sounds like the United States of America is under serious nuclear threat from communist China and so must have a missile defense system to shield herself before it is too late.

In May of 1999, as NATO warplanes were bombing Belgrade in reprisal of Yugoslavian strongman Milosevic's policy of ethnic cleansing toward Kosovo, five missiles hit the Chinese embassy. While the Clinton Administration explained that a mistake had occurred through the use of an out-of-date map of Belgrade, the Chinese government insisted that the embassy bombing was not an accident because the missiles had been fired deliberately. Meanwhile, the military establishment of communist China was especially furious.

At a meeting held on the morning of May 14th 1999, General Zhang Wannian said, "Since the end of the cold war, the world situation hasn't been quiet. U.S. hegemonism, power politics and gunboat policy could become the occasion of war in today's world....On May 8th 1999, U.S. hegemonism launched an outrageous missile attack on our embassy in Yugoslavia. An on-site investigation conducted by our military experts discovered that it had been a deliberate, planned attack on a selected target. Based on the launch angles of the five missiles and their impact point, the attack was neither a target error nor a missile mis-hit. It was a deliberate military provocation and was an attack on Chinese sovereignty....Under the circumstances where the United States pursues its international hegemonism and gunboat policy, there is no way to normalize the relations between China and the U.S. and it is unrealistic to hope for a constructive strategic partnership between the two countries....On the contrary, our military forces will resolutely pursue a hardline against U.S. hegemonism, power politics and gunboat policy, because U.S. hegemonism is Public Enemy Number One to our military forces."

Listen to the rhetoric from the generals of the People's Liberation Army and you'll see how far apart the United States and communist China are in ideological terms. The mistrust and misunderstanding between the two countries is formidable if not unsurmountable. Even assuming that President Jiang Zemin understands America's political structure and Americans' feelings on such issues as human rights, Taiwan, Tibet and the growing U.S. trade deficit with China better than his colleagues in the government because of his knowledge of the English language and the information and analysis provided by his think tank, it is still difficult to imagine how he could come to convince the generals that China should cooperate with the United States. Likewise, it is difficult to imagine how he could come to convince the hardliners of the Communist Party to accept any meaningful political reform program even if he wanted to see democratization to materialize in China.

It is interesting to note that some articles in Hong Kong's Chinese-language political magazines have criticized President Jiang Zemin for leaning toward the left. Perhaps, such criticism of Jiang reflects the views of China's liberal intellectuals, who, having suffered a great deal under communism, now want to see a pluralist democracy emerge as soon as possible but are disappointed with President Jiang's performance in respect of political reform.

Both "left" and "right" are relative terms. Compared with China's liberal intellectual community, President (and party secretary general) Jiang Zemin is definitely to the left. But for that matter, the Communist

Party is supposed to be a left-wing political party, and whoever is in the top party position is supposed to chant Marxist incantations every now and then just to show that he qualifies for it. Can President Jiang Zemin afford to preach Adam Smith like Mrs. Margaret Thatcher?

However, compared with China's classic Marxist theoreticians like Mr. Deng Liqun and company, President Jiang Zemin appears pretty liberal. He speaks English, plays the piano, enjoys literature, European music and Hollywood movies, has a son holding a Ph.D. earned in the United States, has released China's best-known dissident Mr. Wei Jingsheng and best-known student leader Wang Dan, and last but not least, definitely wants China's market-oriented economic reforms to stay on course.

The one big difference between President Jiang Zemin and Secretary General Gorbachev of the former Soviet Union is that Jiang has refused to implement democratic political reforms like Mr. Gorbachev. The question is whether Jiang is able to implement democratization. According to the authors of the said Chinese-language articles, he is. They believe that China's leftist conservative camp which Marxist theoretician Deng Liqun belongs in is too weak to stop Jiang from implementing democratization and that since nearly all the members of the Old Guard (the senior leaders of the communist revolution) are now dead, President Jiang Zemin must be in a position to call the shots. Therefore, they blame Jiang for inaction on the political reform front, convinced that Jiang is unwilling, not unable, to implement democratization.

With all due respect, the liberal intellectuals may have underestimated the strength of the leftist conservative camp, which, in my judgement, includes more than just a few Marxist theoreticians. First of all, even Marxist theoretician Deng Liqun may not be as weak as the liberal intellectuals imagine, despite all the changes that have taken place in China's economic structure over the past two decades. He is not alone. Most likely, he has the backing of the hardliners in the Communist Party and the military.

In October of 1998, Mr. Deng Liqun filed a document entitled "Open Letter to the Third Plenary Session of the 15th Central Committee of the Chinese Communist Party", which was later released by the office of the Central Committee of the Communist Party to the participants in the Third Session. In his open letter, Mr. Deng Liqun said that the current leadership of the Communist Party should wake up to the crisis confronting the Communist Party and adjust its political line and that the Communist Party should launch an internal revolution along Marxist guidelines to purge its organization and change its political line even at the cost of blood.

In the meantime, in the ideological arena, Mr. Liu Ji, a party liberal, had to retire from the Chinese Academy of Social Sciences, an institution believed to be the Communist Party's think tank, even as Wang Renzhi, a well-known party conservative and an ally of Mr. Deng Liqun, remained in the Academy as Deputy Secretary of the Communist Party Committee.

Such developments belie the argument that China's left-wing conservative forces are too weak to prevent political reform. Rather, the reality that confronts China's reformers is that the hardliners have sufficient influence in the government's decision-making process. For reasons best known to himself, President Jiang Zemin seems to have no choice but to listen to the hardliners and decide that he must "nip any destabilizing factor in the bud". One man's meat is another man's poison. What the international community calls human rights is poison to the communist regime, because the communists believe such human rights as the freedom of expression and the freedom of assembly are likely to destabilize their dictatorship and so should be "nipped in the bud". Although they say they are ready to discuss human rights issues, they refuse to define human rights according to international norms. They have their own definitions. For instance, according to the Beijing regime, the freedom of expression is "not absolute", meaning the authorities shall reserve the right to restrict the freedom of expression when they see fit. In other words, Chinese citizens are not free to express anti-communist opinions. The communists are experts at sophistry. One would be very naive if one took their words at face value.

Recent Chinese history shows that after each period of relative political relaxation, the conservatives of the Communist Party would consolidate and then stage a comeback. Toward the end of 1998, a year when there was a lot of talk about political reform in China, Mr. Deng Liqun published a long article entitled "Analysis of China's Economic Reality" in Beijing's "Zhongliu Magazine", saying that the private sector of the Chinese economy accounted for one third of the GDP as of 1998 and was likely to continue to grow even as the state-owned sector kept shrinking. Thus, he went on to call for China's true communists to "struggle against conduct in violation of the Constitution", which stipulates for communist rule based on the dominance of the state-owned sector in the economy. Apparently, in mentioning "conduct in violation of the Constitution", Mr. Deng Liqun was referring to Premier Zhu Rongji's program to revitalize the Chinese economy, since it allows the private sector to grow and the state-owned sector to shrink.

China has been under communist rule for more than half a century, rearing large numbers of people who rely on the old system. And since the old system has become their livelihood, to get rid of it would be tantamount to eliminating their livelihood. Many people, though aware and sometimes even critical of the deficiencies of the old system, find themselves accustomed to the old system and afraid of change, because they fear that reforms will cause uncertainties to their lives. To put it bluntly, reforms, whether economic or political, will make many members of the 50-million-strong Communist Party feel as useless as if they were dumped in the recycle bin of history, because their area of expertise, commonly known in China as "political thought work" which the Communist Party has used to maintain its control of the Chinese society, could not fit into any liberalized environment. Take Marxist Theoretician Deng Liqun as an example. What else could he do, either for a living or for a retirement pastime, if the old system came to an end and the audience to his "political thought work" dissipated? Besides, at every level of the old system there are people like Mr. Deng Liqun feeding on the old system. Hence, the size and the depth of the leftist conservative camp are difficult to fathom and could very well exceed the liberal intellectuals' estimates. At least, one has to admit that China's liberal-democratic forces are not strong enough to convince the hardliners that they must accept political reform.

Chances are that the Chinese leaders know Marxism is erroneous but cannot afford to allow liberal intellectuals to hold open debates on the basic concepts of Marxism like public ownership and one-party rule, since such open debates would certainly expose the absurdity of Marxism, thereby jeopardizing the legitimacy of the communist dictatorship. That is why anyone who asserts the freedom of expression and publicly criticizes Marxism in China would end up in jail. Any Chinese publication which exercises the freedom of the press by publishing anti-Marxist articles would get shut down within twenty-four hours. The communist state apparatus will crush any opposition if need be, though whether it is as effective as it used to be during the leftist Mao era remains to be seen, since some cracks must have developed here and there with the growth in economic freedom and exposure to the outside world.

During the leftist Mao era, the communist state controlled all the economic organizations in the country and tried to brainwash all state enterprise employees through "political thought work" by party secretaries and other party officers. Both financially and ideologically, the employees of the state-owned enterprises were restricted by the communist state. They had no choice. Now, in sharp contrast, the private sector of the Chinese economy is growing while the state-owned enterprises accumulate heavy losses, laying off large numbers of employees. The government is looking to the private sector to create jobs, so as to provide a cushion for the country's high unemployment. Under these circumstances, it is difficult for the communist state to control people financially and ideologically. As large crowds of unemployed people cry out for help, Marxist "political thought work" is clearly irrelevant to the economic realities surrounding them.

However, on the ideological front, well-known liberal intellectuals including Mr. Liu Binyan and Mr. Wang Ruowang have all gone into exile. This should be regarded as a measure of China's political reality and the strength of the leftist conservative forces. In short, if the conservative camp were as weak as the authors of the aforesaid Chinese-language articles believe, China's communist brand name couldn't have lasted to this day.

Still, optimists may want to remind us that the Soviet communist state apparatus started to release and exile political dissidents in the early 1980s before Mr. Gorbachev became secretary general, that is, not very long before communism ended in Russia. They may also want to suggest that since the Chinese communist state apparatus has started to release and exile political dissidents, its days may be numbered. Fair enough, but there's the rub: Whereas Secretary General Gorbachev of the former Soviet Union was under house arrest for only a few days during the 1991 putsch, China's former secretary general Zhao Ziyang has been under house arrest for years since spring of 1989.

While acting as party secretary general, Mr. Zhao Ziyang had a political secretary by the name of Bao Tong. In 1989, Mr. Bao Tong was arrested for his involvement with the student movement and jailed for seven years. After his release in 1996, Mr. Bao Tong remained under house arrest for another two years. In June of 1998, after the house arrest was lifted, he was interviewed by Washington Post and The Voice of America. Mr. Bao Tong expressed his concern that a strong China without democratization might fail to keep its foreign policy behavior in check and thus become a destabilizing factor in the international arena. Immediately after the interviews, the authorities warned him not to grant interviews to foreign correspondents any more.

But later, CBS interviewed Mr. Bao Tong with the help of a translator. Shortly afterwards, the authorities arrested the translator, Ms. Liu Qingyan, claiming she had broken Chinese law. Only after she had signed a confession admitting wrongdoing, was she released. Apparently, the authorities want Chinese citizens to stay away from foreign correspondents, so that unflattering information about the communist state apparatus will not reach the outside world. The methods employed by the authorities to accomplish such goals are still intimidation and coercion, for all the talk of reforms. What happened to Ms. Liu Qingyan should disillusion anyone hoping for political reform in China. As long as "the banner of Marxism" is upheld, talk of political reform will remain just talk.

Each time Westerner reporters ask him about the detention of Chinese dissidents, President Jiang Zemin appears embarrassed. He certainly does not want his moderate image tarnished. But liberal intellectuals point their accusing fingers at Jiang as the man responsible for China's human rights abuses. Of course, as head of the state, President Jiang has to accept responsibility for the conduct of his regime, yet the regime—the communist state apparatus—was set up more than half a century ago by the late Chairman Mao Zedong after the Soviet model. President Jiang and his colleagues in the Politburo only inherited the regime in the spring of 1997 when the paramount leader Deng Xiaoping died. Undoubtedly, President Jiang Zemin shares responsibility with his colleagues. The question is whether he is able to make major political changes singlehandedly even if he wants to. I would say no.

More interestingly, at the same time that liberal intellectuals criticize him for leaning toward the left, President Jiang Zemin has to fend off what sounds like bum raps from the left-wing. For instance, according to reports in Hong Kong's Chinese press, after his visit to the United States in 1997, quite a few critical comments emerged in China's political and military circles to the effect that President Jiang was begging for American support to boost his own position at home. Jiang's detractors on the left were particularly scandalized by reports that during his U.S. visit, President Jiang Zemin spoke and sang in English and even danced to Western music. They were extremely unhappy that President Jiang had granted a number of trade contracts to American companies and, in their view, had made major concessions to the United States on the issue of nuclear non-proliferation.

In the meantime, some high-ranking officers in the People's Liberation Army raised embarrassing questions about President Jiang's various policies:

"Is the current political line of the Central Committee (of the Communist Party) correct?"

"Has the Communist Party betrayed Marxism and changed its nature?"

"Why has the Communist Party lost its cohesion?"

"What has corrupted the cadres of the Communist Party?"

"Has the Central Committee (of the Communist Party) done any soul-searching vis-a-vis these serious issues?"

The fact that such questions have been raised suggests that even as demands for political liberalization mount, President Jiang Zemin feels pressures from the left-wing to uphold orthodox Marxist principles. As a Chinese idiom goes, he faces difficulties on the left as well as on the right. It appears that President Jiang is trying to please everybody, but as the country's social and economic problems accumulate, he may end up pleasing nobody. True, the Communist Party needs President Jiang to mediate between its various factions, but it takes more than mediation to get problems resolved.

Perhaps, at the end of the day, nothing much happens to the status quo. The world may have to wait for the next generation of Chinese leaders to introduce meaningful political reforms. Rumor has it that President Jiang Zemin has already chosen a younger man called Hu Jintao as his successor. Most probably, Mr. Hu Jintao is a party moderate. Since the conservative faction and the liberal faction are unacceptable to each other, the only faction acceptable to all has to be the moderates, that is, middle-of-the-road politicians like President Jiang Zemin himself.

Political dissidents' criticisms of Jiang aside, I tend to see President Jiang Zemin as a political barometer that measures and registers China's overall political atmosphere. If he visits Wall Street and strikes the New York Stock Exchange gavel at the end of the afternoon session, you bet it's good news for the Chinese people since it suggests that more economic freedom, even more political relaxation, may be on the way. On the other hand, if he starts to intone Marxist incantations, you'd better watch out—something naughty might be going on in the Politburo of the Communist Party.

China's liberal intellectuals, however, suspect that President Jiang Zemin's relatively moderate image is designed for international consumption, that is, to fool the international community. They describe President Jiang as wily and ask: If Jiang Zemin is really a moderate, why does he keep former party secretary general Zhao Ziyang under house arrest? Why are there more than two thousand less-known political dissidents languishing in prison?

First of all, the history of the Communist Party shows it is full of wiles. After all, that's how it seized power in China. So its leader has to be wily in order to survive. Only the Communist Party calls wiles "strategies". In the words of the late Chairman Mao Zedong, "Policies and strategies are the Party's life." Put in another way, without "strategies" or wiles, the Communist Party cannot survive.

But the answers to the above questions lie in the fact that Jiang's personal image does not change the monstrous nature of China's communist state apparatus as long as it exists, just as Gorbachev's moderate image did not change the monstrous nature of the Soviet communist state apparatus till it collapsed, not to mention that whereas Mr. Gorbachev proved himself to be a true liberal, President Jiang is eager to prove to his colleagues in the leftist conservative camp that he is not a liberal at all. Thus, he serves as a symbol of the status quo and a symbol of the communist state apparatus. There is no way he can afford to be otherwise. If he acts like a Gorbachev-style liberal, the conservative forces of the Communist Party will probably conspire to get rid of him as they did the previous two party secretaries general, Hu Yaobang and Zhao Ziyang. However, given that China's leaders are all avid readers of history, one would have to presume that President Jiang Zemin must know what has to happen will happen. As far as China is concerned, political liberalization is definitely something that has to happen over time if the Communist Party allows the on-going market-oriented economic reforms to continue.

At a meeting convened in Beijing on June 12th 1998 by the Central Committee of the Chinese Communist Party, President Jiang Zemin made a speech. He said that in the new historical conditions, the political quality, ideology and morals of the members of the Communist Party had already undergone drastic changes and that such changes were being exacerbated. Then he went on to say: "The fact we must face up to is that the organism of the Communist Party is putrefying and dying." He pointed out that many members of the Communist Party, including cadres in leadership positions, were nonchalant toward the possibility that the Communist Party might collapse someday. Apparently, a large number of communist party members just don't care whether the Party will collapse or not. President Jiang warned that if the Communist Party could not function as a political core, thereby losing the ability to rally the people around itself and losing the support of the people, it would collapse and die. Sounds like the Communist Party's swan song.

The speech suggests that President Jiang Zemin is fully aware of the changing circumstances. Perhaps, he knows that one-party dictatorship cannot last forever and that the implementation of democratization in China is only a question of when and how. So-called "People's Democracy" as described and imposed on the Chinese people by the late Chairman Mao Zedong is hardly in line with international standards for democracy. Hopefully, the frequent smiles on President Jiang's face will presage some policy flexibility or readiness to compromise down the road as pressures for change increase.

I still remember the horrendous days of the Cultural Revolution when printed announcements of "The People's Court" were frequently posted in Shanghai's streets listing the names of people either jailed or executed for "counter-revolutionary crimes". Those caught criticizing communism were dead meat. Today, after more than twenty years of "reform and openness", those who openly criticize communist rule are jailed or exiled, not executed. Although Beijing continues to have a poor human rights record, ironically, the fact that it now refrains from executing political dissidents is viewed by some as an improvement in its human rights record. And President Jiang Zemin did order several well-known dissidents like Wei Jingsheng and Wang Dan released during the 1990s.

Does that mean that President Jiang is "a man we can do business with"? Let's hope so. At least, he is a man the Western world has to engage. Besides, it seems that President Jiang enjoys meeting Western leaders. He may have a reason for that. For instance, President Clinton's China visit in June 1998 is believed to have boosted Jiang's position in China's domestic politics. But will President Jiang adopt a cooperative approach toward the West in international affairs? Chances are he will if his colleagues in the conservative camp permit, for he knows that China needs the cooperation of the Western world. The problem is that the hardline conservatives probably disapprove of the moderate faction's attempt to strengthen ties with the United States. Whereas the late paramount leader Deng Xiaoping could pursue his effort to improve relations with the West despite the conservatives' objections, President Jiang may not command the same degree of clout and prestige as Mr. Deng to continue Deng's policy of cooperation toward the United States in the face of pressures from the hardliners.

7

"Join Tracks" with the World Economy? How?

While asserting that modern China has a tradition of strong Western influences, one also needs to be aware that there are large numbers of Chinese who hold strong nationalistic if not xenophobic feelings about the relations between China and the West. As mentioned above, even President Jiang Zemin has annoyed some people because of his frequent use of the English language. But this does not change the fact that more and more Chinese want to learn about the Western world because they believe the Western world is way ahead in terms of its economic and political structures. That is why English-language teachers from the United Kingdom, the United States, Canada and Australia are very popular with their Chinese students and the number of students of the English language in China is increasing rapidly.

It is only fair to mention that since the late 1970s thousands of English-language teachers from the West have spent countless hours of their valuable time in China—often in exchange for very low salaries—helping their Chinese students not only to learn English but also to broaden their horizons vis-a-vis the outside world. In fact, these Western teachers have contributed a great deal to China's effort to open up to the outside world and have enhanced the understanding between ordinary Chinese citizens and the people of the Western world. Their contributions cannot be overemphasized, just as the contributions of the Western Christian missionaries who spent long years in China in the late 19th century and the first half of the 20th century cannot be overemphasized, for both the missionaries and the language teachers have promoted one great common cause—to help China come to the fold (i.e. to enable China to integrate with the rest of the world). The international community (or the Free World) cannot do without China, and sooner or later, China will realize that it cannot do without the Free World. After all, there is only one globe which is getting smaller and smaller with the advances in technology and will eventually become too small to be divided for ideological reasons.

Today, Chinese citizens often use two terms: "jie-gui" and "gua-gou". Literally, "jie-gui" means "join tracks" and "gua-gou" means "hook up". For instance, Chinese officials sometimes would say that the Chinese economy should "join tracks" with the world economy and that Chinese product prices should "hook up" with the international market. Put in plain English, this means that the Chinese economy should be brought in line with the world economy and that Chinese product prices should be determined by the forces of the international marketplace. Since these days, Chinese officials only show interest in the major economies like the United States, Germany and Japan, when they use the term "world economy" they apparently refer to the capitalist economies of the world, not the ridiculously inefficient economies of communist North Korea and Cuba.

The frequent use of the two terms ("jie-gui" and "gua-gou") by Chinese citizens is a strong indication that more and more Chinese now believe that the Chinese economy is not on the right track because it is based on the Soviet model and that only economies like the United States are on the right track. Although "jie-gui" or "gua-gou" is easier said than done, Chinese officials have indeed tried various ways to make the Chinese economy "join tracks" with the world economy, though without much success, because what is on the wrong track cannot be easily lifted and then put on the right track. Nor would it work if the wrong track is artificially joined to the right track. Besides, efforts to integrate China's economy with the global economy tend to increase pressures for political reforms to integrate China with the rest of the world on an ideological level. Apparently, the ruling Communist Party is sure to resist such pressures as long as possible.

In the early 1990s, Chinese officials indicated that they had a plan to make the Chinese currency, the (Renminbi) (RMB) yuan, convertible. But the Asian financial crisis which started in summer of 1997 suggested to the Chinese authorities that if the (RMB) yuan became fully convertible, it would inevitably come under the same kind of selling pressure in the international financial markets that Asia's other currencies had experienced. As a result, the Chinese government decided to put the plan on hold. Since the World Trade Organization (WTO) requires its member countries to have convertible currencies, the (RMB) yuan's non-convertibility could become a roadblock to China's effort to join the WTO in the foreseeable future. The question is: How can any economy integrate with the world economy if its currency remains non-convertible?

It seems that although Chinese officials know the economic model transplanted from the former Soviet Union after the 1949 revolution hinders China's economic growth and are looking to the West for help, the country's Marxist ideology which stresses the state's control of the economy prevents them from introducing thorough and fundamental reforms such as a total privatization of industry, commerce and banking. A case in point is China's restrictions on foreign investments in its telecommunications sector which includes its Internet industry. In the eyes of the Communist Party, foreign investments in the Chinese Internet industry could facilitate foreign infiltration of a strategically important sector it must control. As we all know, the Internet is about information flow. Yet, information flow is exactly what worries the

Communist Party. Some overseas Chinese-language Internet publishers like VIP Reference keep releasing information very unflattering to the communist regime through the Internet, and Chinese Internet users can now access such information and print it out for others to read. The authorities know if more and more people get to know the truth about the workings of the communist state apparatus, their grip on the people would slip.

Between control and business common sense, the Communist Party has chosen control. In September of 1999, during a communist party central committee meeting, President (and party secretary general) Jiang Zemin asserted the Communist Party's determination to uphold its "basic socialist economic principles". What does that mean? Well, in the communist jargon, the term "socialist" refers to communist control. It means the Communist Party will continue to control a large chunk of the economy, the so-called state-owned sector which includes all the industries that the Communist Party considers to be of strategic importance to the survival of its dictatorship. At the meeting, President Jiang stressed that the Communist Party would absolutely prohibit the privatization and foreign investment infiltration of any strategically important industries such as the telecommunications sector.

But if China keeps its telecom and Internet markets closed to Western businesses, why should the United States and other Western countries agree to admit China into the WTO, enabling it to take advantage of their open markets? So, Beijing has made some "concessions". Now, under the U.S.-China WTO deal, foreign companies shall be allowed to hold a 49% interest in a Chinese telecom enterprise. That means the Chinese partner (usually a state-owned firm) will have a controlling stake, no matter how much money the foreign partner has invested.

More interestingly, the term "jie-gui" ("join tracks") is mentioned not only in the economic area but also in other fields. A friend of mine (a school teacher) writes to me from Shanghai, complaining that although the authorities have kept talking about making China's educational system "join tracks" with international standards (meaning China's educational system should be brought in line with international standards), his classroom is filled with far more students than is allowed in the West. The term "international standards" definitely refers to Western standards. In short, the Chinese people are now convinced that anything which is not up to Western standards is not on the right track and so should "join tracks" with "international standards". Yet the reality remains that there is no way for China to meet Western standards unless it scraps its Marxist ideology that provides for state control over everything.

To be objective, I would define China as a country in transition from the Soviet model transplanted after the 1949 revolution to what appears to be a "new model", a look at which may help us determine whether China remains a communist country.

For all the market-oriented economic reforms that Western media has reported, China continues to have a socialist economy, that is, a state-led economy. Chinese officials now claim that China has a "socialist market economy". Do not think they are just kidding when they use the word "socialist", because all of China's major industries including the import and export business are controlled by the state, though at least fifty percent of its state-owned enterprises are losing money. The heavy losses accumulated by the state-owned enterprises are the single most important factor compelling the state to relax its grip on small and medium-sized state enterprises and adopt certain reformist measures. For instance, the government now allows the state-owned enterprises to form joint ventures with Western businesses or to become joint stock companies through their initial public offerings (IPO's) to domestic and overseas investors. In addition, loss-making state-owned enterprises can now declare themselves bankrupt.

However, a close look at these measures will reveal that they are neither designed to bring about a total privatization of the state-owned sector nor intended to create a real free market economy. Some of the so-called reforms are clearly designed to suck in capital to prop up the ailing state enterprises. For instance, after an IPO to domestic and overseas investors, a state-owned enterprise tends to remain under state control since it continues to be run by the same management team that created the poor track record of performance in the first place. The man who used to be the communist party committee secretary of the state enterprise now probably has a new title "Chairman of the Board of Directors", even as the other officials on the communist party committee distribute their name cards as "Directors". Ordinary shareholders do not have much say in deciding how the enterprise should be managed. If the state-run enterprise continues to perform badly, it's going to be private investors' money that is at stake this time.

All Chinese-foreign joint ventures in China are incorporated under Chinese laws and in accordance with joint venture contracts which often stipulate that the Chinese partner (usually a state-owned enterprise) shall hold a 50% or even 51% interest and that the foreign partner cannot pull out its investment without the prior consent of the Chinese partner and the Chinese government authorities. What if things go sour? Most probably, the foreign partner will have to remain stuck with all its capital tied up in the joint venture project. It is worth noting that in many if not all cases, the Chinese partner only provides a certain number of years of land use rights plus factory premises use rights as capital investment while the foreign partner contributes cash in hard currency to the registered capital of the joint venture. If the joint venture fails to perform as expected, it's going to be the foreign partner's money that is at stake, because the Chinese partner didn't come up with any cash in the first place.

As to the land use rights, since all land in China belongs to the state, the state-owned enterprises do not own any land. They only hold the land use rights to the land under their control. If a state-owned enterprise forms a joint venture with a foreign company, it shall allow the joint venture to use the land and the factory premises under its control for a certain number of years. In the process of the establishment of the joint venture, the value of the use rights to the land and the factory premises is assessed by a Chinese accountant office, not determined by the forces of any free market. This value, fair or not, is then used by the Chinese partner as its capital investment in the joint venture. If the performance of the joint venture turns out to be less than satisfactory, it won't hurt the Chinese partner as badly as it does the foreign partner, because only the foreign partner needs to pay interest on the money it has borrowed and invested in the joint venture.

For all the strong evidence that state control of enterprises doesn't work, the Chinese authorities still want the state to control the country's industry, commerce and banking, because they know that the survival of the communist state apparatus relies on the state's control of the economy. Hence, so many joint venture contracts provide that the Chinese partner shall have a major interest. Since every joint venture project has to be submitted to the authorities for approval, proposals which fail to provide for a major stake for the Chinese partner may get turned down.

Yet it appears that joint ventures where Chinese partners have major stakes are doomed to become mismatched marriages that futilely attempt to put communism and capitalism in the same bed, because there could be few synergies between a Western business and a communist-controlled state-owned enterprise with regard to corporate culture and business philosophy. As a result, there is likely to be more contention than cooperation.

To be sure, it would be much better if a Western businessman could buy the land use rights and set up a wholly-owned enterprise on Chinese soil. But to do so, he would need the approval of the authorities. Then he would come to realize that things could become easier if he had a Chinese partner (usually a communist-controlled state owned enterprise) with the necessary connections to the authorities to ensure the obtainment of the approval. Thus, he would conclude that whether he likes it or not, he has to have a Chinese partner anyway. At the end of the day, he has to ask himself whether he is ready for the risks in case his Chinese partner fails to cooperate, because if that happens, he would find himself hostage to a situation completely out of his control, once his money is invested in China. For he would find himself overly dependent on his Chinese partner and in the event of a dispute between himself and his Chinese partner, the regulations may not be in his favor and the cost of litigation could be very high since the lawyers he might have to hire from Hong Kong would certainly charge exorbitant fees. Besides, everything in China including the law is under "the leadership of the Communist Party". That means even the law could be somehow manipulated by party officials and bureaucrats. What if his partner (a state-owned enterprise controlled by party officials) has some kind of "guanxi" (connection) to the court?

As mentioned above, it won't be easy for the foreign partner to pull out if things go sour. For instance, if the Chinese partner fails to cooperate on the board of directors, the foreign partner sure is caught in a dilemma. Remember the Chinese partner is a state-owned enterprise which may have lost money in the past. What it needs now is capital from the foreign partner, whereas all it can contribute is land use rights and factory premises use rights, plus perhaps some used equipment only fit for the scrap dumps. But since the Chinese partner has a 50% interest in the joint venture, the foreign partner cannot run the business of the joint venture as he sees fit unless the Chinese partner cooperates. If the foreign partner allows the joint venture to be run in the Chinese way, the risk of losing money could be pretty high. Besides, there is a big difference in mentality between the Chinese partner and the foreign partner. It won't take a genius to figure out what that difference is: The foreign partner is certainly worried about any possible losses because he has invested borrowed money in the joint venture and will have to pay interest to his banker, whereas his Chinese partner (a state-owned enterprise) is not because it only contributed land use rights and factory premises use rights and need not be concerned about interest payments and principal repayments.

As an economic philosophy, Marxism may very well be labeled as the quintessence of wishful thinking, in accordance with which, the state has to own the enterprise and the enterprise has to be run by the officials of the Communist Party on the assumption that as devout believers in "the great communist ideal", they will work ever so diligently to make the enterprise a success story and will not be corrupted by the power in their hands, as if they were thoroughly purified angels with none of the seven deadly sins that have plagued the human race since the beginning of time. Yet the realities of China's ailing state-owned enterprises paint a completely different picture.

In both psychology and behavior, communist party officials are completely different from business people, when it comes to business. Whereas business people do business at their own risk, party officials run state-owned enterprises at the risk of the state. When a state-owned enterprise makes money, the party officials in charge tend to pay out bonuses to workers so that they can justify granting themselves a big piece of the action. If the enterprise loses money, the party officials do not risk anything that belongs to themselves. Instead, they can count on some state bank to grant them a loan, on which they might default later when it becomes clear that their enterprise will never be able to turn around.

If a state-owned enterprise plans to form a joint venture with a Western company, the party officials in charge of the state-owned enterprise, as a rule, would submit a proposal to the government authorities. More often than not, the proposal would say: "Through this Chinese-foreign joint venture project, we expect to learn the scientific management practices of modern enterprise during the joint venture period, so that we will be able to run the business efficiently when the joint venture period expires." Sounds good, but is it realistic? Chances are that the party officials will never learn "the scientific management practices of modern enterprise" as long as they continue to be party officials. The truth is only private business people will learn how to run their private businesses efficiently, because if they don't, they will lose their own money.

Although there have been numerous media reports about the heavy losses incurred by China's state-owned enterprises, people in the Western world may have difficulties in figuring out what a state-owned enterprise is like and why it loses money. One Chinese researcher, however, made an investigation into a state-owned enterprise with more than seven thousand employees. The findings of the investigation may shed new light on the causes of the state-own enterprises' poor performances.

The subject of the investigation is a factory that boasts a four-storied office building. To the surprise of the researcher, half of the factory's office building is occupied by communist party organizations. As with all local committees of the Communist Party, the party committee of the factory maintains a number of offices as follows: (1) Party Committee Office; (2) Organization Department; (3) Propaganda Department; (4) United Front Department (a section whose job it is to project a friendly image for the Communist Party to those not yet controlled by the Communist Party, e.g. the people of Taiwan); (5) Party Discipline Committee; (6) Party Committee Confidential Materials Room; (7) Party Committee Investigation Office; (8) Policy Implementation Office; and (9) Party Committee Printing and Typing Room, which is staffed by full-time party work officers. In addition, the party committee of the factory has three "mass organizations" under its direction: (1) the Trade Union; (2) the Communist Youth League; and (3) the Women's Association.

Each of the above-mentioned sections has one chief and several deputy chiefs plus a number of officers. In addition, each of the factory's workshops, administration offices and production management offices has a full-time communist party cell secretary and a full-time deputy party cell secretary. Though these full-time party cell secretaries and deputy party cell secretaries do not engage in any productive activity, they are all on the factory's payroll. The other communist party personnel who staff the sections listed above also receive wages from the factory.

This is only one among China's many state-owned enterprises which are structured more like government bureaucracies than like business enterprises. It is hard to imagine how such state-owned enterprises could become profitable, as long as they remain so bloated and so burdened with mechanisms completely irrelevant to business operations. But the state ownership system serves one practical purpose for the Communist Party: Since it allows enterprises to feed so many party officials and officers, the state ownership system has certainly generated a formidable level of support for the communist system. Whether this state of affairs will help Western joint venture partners to make money or not is a different kettle of fish.

In the second half of 1997, the Chinese government began to focus its energies on China's five hundred large state-owned enterprises which accounted for 82% of the total value of production of all state-owned enterprises. Of the five hundred large enterprises, fifty were leviathan-like state-owned conglomerates, which accounted for 78% of the value of production of the five hundred large enterprises. The performances of these large state-owned enterprises were far from satisfactory. As of the end of the first half of 1998, two hundred eighty-nine of the five hundred large enterprises were in the red (or almost in the red). Of the fifty leviathan-like conglomerates, twenty-one were in the red. In January of 1999, China's State Statistics Bureau admitted that the country's state-owned enterprises suffered an aggregate loss of RMB 92 billion yuan (about US$11 billion) in 1998, up 28% from 1997, and that these loss-making enterprises had accumulated a total of RMB 715.50 billion yuan (about US$86.20 billion) in unsalable goods in their warehouses.

It appears that since the government can no longer take care of China's numerous small and medium-sized state-owned enterprises, they are now allowed to go private. But who would care to purchase them? These small and medium-sized state-owned enterprises have nothing but heavy losses to show for it. A survey conducted by the China Social Investigation Office in 1998 suggested that many enterprises had pressurized their employees to purchase their shares, causing serious grievances among the employees. The organization investigated a total of 640 enterprises in Shandong Province, Qinghai Province, Sichuan Province and Liaoning Province. Finally, it estimated that 60% of these enterprises had exerted various degrees of pressure on their employees in order to make them accept the shares. The most common tactic used by the enterprises was to tell their employees that those who refused to buy the shares would get sacked.

The harsh economic realities in China have inevitably inflated the ranks of the unemployed. According to China News Agency, by the end of the first quarter of 1998, ten million one hundred thousand workers had been laid off by various kinds of enterprises. Out of this figure, six million five hundred and seven thousand had been laid off by state-owned enterprises, accounting for 9.2% of China's state-owned enterprise employees. Based on a report about urban unemployment released by China's State Statistics Bureau on August 11th 1998, while the average unemployment rate in China's urban areas was 22.5%, joblessness in Sichuan Province, Guizhou Province and Shaanxi Province was much higher, ranging from 38% to over 40%. Things were somewhat better in major cities like Beijing and Shanghai, where joblessness ranged from 7.5% to 8%. By some experts' estimates, at the end of the 20th century, China had an unemployed population of more than 30 million, not counting the 130 million-strong surplus labor force in the countryside.

In the meantime, since the private sector of the Chinese economy creates jobs for society, absorbs some of the workers laid off by the failing state-owned enterprises and poses little threat to the regime, the authorities allow it to exist and grow for now, which fact in turn has provided the Chinese people with the highest level of freedom they have ever known since the founding of the People's Republic.

According to Mr. Yuan Ming, an expert on Chinese affairs who at one time worked for the Chinese government but left China in the 1980s, the state-owned sector of the Chinese economy can no longer play the dominant role stipulated in the country's communist constitution. Mr. Yuan believes that in the China market, the really active players today are the foreign-invested companies, not the state-owned enterprises. There are about three hundred thousand foreign-invested companies, which own a total of US$250 billion in assets and employ about twenty million Chinese workers. Accounting for 45% of the exports from China in 1998 up from 1% in 1985, the foreign-invested companies now play an increasingly important role in the Chinese economy. These figures suggest that China's economy relies heavily on foreign investments, foreign technology, foreign designs, foreign management skills and foreign marketing methods. On the other hand, with an ample supply of cheap labor from the vast countryside, the foreign-invested companies are able to manufacture large quantities of inexpensive but good-quality products in China and then sell them in the international market.

If Mr. Yuan's figures and estimates are correct, a certain degree of optimism may be warranted, because the Chinese government now has strong economic reasons to cooperate with the Western world. Apparently, cooperation will make life much easier not only for America's multinational corporations, but also for the Chinese leaders themselves since they have to find ways to feed a 1.3 billion-strong population. And needless to say, more cooperation from China would mean less trouble for the West.

Will the changes in the economic arena lead to changes in the nature of the communist state apparatus? So far, that has not happened. Despite the economic reforms, China's communist state apparatus remains intact. Its prisons hold not only common criminals but also political prisoners (of conscience) and underground Christian preachers. Its communist-controlled judicial system metes out punishment to political offenders according to laws formulated on the basis of Marxist ideology. Its KGB-style intelligence establishment continues to operate numerous mail inspection stations (workshops) where, with the help of the post offices around the country, intelligence officers could secretively open and read letters mailed to Chinese citizens from overseas. The communist state continues to control all the newspapers, magazines, radio stations and TV stations in the country to ensure that public opinion is influenced and controlled by the authorities and that dissenting voices are contained. Most importantly, it has a military establishment always ready to respond to the call of the Communist Party in case of popular uprising, as was demonstrated during the June 4th 1989 Tiananmen Square crackdown. So, is China a communist country? It certainly is—at least for now. That is because the left wing of the Communist Party remains strong, whereas the liberal faction is far from fully fledged and the moderates just want to play safe.

Nonetheless, the communist regime needs to project a moderate image to the outside world in order to attract investment dollars. Look at President Jiang Zemin. He is doing a terrific job suggesting to the West that he is a man the West can do business with. When meeting Western politicians or reporters, he would wear a superbly tailored suit and a tasteful silk tie, speak English and beam with warmth. His personal image is impeccable to the point where a Westerner politician would tend to think, "Well, perhaps, President Jiang is a man we can do business with." At least, President Jiang does have a Western veneer.

But all this doesn't change the fact that President Jiang Zemin is the leader of a communist country and as such he has to play by the rules of the communist state apparatus. He is not allowed to step out of the party line. If he does, his colleagues on the left would jump upon him and come down like a ton of bricks. Therefore, sometimes he talks Marxist politics while at other times he promotes market-oriented economic reforms. This way, the left-wing conservatives cannot blame him for not being a Marxist, and the liberals cannot blame him for not promoting economic reforms. Whether or not he wishes to make fundamental changes to the old system in order to bring China in line with the rest of the world on both the economic level and the political level, his hands are tied anyway. As a result, while China's reformers do want to see the Chinese economy "join tracks" with the world economy, pessimists may want to ask: "How?"

8

Moderate Forces Are Growing—Their Strength May Be Underestimated

Given the ferocity of the communist state apparatus, I cannot help but view China's political dissidents as very courageous people. In the meantime, I tend to believe that I understand why the liberals (and perhaps the moderates) in the Communist Party cannot afford to say what they might be thinking about the communist system. Many of the liberals and the moderates are well-educated (even well-intentioned) people. To say that they don't know the problem of the old system is to insult their intelligence. Yet, should they act as if they were living in a free country, they would risk losing everything: position, remuneration, benefits, even personal freedom. In which case, who would look after their families? If the economic reform programs fail, the reformers' heads would roll while the leftist conservatives gloat. It has always been that way in recent Chinese history.

From the mid-1980s till the 1991 putsch in the former Soviet Union, Mr. Gorbachev did everything in his power to push his glasnost political reforms. He definitely knew the problem of the old system. But never once did he openly challenge Marxism in his speeches, because as secretary general of the Soviet Communist Party, he could not afford to do so. Still, the hardliners in the Soviet communist state apparatus decided that they could no longer tolerate his reforms and had to put him and his family under house arrest. That was really a scary moment. Now, by the same token, I don't expect China's reformers to come out into the open and criticize Marxism as I wish they would.

I have heard people in the West ask: Why must the Chinese keep their communist brand name, which is so offensive to the rest of the world? The answer is they cannot scrap it. The left-wing is so strong that the ruling party remains communist in nature at least for now. The hardliners know that without the communist brand name they would have a lot to lose. As to the liberals, although they do not think much of the old system, the old system feeds them too. In fact, the old system controls them and would not allow them to scrap its communist brand name.

The brightest minds in China are the liberal intellectuals who represent the conscience of the country. Their influences in the Chinese society are strong. Although they are unable to publish their views in China's state-controlled media, they have various ways to spread their ideas about free-market economics and democratization. They are a formidable force for the future of China. The fact that many liberal intellectuals now live in exile is a great loss to the country. In early 1992, while touring southern China, the late paramount leader Deng Xiaoping called upon young intellectuals to return to their homeland, whatever their political views. He knew that liberal intellectuals had played an important role in promoting his reforms. Out of China's 1.3 billion-strong population, only a small minority are very well-educated. Yet over the years, the old system has shown little tolerance toward the cream of society, resulting in a serious brain drain. While the authorities expect loyalty from the intellectuals, the intellectuals tend to ask themselves why they should be loyal to a regime that has humiliated them by suppressing their freedom of expression. Over the centuries, Chinese intellectuals have been sensitive people with complicated sentiments toward their rulers. Reared in a strong Confucian culture, they have pledged their loyalty to various dynasties in exchange for respect, not humiliation.

When Western business people visit China, they will certainly see the five-star hotels in the major cities, the small stores operated by private business people, the illuminated signs and advertisements on the street, the McDonald's restaurants in town and the crowds of people drinking Coca-Cola. If they compare these aspects of Chinese life with the lifestyles in other Asian countries, they are likely to find similarities between China's open coastal cities and Asia's capitalist countries. This may lead them to conclude that China is different from communist North Korea and, therefore, "is not a communist country", as Mr. Mark Mobius of Templeton Investment said in 1997.

Thank God, the situation in China is indeed different (and much better) than in North Korea. This is because while North Korea continues to practice orthodox Marxism, China is practicing "socialism with Chinese Characteristics", a kind of reformist or revisionist communism that allows the marketplace to play an increasingly important role in the economy. That's where the difference lies. But reformist or revisionist communism is also communism. It is a new variety of communism which calls for the Communist Party to continue to control the economy as well as the marketplace. At least for now, this new variety of communism appears to be acceptable to a large proportion of the people in China, because Deng Xiaoping's economic reforms have indeed benefitted a lot of people since 1979.

According to China's well-known liberal intellectual in exile Mr. Liu Binyan, about one third of the population are content with the status quo because their lives have improved substantially due to the economic reforms. I must hasten to say that there are also a large number of disgruntled people who criticize the political system, the official ideology and the economic realities surrounding them. But this new variety of communism could turn out to be a transition between communism and free-market capitalism, if the moderate and liberal forces keep growing.

Between the three factions of the Communist Party (the leftist conservative faction, the moderate faction, and the liberal faction), there is some kind of a balance of power. If the conservative faction is excessively strong, the balance of power will tilt in its favor and the reforms will have to be put on hold. If the liberal faction becomes stronger than the conservatives, the scale will tilt in the liberals' favor, allowing the economic reforms to continue and political liberalization to emerge. The moderates are in the middle, trying to keep the boat steady. And President Jiang Zemin, a moderate in my opinion, basically reflects the status of the balance of power. As things stand now, there is no reason to believe that the liberals have sufficient strength (or prowess) to coopt the moderates and transform the communist state apparatus into a democratic pluralist mechanism. Even if such a transformation is ever set in motion, it could be a very long process and would require one essential precondition: a market economy free from communist control. But as Western investors must have learned by now, the China market is far from open and free.

China is a country with a 5000-year history of civilization and an extremely patient people. If the ruling party promises to establish a free-market economy under a real democracy in ten to twenty years' time, I believe the Chinese people would be happy to give it that amount of time to deliver on its promise. A slow and smooth transition from communism to free-market capitalism might be in the best interest of the country, since it would cause less pain to the large numbers of people who depend on the old system for a living. Besides, it would certainly be in the best interest of Chinese leaders themselves, since it would allow them to preside over a booming economy in a stable situation. The question is: Do they have the vision, farsightedness, political will and intention to allow such a slow and smooth transition to happen?

My assumption is that the liberals in the Communist Party may have plans to bring about further economic and political liberalization. They are very well-educated people. Just because they have to quote from Karl

Marx occasionally does not mean they have never heard about Adam Smith. But the present state of China's economy does not favor political changes toward a real democracy. It favors authoritarianism. The state controls most of the country's economic resources plus an excessively large (though inefficient) chunk of the economy and is not prepared to completely privatize China's industry, commerce and banking sector. After all, that is what communism is all about: through the control of economic resources, the communist state controls the people.

So, it is necessary to point out that China's "socialist market economy" is not a market economy at all by Western standards. Will the failure of the public ownership system eventually force the authorities to implement a total privatization program? Only time can tell. Currently, there are signs that the Chinese government is ready to make concessions to foreign businesses. For instance, Chinese laws no longer require that a foreign business must have a Chinese partner in order to run an operation in China. Thus, multinational corporations like General Motor, Dow Chemical and Procter & Gamble have succeeded in assuming full control of their China operations by buying out their Chinese partners. But these are among America's strongest corporate giants. Smaller Western companies may not be able to flex their muscles with equal success. Government intervention remains strong. For instance, in 1997, it was partly due to pressure from the Chinese government that Motorola decided to build a US$750 million silicon-wafer fabrication plant in China and then share revenues with the Chinese through several joint ventures. As Motorola must have learned, goodwill from the government is essential to even wholly foreign-owned enterprises.

But the harsh economic realities are challenging Chinese leaders to take action. If they balk at the necessary structural changes that the economy now requires, such problems as weak demand, stagnation, industrial inefficiency, high unemployment, and bureaucratic corruption could snowball into a crisis beyond control, hurting everybody ranging from Western investors to Chinese leaders themselves, not to mention the tens of millions of workers who tend to be vulnerable in any chaotic situation.

Fortunately, China's moderate forces appear to be growing. Since the late 1970s, economic reformers have moved into important positions. A case in point is the fact that China's economic czar Zhu Rongji, who fell victim to Mao's 1957 crackdown on liberal intellectuals and was dubbed "China's Gorbachev" by Western media in the early 1990s, replaced Mr. Li Peng in March 1998 as China's premier. The position of premier is a very powerful one. But this does not mean Mr. Zhu Rongji will have the last word on every major issue, though he certainly has a bigger say in both economic and political matters now. In addition, Mr. Zhu Rongji's promotion indicates that he is extremely useful to the communist state at a time when it is confronted with quite a few serious issues:

(1) Hundreds of thousands of state-owned enterprises are on the verge of bankruptcy and depend on loans from state-run banks to pay wages to their employees.

(2) The state banks themselves are insolvent by Western standards because they are unable to collect the hundreds of billions of dollars worth of loans extended to the state-owned enterprises.

(3) The options available to the government in resolving these problems are all difficult. Either it keeps the failing state enterprises open with more bank loans, or it shuts them down, thereby turning tens of millions of workers out on the streets at the risk of social unrest.

As of this moment, Mr. Zhu Rongji is probably the only man available to tackle the legacy of decades of economic mismanagement under the Soviet model. Rumor has it that Mr. Zhu Rongji had the trust of both the late paramount leader Deng Xiaoping and the ruling party's late senior economist Chen Yun. It is certainly not easy for the party to find another man as capable and trustworthy to handle a job of such magnitude.

Mr. Zhu's predecessor Mr. Li Peng, who declared martial law in the spring of 1989 before the military crackdown started, is considered to be a conservative by China's liberal intellectuals. In March 1998, Mr. Li Peng stepped down as premier and became Chairman of the Standing Committee of the National People's Congress. But since the National People's Congress is only a rubber-stamp parliament, all major issues being decided by the Politburo of the Communist Party, Mr. Li Peng's role in Chinese politics may have diminished. Besides, Mr. Zhu Rongji seems far more popular than Mr. Li Peng in Chinese politics. An opinion survey conducted by the Policy Research Office of the Central Committee of the Communist Party in spring of 1998 indicated that Premier Zhu Rongji's approval rating was as high as 85% at the time.

Still, one thing is for sure: The conservative hardliners will look closely at Premier Zhu Rongji's every move in order to find anything that they may consider non-socialist. Over the years, they (the hardliners) have declared almost every effective reformist measure non-socialist. Ironically, they may be right. Since all the socialist economic measures endorsed by the hardliners in the past have proven to be ineffective, whatever effective economic measures Premier Zhu is going to introduce now cannot be as socialist as they might wish. The simple truth is that if the so-called "socialist economic measures" are allowed to continue, the economy will collapse as depositors start a run on the state banks.

On the other hand, as a cautious reformer, Premier Zhu is unlikely to implement any program without the prior approval of the Central Committee of the Communist Party and President Jiang Zemin. Thus, he can always claim to have the full support of the party and the people behind him, no matter how capitalist his economic reforms might appear to the hardliners. Although many capitalistic market-oriented reforms have been introduced since the late 1970s, the reformers claim that their economic measures are completely in keeping with the principles of

Marxism. Apparently, they are doers (not theoreticians) and as such, they avoid involvement in ideological debates.

It would be most interesting to know what attitude China's military would adopt toward Premier Zhu Rongji's economic reform programs in the future, since the military has always played an important role in Chinese politics. Without the support of the military, no reforms, whether economic or political, stand a chance to succeed. Yet there is no evidence that the military is not concerned about the heavy financial hemorrhage caused by the state-owned enterprises, which have drained the country of useful resources and failed to create a reasonable level of tax revenue that the country needs to modernize its military. In theory, the transformation of China's state-owned enterprises will help save resources, which in turn could be funneled into the military.

In the 1980s, in order to let the military have an extra source of income, the Communist Party gave China's armed forces permission to run businesses. The Central Committee of the Communist Party, the State Council and the Central Military Commission issued a number of directives to provide for military-controlled businesses in May 1986, March 1989, July 1992 and July 1997 respectively. Gradually, the military became some kind of a conglomerate, operating various franchises including rocket-launching, real estate, pharmaceutical manufacturing, telecommunications services, civilian durable goods manufacturing, foreign trade, kareoke night clubs etc. By expert estimates, at one time, there were more than 15,000 military-controlled enterprises around the country. 5 to 10% of these enterprises boasted pretty large scales, while the rest were of small and medium sizes. These military-controlled enterprises had a total business turnover of US$10 to 18 billion per annum, equivalent to China's annual military budget. Their total profits amounted to US$1 to 3 billion per annum. Clearly, the military has benefited from the economic reforms.

However, since the People's Liberation Army (the PLA) had various privileges, the military-controlled enterprises had many advantages that no ordinary business organizations could even dream of. As some of the officers involved in business activities were corrupted by money and power, the PLA created a bad image for itself and weakened its fighting ability. Thus, on July 11th 1998, President Jiang Zemin declared at a politburo meeting that the armed forces had to stop their involvement in business activities and hand over their enterprises to the civilian authorities. Only time can tell whether this order has been faithfully executed by the various military units that were busier in making money than in honing their military skills during the 1980s and 1990s. If the military-controlled enterprises have really been handed over to the civilian authorities, the PLA must have lost an important source of income and so will have to depend completely on the central government's appropriations for its modernization. That means the profitability of the state-owned enterprises and their ability to generate tax revenues for the government will become an important factor for the PLA generals to consider when they decide whether they should support Premier Zhu Rongji's economic reform programs or not.

Currently, the decision-making process at the state-owned enterprises and the way in which they are managed are far from rational by the standards of modern industry and commerce. For instance, in 1996, China's steel production exceeded one hundred million tons for the first time, but only 10% of the steel produced met international standards, and the capacity utilization rate of the steel industry was as low as 56.2%. While the motor-cycle manufacturing industry had a production capacity of 14.8 million per annum, the utilization rate was only 44.3%. The washing machine industry was capable of producing 21.38 million washing machines per annum, but only 43.4% of the capacity was in use. China's refrigerator manufacturers had an aggregate production capacity of 18.21 million refrigerators per annum, but only 50.4% of that capacity was utilized. The air-conditioner manufacturing industry was operating at 33.5% of a capacity of 2.03 million. The textiles industry boasted a total of 41.9 million spindles, of which only 77% were utilized.

All this means the demand for manufactured goods has been weak. As a result, unsold products have kept piling up in the state-owned enterprises' warehouses. For instance, in 1997, China's watch manufacturers had more than ten million unsold watches stored in their warehouses. The bicycle industry had more than twenty million unsold bicycles in its warehouses. And the auto industry was stuck with more than one hundred thousand vehicles it couldn't get rid of. Both the electric home appliances industry and the textiles industry were in a recession.

The mismanagement of the state-owned enterprises and their low productivity have led many experts to call for their transformation. But after years of discussions on how to transform and upgrade the state-owned enterprises, statistics show that the quality of China's enterprise management has been sliding downhill ever since 1993. At least 45% of the state-owned enterprises are poorly managed, incapable of generating reasonable profits and tax revenues.

For instance, in 1993, China's well-known state-owned brewery Tsingtao Beer transformed itself into a stock company through its initial public offerings (IPO's) in both China and Hong Kong, raising a total of RMB 1.6 billion yuan (about US$192 million). With this money, Tsingtao Beer bought two production lines from Germany and another two production lines from the U.S. to double its production to 280,000 tons. In 1994, Tsingtao Beer set up a new plant with a capacity of 250,000 tons per annum. But the company's profitability fell sharply, even as its size grew. In 1993, its earnings per share (EPS) was RMB 0.25 yuan. By 1996, its EPS had fallen to RMB 0.07 yuan. By 1997, its EPS had plunged below RMB 0.07 yuan. Of the RMB 1.6 billion yuan raised through the IPO's, more than RMB 1.4 billion yuan was used to repay bank loans. Only somewhat more than RMB 1 billion yuan of the IPO money was spent on capital construction and technology upgrading.

Certainly, Premier Zhu Rongji knows the seriousness of the problem of the state-owned enterprises and the difficulties in transforming them. For one thing, his reform programs will estrange the conservatives. But at least on the surface he appears to have the support of President Jiang Zemin, whose political strategy is basically an effort to maintain a mid-of-the-road image which suggests to the various factions of the ruling party that he is neither leaning toward the left nor leaning toward the right. In doing so, he has the benefit of being capable of receiving support from both the leftist conservatives and the liberals, thereby striking a balance of power to ensure political stability. That is why President Jiang Zemin sometimes has to brush up on the Marxist rhetoric that he must have learned years ago in the Senior Cadre School of the Communist Party to appease his comrades in the conservative camp, while preaching market-oriented economic reform and Deng Xiaoping Theory on other occasions to assure his colleagues in the liberal camp that he will continue to endorse their reform programs. Perhaps, he is doing what any savvy politician would do in the kind of political environment that exists in today's China.

However, in case anything goes wrong, be it political or economic, the fall guy would most likely be Premier Zhu Rongji, not President Jiang Zemin, though that sounds outrageously hypothetical, given that China's dire economic realities definitely justify any drastic reforms that the premier might consider necessary. Fortunately, after years of the late Mr. Deng Xiaoping's reform-and-openness drive, the ideological branch of the leftist conservative camp is significantly weaker than before. Since the principal members of the Old Guard are all dead now, the conservative faction has certainly lost some major supporters. Thus, they may not have sufficient strength to unseat Premier Zhu Rongji now. On the other hand, the premier seems to be fully aware of the risks in front of him and has declared that he is prepared to step down if his programs fall through.

In fact, Premier Zhu Rongji's reform programs face stiff resistance from the vested interests in the Communist Party. For instance, the premier intends to reduce the size of China's bloated bureaucracy by 50%. But this means that eleven million communist party officials will be made redundant. Statistics show that a total of twenty-two million communist party officials were on government payrolls as of March 1998. In addition, there were more than ten million cadres (officers) working for various communist party committees around the country. Altogether, as of March 1998, nearly thirty-five million communist party officials and officers depended on the old system for a living. Once out of office, the eleven million ex-party officials will lose the influence they have wielded over the years. Needless to say, that would not make life easier for them, since influence is a kind of currency without which one can hardly get anything done in China. Such being the implications of the reforms, no wonder they meet with resistance.

Moreover, China's state-owned enterprises are run by party officials, many of which are in the red but continue making payments to workers as if they were welfare institutions. Should the government shut down such loss-making state-owned enterprises, not only tens of millions of workers but also hundreds of thousands of party officials would have to be laid off. This indicates that the state-owned sector of the Chinese economy is like a parasite that lives on the fruit produced by the booming private sector. In the meantime, it also explains why Premier Zhu Rongji's reform programs are difficult to implement. No matter how unreasonable the old system may be, it feeds a lot of people. To reform the old system will hurt all those who feed on the old system. The government is certainly aware of the issue and seems to be ready to provide some kind of a cushion for those affected by the reform programs. For example, according to media reports, party officials laid off under the reform programs will receive an allowance equivalent to 80% of their original wages for a period of four years.

A report written by the Central Policy Research Office of the Communist Party in the spring of 1998 on the restructuring of the Chinese bureaucracy said that some high-ranking party officials with vested interests were likely to pose problems for the restructuring program of the State Council and that since corruption among party and government officials was rampant, some of the officials leaving office under the program might take advantage of their connections and influences to advance their own interests, thereby creating a new form of corruption that the existing government supervision mechanisms could hardly find out.

The restructuring program required that proper arrangements be made so that officials leaving office could move into positions on the standing committees of the various People's Congresses and Political Consultative Conferences around the country or on the boards of directors of the state-owned enterprises. But the report said that the existing government sections and state-owned enterprises were unable to accept so many ex-party officials. So, just how many party officials would be made redundant by the restructuring program? According to the report, the number of high-ranking party officials who had to leave office under the State Council program would exceed 2.3 million nationwide.

At a meeting held on July 14th 1998 with China's provincial and regional officials, Premier Zhu Rongji said that the central government's reform programs had met with resistence and were under pressure from people inside the Communist Party. He said that some high-ranking party officials were resisting the implementation of the central government's policies because they continued to believe in outdated ideology and bureaucratism , that the country's outdated structures and mechanisms were hampering the economic reforms, that sectarian local forces were resisting the reforms, and that the Communist Party's cohesive power had weakened and was being seriously tested. Again, he said he was prepared to resign if his reform programs fell through. Apparently, he knows the reform programs will hurt the vested interests of millions of communist party officials.

In order to enable the state-owned enterprises to operate like real business organizations, Premier Zhu Rongji's restructuring program would force many of the industrial dinosaurs to either close or down-size and lay off tens of millions of their employees in the process. In fact, large numbers of workers have already been laid off around the country by the state-owned enterprises, and the level of unemployment thus exacerbated has created a destabilizing factor in the Chinese society. According to a June 13th 1998 telephone conference convened by the State Council, the number of demonstrations staged by laid-off workers started to rise in early 1998, and the people involved in the demonstrations included not only laid-off workers, but also grassroots communist party officers and retired party officials.

During some demonstrations, the protestors broke into government and communist party offices, destroying (or burning) government properties such as vehicles. On other occasions, the demonstrators clashed with the police, causing casualties. In certain parts of the country, people took to the streets to stage petition processions outside government offices. (The Chinese government must be very nervous about such petitions since they may have political implications.) Between January and May of 1998, seventy-five Chinese cities saw laid-off workers and urban residents staging protests. More than 270 of these protests led to violence. In more than ninety of these protests, the demonstrators clashed with the police. As a result, more than 3500 people were either wounded or killed. The telephone conference disclosed that more than 270 public security personnel and armed police had been killed in the clashes. During thirty-two demonstrations, the protestors openly condemned the Communist Party and the country's socialist system. Furthermore, the telephone conference revealed that some local party officials had secretly provided their support to the demonstrators as a signal of their displeasure with the central government's enterprise restructuring program.

In the meantime, amid signs of social unrest, high-ranking officials of the Communist Party may have embarked on a debate among themselves as to the wisdom of Premier Zhu Rongji's enterprise restructuring program. For example, in June 1998, thirty-five members of the Standing Committee of the National People's Congress submitted an emergency bill to the Chairman of the Standing Committee with regard to the issue of social unrest caused by the large number of workers laid off by the state-owned enterprises.

The emergency bill claimed: (1) that the measures to lay off workers as stipulated by the state-owned enterprise restructuring program had infringed upon workers' right to a livelihood; (2) that the lack of social security for the large number of workers laid off by the state-owned enterprises was a breach of the system of the People's Republic of China which was based on a union of the working class and the peasant class; (3) that the merits of the socialist system embodied in workers' rights were under threat; (4) that the people of the country and the members of the Communist Party did not support the measures used by the state-owned enterprises to lay off their employees; (5) that the petition processions and demonstrations staged by laid-off workers and the incidents involving protestors who broke into government and communist party offices were an indication of escalating social unrest and political instability; (6) that public discontent with the Communist Party and the government was becoming more and more visible; (7) that confronted with high unemployment and large crowds of laid-off workers, some local government authorities had lost control of the situation; (8) that in a number of places hostile forces were taking advantage of the mounting problems created by the enterprise restructuring process, instigating disturbances with political implications; and (9) that the central government had failed to resolve the unemployment issue.

Among the thirty-five members of the Standing Committee of the National People's Congress submitting the emergency bill were ex-government ministers, army generals, ex-provincial communist party committee secretaries, and ex-provincial governors. I am tempted to deduce that some serious differences of opinion might have emerged among the Chinese leaders with regard to the consequences of possible social unrest likely to be induced by the state enterprise restructuring program. According to sources in Beijing, some Chinese leaders worry that if disturbances break out in a major city because laid-off workers protest the loss of their livelihood, the public of that city may sympathize with the protestors, and then the people of other cities may also take to the streets, triggering nationwide unrest. Under such circumstances, urban residents might spontaneously form their own organizations, which would then liaise with each other, triggering further disturbances with far more profound political implications.

Between April and June of 1998, at least twelve provincial governments sent reports to the State Council and the Central Committee of the Communist Party, demanding that the central government should stipulate specific measures to address social unrest in the provinces brought about by the enterprise restructuring program. Among other things, the provinces requested: (1) permission to formulate their own economic policies; (2) tax reductions and remissions; and (3) most importantly, loans from the central government to ease the hardships afflicting the laid-off workers. Some provinces even wished that the central government would order the state-owned enterprises to stop laying off employees.

The report from the government of Liaoning Province said that the central government should review the state enterprise restructuring program and find out whether the policies and measures stipulated by the program were correct under the circumstances of the nation. In its report, the Communist Party Committee of Heilongjiang Province mentioned that laid-off workers and jobless people in the province had been shouting extremely disturbing slogans at their gatherings such as: "Down with the new exploiting class!" "Fight for the livelihood of the working class!" "Bury the new privileged class and establish a republic with a real regime for the people!"

The government and the Communist Party Committee of Shanxi Province told the central government that the province's laid-off workers had spontaneously set up such organizations as "committees to safeguard the factories", "committees for employee self-salvation", and "congresses to represent employee rights". What is worse, these organizations had won sympathies and support from the public, including communist party members, retired workers, members of China's "democratic parties" and even party officials.

At a conference convened on May 14th 1998 by the Central Committee of the Communist Party and the State Council, Secretary of the Communist Party Committee of Hunan Province, Wang Maolin, said that his province had one million jobless people, plus 850,000 recently laid-off workers and nearly three million under-employed people. He said that each day more than forty petition processions or demonstrations took place in his province, that on a daily basis his province witnessed more than ten incidents involving protestors who broke into government offices or state enterprise communist party offices, and that many grassroots communist party officers and state enterprise officers had participated in the demonstrations.

At the same conference, Secretary of the Communist Party Committee of Sichuan Province, Xie Shijie, said that if the restructuring of the state-owned enterprises continued under the current program, more social unrest would emerge, triggering possible disturbances with political implications. He expressed his concern that the situation might get out of control, if political disturbances erupted.

Even as Chinese workers struggle for their livelihood, corrupt party officials have been robbing the state for quite a while. Data gathered by the State Statistics Bureau in Beijing suggest that during the five-year period from the beginning of 1993 to the end of 1997, a total of RMB 355 billion yuan (about US$43 billion) in state assets and state funds went missing, of which RMB 250 billion yuan (about US$30 billion) had left China. Thus, although employees understand that it is necessary to restructure the failing state enterprises, the rampant corruption among party officials has raised a serious question: If those responsible for the failure of the state-owned enterprises can continue to feed on the old system, why should the workers be the ones to bear the brunt of the economic hardships brought about by the restructuring program?

According to the State Statistics Bureau, by April 1998, the country's state-owned enterprises had laid off a total of 18.31 million employees, of whom only 4.185 million were fortunate enough to have found work with other employers. Since the laid-off workers are eligible to receive small amounts of financial assistance for a limited period of time, they are not included in the joblessness numbers compiled by the government. Even so, these official numbers are very alarming. For instance, as of April 1998, a total of 7.353 million people in China were registered as being unemployed. In the rural areas, large crowds of peasants are unable to find any work to do. The figures on China's rural joblessness are so huge that I do not believe anybody (that is, anybody except Almighty God) has a solution. Based on media reports, the country's rural areas have an aggregate surplus of labor in excess of 114 million peasants. What is more, this number will increase by nearly 5 million per annum. By rough estimates, more than 68 million peasants have already left their homes in the countryside for the cities to seek their livelihood.

Which way China will go remains to be seen. Long term, there is certainly reason for optimism about the country's economic reforms. At least, conventional wisdom says that economic freedom will eventually lead to political freedom. During one trip to Asia after he had left office, former U.S. President George Bush said to the press that he was bullish on China (and Hong Kong as well). Yes, he used the word "bullish".

Apparently, he was looking at the long term. Mr. Bush spent quite a few years in Beijing in the 1970s when he served as head of the U.S. liaison office before the United States granted diplomatic recognition to China. Not forgetting about his strong intelligence background, I tend to have a lot of faith in his expert judgement. Somewhere down the road (that is, long term), China will have to come back to the fold of the Free World, if it is to bring its economy in line with the world economy.

But for now, China remains a communist country with a complete communist state apparatus and a complete system of state controls over the economy despite the existence of a small-scale private sector. To be fair, I must admit that things have improved a great deal since the late 1970s when China's late paramount leader Deng Xiaoping initiated his reforms, which have enabled the ruling party's moderates and technocrats (and even liberals) to move into important government positions. In addition, Mr. Deng Xiaoping's policy of "reform and openness" has indeed provided the Chinese people with certain economic freedoms and has reduced government interference in their private lives.

As a measure of the economic freedom currently enjoyed by ordinary Chinese citizens, U.S. dollars are now available to them on the black market in major Chinese cities. Although the Chinese currency (the "RMB yuan") is non-convertible, joint ventures between Chinese enterprises and foreign businesses are allowed to purchase limited amounts of U.S. dollars with the "RMB yuan" at China's foreign exchange swap centers, if they need U.S. dollars to import equipment or materials from overseas for their business operations. Furthermore, Chinese citizens are allowed to carry a maximum of RMB 6000 yuan per person out of the mainland when they visit Hong Kong, where they can convert the Chinese currency in their possession into Hong Kong dollars or U.S. dollars at any China-backed bank there.

In short, Deng's reforms have brought about relaxation and liberalization in certain areas without causing the ruling party to lose its grip on state power. Hopefully, the private sector of the Chinese economy will grow to such an extent that the ruling party feels that to cooperate with private enterprises will better serve the state's tax revenue interests, since the old practice of appointing party officials to run state enterprises has resulted in heavy losses of capital and tax revenue. Such a cooperation between the private sector and the ruling party (if it ever materializes) could accelerate the process of change in the ideology of the ruling party toward further liberalization, which in turn would foster the growth of the moderate (and liberal) forces in the ruling party. Then what? Will they scrap Marxism as a moribund economic theory? Let's see.

At the end of the day, politics is about money. It is about who shall manage China's resources. It is about who can balance the country's accounts. It is about who can enable the economy to grow at a sustainable pace. If the economy fails to perform, it would be impossible to improve the quality of the country's balance sheet. That in turn could jeopardize political stability, no matter how hard President Jiang Zemin tries to maintain the balance of power between the reformist camp and the left-wing conservative camp.

Throughout the history of the Communist Party, the reformist forces and the conservative left-wing forces have struggled with each other for political control. But as China's late paramount leader Deng Xiaoping admitted in early 1992, traditionally, the influences of the Party's left wing have been very strong and scary. The problem is that the left-wing's influences have never helped to balance the country's accounts. Why? Because the basic Marxist concept of public ownership of the means of production, endorsed by the left wing without reservation but questioned by the reformers at heart, has been rejected by the unsurmountable forces of the marketplace. Now, the economic reforms offer the reformers an opportunity to tip the balance of power in their favor. It is up to the reformers to decide when to declare to the Chinese people that Marxism is wrong. Sooner or later, this has to be done, because the Marxist ideology of the Communist Party is the single most colossal obstruction to the reformers' efforts to improve the country's balance sheet.

9

Marxism-Leninism or Corruption? But Who Cares?

It is important to note that while China maintains a one-party dictatorship with all the trappings of a Soviet-style communist regime, the ruling party includes people of various views and opinions, a certain number of whom are moderates and liberals with strong reformist ideas. For example: In early 2000, former director and editor-in-chief of The People's Daily (the Communist Party's organ) Hu Jiwei, a long-time party member living in retirement in Beijing, somehow published a long article entitled <<"Socialism" Without Democracy—Words From My Heart In The New Century>> in a San Francisco Chinese-language newspaper.

The article condemned the Communist Party's ruling philosophy, saying, "The theory and practice of proletarian dictatorship is similar to the theory and practice of fascism.....The root cause of despotic autocracy lies in the organizational principles of the Communist Party." Mr. Hu asked, "How can we have socialism if we do not have democracy? Is it true that the kind of socialism with Chinese characteristics which we want to build is nothing but socialism without democracy indeed?"

What a courageous old man! In the late 1970s and early 1980s, Mr. Hu Jiwei (84 in 2000) served as a key aide to Mr. Hu Yaobang (the late liberal-minded secretary general of the Communist Party) and played an important role in the "thought emancipation" drive of that period. Anyone who thinks there are only "bad guys" in the Communist Party needs to think twice. At least, it is difficult to call Mr. Hu Jiwei a "bad guy". My guess is there must be many other party members who have similar views and opinions about the old system. We just don't know how many party members are as liberal-minded as Mr. Hu Jiwei is.

As the economic reforms continue, China's middle class, which includes ordinary citizens as well as members of the Communist Party, is growing rapidly. In fact, many of the well-off today are party officials' relatives and close friends who have taken advantage of their special connections with the bureaucracy to get rich quick. A certain number of the new rich have already transferred their wealth to Hong Kong, which, though under communist control now, continues to have a free-market economy, or to counties in the Free World such as the United States, Canada and Australia. In 1996 and early 1997, when Hong Kong's stock and property markets rallied strongly, rumors began to circulate that large amounts of money had flowed into Hong Kong from China's new rich, helping push up stock and property prices to unsustainable levels. In fact, some of the new rich have already left China and settled down in North America—either in the United States or in Canada. Obviously, the new rich, some of whom are the sons and daughters of the old communist revolutionaries, neither believe in communism nor see communist China as a safe place for their wealth.

So, needless to say, China's current business environment or business culture is a hotbed of corruption where "guanxi" (connections) and back-door practices provide the key to success. Indeed, bureaucratic corruption has already caused bitter grievances and resentment among the unfortunate who have difficulty even in finding work to support themselves. The social injustice created by corrupt communist party officials is evident.

But let us look at the issue from a different perspective. The Communist Party was founded in the summer of 1927 as a proletarian revolutionary party, a party for the poor, "committed to digging a grave for the bourgeoisie" by confiscating their wealth, I guess. But look at the Communist Party today. It is so intertwined with the new rich that its class nature must have changed to a certain degree, though its name has not changed at all. Besides, the entire system appears to be moving from totalitarianism (i.e. a system by which the government has a complete control of both political power and economic resources) toward a new kind of authoritarianism which allows the private sector of the economy to grow but suppresses political dissent. This new authoritarianism seems to be the Communist Party's new philosophy of governance.

Is the party still "committed to digging a grave for the bourgeoisie"? Probably not. According to a 1999 State Council document entitled "Opinions About How to Better the Lives of the Elderly Cadres of the Party, the Government and the Military and Their Families", the government shall grant pricey residences and handsome allowances to high-ranking officials and their families. Since these items, once granted, will become private properties, the children of the officials shall be able to inherit or sell the luxury residences. In other words, based on their financial status, the high-ranking officials of the Communist Party and their families belong to the moneyed class, rather than the proletariat.

The sons and daughters of the old communist revolutionaries now have enough wealth to live the kind of lifestyle that only the bourgeoisie can afford. So, who are the bourgeoisie? If the Communist Party still wants to "dig a grave for the bourgeoisie", I would say, "No problem, go right ahead. But remember that would hurt the well-off in the Communist Party too." The question for the ruling party is whether it is wise to continue to promote Marxist ideology, a philosophy that urges the poor to confiscate the wealth of the rich, when many of the important members of the ruling party are now the owners of wealth?

Although there are critics of the above-mentioned State Council document, I see it as an effort by the moderate faction to tone down the radical Marxist philosophies of the ruling party. Perhaps, that is the best way to pacify those Marxist theoreticians in the conservative leftist camp. The rationale behind the move is: Give them a sop and they will quiet down.

As the number of the well-off grows, the urge among the new rich to find a way to protect their wealth and rights will grow as well. At present, the usual way to get protection is to try to establish "good relations" with the bureaucracy, i.e. people in power. Going forward, the ruling party might have to make concessions to the new rich by allowing the country's rubberstamp parliament (The National People's Congress) to pass legislation that provides more protection for private wealth. But as long as China does not change its communist brand name, the new rich will not feel safe, no matter how many laws are passed by the NPC. Still, optimists would remind us that both South Korea and Taiwan used to have authoritarian regimes, too, which allowed the private sectors of their economies to grow but suppressed political dissent. Eventually, however, pluralist democracies emerged in both countries. The same thing might happen in China over time, though it would be unwise to count the chickens before they are hatched.

During the Mao era which ended in 1976 with Mao's death, the Communist Party recruited only from the working class and the peasant class. It investigated the family background of each would-be recruit to ensure that his or her parents were workers or peasants. This procedure was designed to preserve the purity of the proletarian nature of the Communist Party. After Mr. Deng Xiaoping consolidated his position in Chinese politics in 1979, the Communist Party's recruiting policy underwent fundamental changes. Soon, it started to recruit heavily from the well-educated, thereby accepting many people of non-working-class family backgrounds. It is worth mentioning again that China is a country with a very long history of culture and civilization where, traditionally, the well-educated have come from the upper class and the middle class, not from the working class and the peasant class. Thus, the practice of recruiting from the well-educated may have served as a catalyst in the process of change to the class nature of the ruling party. The following is a true story that I wish to tell to illustrate my point:

It was toward the end of 1948, not very long before the Communist army marched into Shanghai, that W (false name) arrived by air from Xian, a city on the front of the civil war between the Nationalists and the Communists, with his mother, a devoted Christian who read the Bible every day. W and I became playmates but were too young to understand what was happening in the country. Later when I was older, I learned that W's father had served as a general with the Nationalist army.

I admired W because he could learn any subject far more quickly than I did, be it language or math, though we were the same age. I had barely finished my primary school when he began to attend high school. When I was attending my junior middle school with great frustration at those difficult text books on contemporary Chinese and ancient Chinese, I noticed that W was reading classical Chinese novels. I kept wondering why W was so quick and I was so slow. By the time I completed my senior middle school, W had already left Shanghai to study at one of the best universities in Beijing. What a genius, I thought.

I met W again in the early 1970s when the Cultural Revolution started to cool down after the death of Marshal Lin Biao, who had been Mao's heir apparent earlier at the beginning of the movement but had fallen victim to the intramural power struggle in part of his own making. At the time, W appeared to be very cautious not to touch upon any politically sensitive topics. Then, more than twenty years later, in summer of 1997 shortly before my departure from Hong Kong for North America, a relative of mine from Shanghai told me that W was a member of the Communist Party and held an important position with a government agency. I was quite surprised at the news. For it would have been completely unthinkable during the Mao era for the Communist Party to recruit a man whose father had been a general with the Nationalist army fighting the communists during the civil war.

However, it would be very naive of me to presume that the organization department of the Communist Party's local committee had failed to examine W's family background before appointing him to his position. As a man who once lived under communism for extremely long years, I know quite well that the organization department keeps files and is highly efficient in gathering information about any party member's family background. The story about Mr. W is an indication that the Communist Party now attaches more importance to education and ability than family background in recruiting new members. Only it would be inconceivable if smart, well-educated people like Mr. W had joined the Communist Party because they believed in Marxism-Leninism. I for one certainly do not believe that "faith in the communist ideal" were their motive for joining the Communist Party. Rather, I would presume that they have joined the Communist Party in order to advance their personal interests.

Please do not get me wrong. I am not blaming Mr. W or any other people who have joined the Communist Party because they need to look after their own interests. Rather, I see their decision to join the Communist Party as very human in the light of the political and economic realities in China. Since the Communist Party controls the power of government as well as most of the country's resources, the easiest way to get a piece of the action is to join the Communist Party. Now that the economic reforms require the ruling party to recruit well-educated people to work for it, I guess many of the well-educated must have realized it is in their best interest to jump on the band wagon. In the meantime, as the number of well-educated party members increases, their impact on the ruling party's domestic and foreign policies will become more and more visible as time goes by. Historically speaking, throughout China's various dynasties, well-educated Chinese have always regarded selling their services and talent to the authorities as a secure route to success.

So, now the question is: Just how many party members still believe in Marxism-Leninism, even though it remains the ruling party's official ideology? In effect, few people in today's China really believe in Marxism. Nor does the ruling party give a damn whether Chinese citizens believe in Marxism or not, as long as they do not make trouble for the authorities. If CNN reporters are allowed to conduct opinion surveys on the streets of China's major coastal cities, they will realize that the most difficult task to fulfill in today's communist China is to find someone who truly believes in communism. It would be a miracle if CNN reporters found a Chinese citizen reading Karl Marx and nurturing "the great ideal" of the communist Utopia while so many of his fellow countrymen are looking to make a quick buck. I would not be surprised if there is as much greed in Beijing or Shanghai or Guangzhou as on Wall Street. Is Marxism relevant any more? Probably not, as far as the economy is concerned.

I would rather presume that in China's current economic environment, the moderate forces in the Communist Party will continue to grow and eventually conclude that without fundamental changes to the country's economic and political structures, it would be impossible to bring the Chinese economy in line with the world economy. Although it is well known that Chinese leaders want to see their country catch up with the rest of the world, the catch is that their goal could become unattainable if they allow the Marxist principles of the ruling party (such as the concept of "socialist public ownership" and the philosophy of "proletarian dictatorship") to continue to restrict the growth of the Chinese economy.

Firstly, "socialist public ownership", that is, the nationalization of industries, simply does not work anywhere on this planet, so any further experiments in this respect should now be moved on to the Mars before they cause more damage. Secondly, I can hardly believe my ears when the officials of the ruling party tell the world they represent the proletariat. Look at the fine suits and silk ties they wear. Look at the luxury saloons and limousines they ride in. Look at the college diplomas and degrees they hold. I would say: Come on, give me a break! At least in North America, no proletarians have such educational backgrounds and live such lifestyles. This myth of "proletarian dictatorship" in China needs to be toned down to convince the well-off to keep their new-found wealth inside rather than out of the country.

The fact of the matter is that even as the ruling party preserves its communist brand name in an attempt to stabilize its control, quite a few of its members take advantage of the one-party system to serve their own interests. Since the communist state controls most of the country's economic resources, needless to say, it is the officials of the Communist Party who have access to the resources as well as the business opportunities related to the resources. Furthermore, they also have the power to determine how to allocate the economic resources and business opportunities under their control.

On the other hand, a large number of business people are out there, eagerly seeking to establish "guanxi" (connections) with the officials of the ruling Communist Party in the hope that the officials will grant them lucrative business opportunities. Would they be willing to pay handsome kickbacks to the officials? You bet. So, ironically, to join the Communist Party must have become a fashionable route toward power and financial success in China, rather than an effort "to realize the great ideals of the proletarian revolution". I guess Karl Marx (author of Das Kapital) and Friedrich Engels, the two founding fathers of the communist movement who published the Communist Manifesto in 1848 calling for the proletariat to seize power from the bourgeoisie and nationalize society's resources as a way to bring about the Utopia of their fancy, must be turning in their graves with discomfort and embarrassment.

Let us hear what China's best-known Marxist theoretician Deng Liqun had to say about his own party at a meeting convened on June 29th 1999 by the Secretariat of the Central Committee of the Communist Party in relation to the party's propaganda affairs:

"Because Deng Xiaoping (China's late paramount leader) was only focused on economic affairs, allowing money matters to prevail over political issues, the country and the Communist Party are now in serious trouble. Corruption in the Communist Party has destabilized its leadership position and alienated the people and is likely to cause the demise of the party. The problem currently confronting the Communist Party is not that some sections, some local authorities, or some senior officials have degenerated through disorientation, but that the entire party including its leading cadres has lost faith in the communist ideal. Now the party is Marxist only in name, not in essence. Which way is our country moving? Our party has degenerated and is virtually on the verge of collapse. Shall we reflect upon this reality? It is going to be a serious historic test to the leadership of the party....

"Various kinds of social problems are deteriorating, challenging the party and the government, challenging the leadership of the Communist Party. From the departments and commissions of the Central Committee down to the local committees, the grassroots party organizations and the rural party cells, the organism of the Communist Party is already putrid. This in turn could trigger a political crisis in the country and the collapse of the Communist Party's leadership position. But that is exactly the kind of price the party will have to pay for the failure of Deng Xiaoping's theory."

What a moving swan song by a true believer in the communist Utopia. But who cares? The Chinese people, including the members of the Communist Party, are apparently far more interested in advancing their financial interests than in Mr. Deng Liqun's "faith in the communist ideal". Perhaps, among those who show the least respect for "the communist ideal" are the sons and daughters of the officials of the

Communist Party. As a rule, it is much easier for them to join the ruling party. It is much easier for them to get promotions if they work for the government. And more importantly, it is much easier for them to become successful business people. Critics would certainly cry "outrageously preferential treatment for the privileged" or even "foul play".

But again, let us look at the issue from a different perspective. Since many of the sons and daughters of the high-ranking officials of the Communist Party are well-educated or very well-educated with extensive exposure to Western cultural influences, their participation in Chinese politics and business could become a positive development in Chinese society, which needs well-educated people to provide leadership and new ideas for the future.

As to the officials of the Communist Party, it is by now known not only to ordinary Chinese citizens but also to the rest of the world that it is somehow much easier for them to become financially successful. I have no objection whatsoever to party officials becoming financially successful. Rather, I hope they will all have a taste of wealth, freedom and good life and then tone down their Marxist rhetoric. Perhaps, as people begin to wonder whether the ruling Communist Party is still proletarian in nature, party officials will find it difficult to call themselves "the vanguard of the proletariat", especially if fat bank accounts are hidden under their mattresses. Anyway, it is getting more and more difficult to justify one-party rule in the name of "proletarian dictatorship" when the officials of the ruling party act like capitalist big shots.

Under the current one-party system, corruption has become a way of life in China, because no effective supervisory mechanisms seem to be in place to check the officials of the ruling party which controls the various sections of the government and the entire state-owned sector of the economy. Although the party claims that it has only the people's interests at heart, I cannot help wondering whether it is kidding itself. Since party officials are normal human beings with normal inherent human weaknesses that all other normal humans are guilty of, the above-mentioned claim by the ruling party lacks credibility. Rather, it sounds hypocritic to me. It may even sound hypocritic to the members of the ruling party as well. At a meeting convened by the Politburo of the Communist Party in early March of 2000, Politburo member Wei Jianxing (the man responsible for party discipline) disclosed that during 1998 and 1999, more than seven thousand and three hundred party members had proposed to quit the party, because they thought it was no longer worthy of them. In the judgement of these party members, the corrupt behavior of party officials had already cost the Communist Party its support base among the people.

I am not saying that the Communist Party has never done anything in the interest of the people. The market-oriented economic reforms initiated by the ruling party in the late 1970s under the stewardship of the late paramount leader Deng Xiaoping have certainly benefited the people big time. What I can hardly believe is the suggestion that the ruling party does not have an axe to grind, because the one-party system undeniably safeguards the privileges of the officials of the ruling party. That is why most party officials are not interested in pursuing political reforms. They know very well that real democratic political reforms would result in the elimination of their privileges. Just because they call themselves communists does not mean they do not know which side their bread is buttered.

Privileges are the livelihood of the officials of the Communist Party. Since nobody would allow their livelihood to be taken away without a fight, it would be very naive of me to expect the Communist Party to end the current one-party system which safeguards the privileges of party officials any time soon. Take China's late dictator Mao Zedong as an example. After the Great-Leap-Forward-and-People's-Commune Drive launched by Mao in 1958 turned out to be an economic disaster resulting in the starvation of millions of people, the moderates of the Communist Party came to express their disapproval of Mao's economic policies, though in a very polite manner. Still, it was completely intolerable to the narrow-minded Mao.

First, in 1959, Mao replaced Minister of Defense Peng Dehuai, who had earlier submitted a long report on the disastrous consequences of the Great-Leap-Forward Drive, with his protégé Marshal Lin Biao. By doing so, Mao put his colleagues on notice that they were not allowed to criticize his policies. Then, as if that was not enough, Mao developed strong suspicions that his political rivals were plotting a coup d'etat against him and decided that he had to take pre-emptive action to protect his privileges. So, apparently on Mao's instructions, Marshal Lin Biao made a speech to the members of the Politburo of the Communist Party on May 18th 1966, claiming that some people were plotting a coup d'etat against the Chairman. Almost immediately, Mao launched his Cultural Revolution to purge the party. Inevitably, many of his potential rivals like State President Liu Shaoqi and the then Secretary General Deng Xiaoping fell victim to the political purge that ensued in the name of "culture"—nothing could have been further from the truth!

As a result of the Cultural Revolution, the country was thrown into a state of complete chaos, countless families were broken, and the president of the country, Mr. Liu Shaoqi, was persecuted to death. However, Mao's privileges were preserved till the end of his life. In that sense— and only in that sense, the Cultural Revolution was Mao's greatest achievement in life, for it served his personal interests to the uttermost. No wonder he told his followers that the Cultural Revolution was absolutely necessary and his followers kept telling the public that the Cultural Revolution was very good. Yes, the Cultural Revolution was "absolutely necessary" and certainly "very good" to Mao and his followers, in so far as their interests were served. Human nature is selfish, and so was "the Great Leader" Mao Zedong, who was as great a hypocrite as he was a despot. Throughout his life, Mao successfully sold himself as a selfless revolutionary leader to so many suckers who helped make him emperor of the Middle Kingdom without even suspecting that he could be as selfish at heart as anybody else, until the Cultural Revolution broke out and hurt them as well. What an irony of life!

In the final analysis, politics is about money, that is, about the control of resources. However, at least on the surface, Chinese politics appears to be about power and privilege. Only, without power and privilege, life would not be easy for the officials of the Communist Party. That is why they want to keep their one-party system and tell the world "socialism is great", even as corruption runs wild in the People's Republic. They are normal human beings with normal human emotions and normal human desires just like us in the Free World. The difference is that they wear a Marxist mask (which we do not wear), trying to fool others into believing that they are true believers in "the great ideals of the proletariat" caring "only for the interests of the people". In doing so, they may have fooled themselves as well. If it is true that the Communist Party cares "only for the interests of the people", why so many Chinese including myself have left China or escaped from China for good? Why are there so many Chinese who want to leave their "beloved socialist motherland" right at this moment?

However, I believe I understand the officials of the Communist Party. I even sympathize with them. I know they wear that Marxist mask, because they have to in order to survive. For decades, I lived in Shanghai, China, under communism till 1986 when I left for the then British crown colony, Hong Kong. I fully understand why communist party officials have to wear their Marxist masks.

Perhaps, because I was born in a businessman's family, the propaganda of the Communist Party could not fool me at all even when I was a kid. I remember that quite a few of my primary school mates and my middle school mates did not give a damn what the Party had to say. One afternoon in 1953 or 1954 when I was only nine or ten years old, one of my classmates and I were reviewing lessons after class on the veranda of our school building. Ding was his surname. He was from a wealthy business family living in a nice residential quarter on Shanghai's Nanjing Road West. Somehow, he took out a notebook. When he opened it, I saw a Mao picture printed on the first page. Young as I was, I knew it was unsafe for me to mention the name of the chief of the Communist Party to anyone in a negative tone, so I said nothing. But I was pleasantly surprised when Ding made his comment about Mao, the man portrayed by the Communist Party as "the savior": "It's all because of him." Then he forcibly flicked his forefinger against the Mao picture with a sullen look on his face to make his meaning clear to me. He meant to say that Mao was the cause of disaster. I knew many wealthy families had suffered a lot under Mao's reign, so I understood why Ding was angry. Still, I said nothing. Maybe, I gave a nod of agreement to appease him, but I have no recollection of that. What I can recall clearly is I did not say a single word of disapproval about Mao.

In retrospect, I must admit that I was a very shrewd Shanghai kid, but that is how I survived under totalitarianism. During all the long years I spent in communist China, never did I utter a word of condemnation against communism or Marxism in public, for fear I should land myself in jail. Even if I had been bold enough to criticize communism in public, it would not have made any difference. So, now, do I have the right to demand that the officials of the Communist Party take off their Marxist masks? I don't think so. Yet, I guess that when such well-known communists as Marxist Theoretician Deng Liqun preach Marxism-Leninism and "the great communist ideal" in Beijing, many Chinese citizens would wonder, "What great communist ideal? My foot! Hell with it!"

Is socialism great? It sure is, provided that you are a communist party official. Socialism (or collectivism), while restricting individual freedoms, guarantees the officials of the Communist Party powers and privileges to control the resources of society. I would love it, if I were a communist party official myself! I would sing the famous Mao-era song entitled "Socialism Is Good" every morning to cheer myself up. Why shouldn't I, since "socialism" would make life very easy for me? In addition, I would certainly hate any reform program, be it economic or political, because it would hit me where it hurts!

Vertically, corrupt behavior could happen between a communist party-controlled institution at a higher level and a communist party-controlled institution at a lower level. For instance, in order to get anything done, a lower-level institution has to apply to a higher-level institution for funds, and in order to ensure that its application will be successful, the lower-level institution might have to bribe the officials of the higher-level institution. Otherwise, the application might never be approved.

Horizontally, corrupt behavior could happen between two communist party-controlled institutions at the same level. For instance, when the officials of the Administration of Industry and Commerce of Province A visit Province B, they are often treated to expensive feasts and given expensive gifts by the Administration of Industry and Commerce of Province B, and vice versa. The question is: Whose money is it that is spent on such expensive feasts and gifts? The answer is: The Chinese taxpayers' money. Outrageous! Yes, it is, but that is a way of life in the People's Republic, because the country's "socialist system" has generated such a deep-rooted bureaucratic culture over the years.

Corrupt behavior could also happen in the dealings between two completely different organizations. For instance, a school may find itself in an embarrassing situation where it must accept certain students who fail to meet the entrance requirements set by the school authorities, because their parents are among the officials of the relevant government agencies of the jurisdiction in which the school is located. To refuse to do a favor to these students of special family backgrounds would put the school in an unfriendly environment.

Based on media reports, an unknown (but pretty considerable) number of officials in charge of personnel, funds and materials are involved in corrupt activities, such as bribe-taking and misappropriation, since they have the power to approve personnel promotions, loans, projects, project contracts, as well as the amount needed to finance a specific project. It is alleged that tax officials in China are frequently bribed. Some business operators claim that if they do not bribe the tax officials with jurisdiction over their businesses, the profits from their business operations would not be enough to cover their tax payments. To report corrupt tax officials to any higher authorities could become a suicidal undertaking that would make things worse rather than better, because once a tax official is punished for corruption, his successor will not dare to accept bribes, and as a result, the businesses in the new man's jurisdiction will have to pay higher taxes and even penalties, in which case, the business operators won't have much money left to pay bonuses to their employees.

Corrupt behavior could happen in an invisible manner. For instance, the head of a tax office could become rich very quickly without apparently accepting even the smallest gifts or invitations to dinner parties. How? Here's the secret. He could let a relative of his to open a garment-and-furniture factory in his jurisdiction, so that the businesses that operate in his jurisdiction may become the customers of his relative's factory. Companies that buy workshop outfits and furniture from his relative's factory will make his preferential tax treatment list, while those who don't will have a hard time. Again, for instance, the manager of a large state-owned enterprise may not receive any kickback when granting project contracts, as far as the records can tell, but he can become rich very quickly too. How? The secret is that the contractor to whom the project contracts are granted is his relative.

In recent years, many officials of the Communist Party have become rich very quickly through the initial public offerings (IPO's) of the state-owned enterprises. How? For instance, before a state-owned enterprise receives government permission to make its IPO, the officials of the various sections of the local government which controls the state-owned enterprise may receive options to purchase its shares at the IPO price, say RMB3 yuan. In the meantime, the state-owned enterprise launches its hype by telling sucker investors about its "great long-term earnings potential". So, within a week after the IPO, the share price of the state-owned enterprise goes up to RMB24 yuan, allowing the officials of the local government to take hefty profits before the stock falls back down to earth. Where is the level ground for ordinary investors? Or, does it mean that sucker investors do not deserve any level ground?

In order to keep business operations going smoothly, companies may have to bribe the officials of certain relevant entities. For instance, if a construction company does not try to bribe the officials of a state-owned enterprise which plans to build a project, it (the construction company) will fail to establish "guanxi" (a good relationship) with the state-owned enterprise, thereby losing the contract to a competitor. As a result, the construction company will have a difficult time paying wages to its employees. Such harsh realities have forced many business managers to become smart public relations experts who know whom to bribe in order to establish "constructive business ties". While one may regard corruption as part of the country's business culture, the corrupt business practices mentioned above could lead to grave consequences.

In summer of 1998, one of China's major streams, the Yangtze River, overflowed and breached the retaining walls four kilometers west of the city of Jiujiang, Jiangxi Province. Later, investigators found out that the retaining walls were not made of reinforced concrete with imbedded steel bars. Instead, they contained bamboo sticks! Of course, these poor-quality retaining walls were not strong enough to confine the flood water of the roaring Yangtze River. In order to cut costs, the contractor building the retaining walls had substituted bamboo sticks for steel bars. But why was it necessary for the contractor to cut costs in this manner? Because the contractor had incurred "extraordinary expenditures" while maintaining "constructive business ties" with officials.

On January 24th 1998, a main bridge in Liuzhou, Guangxi Province, suddenly collapsed. Built in 1994 over the Liujiang River, it was known as the Huxi Bridge and was several hundred meters long. At the time of the collapse, a 240-meter-long and 6-meter-wide block of reinforced concrete plunged to the river, crushing three freight boats anchored under the bridge. In the accident, three people were killed and three seriously wounded. It was not until July of 1998 that a report on the accident appeared in Liuzhou's state-run newspaper "The Liuzhou Daily", saying the Huxi Bridge accident had been caused by "design errors and construction errors". However, the report didn't mention who was responsible for the design and the construction of the bridge. Nor did it say a word about who was liable for compensation to the victims of the accident.

Yet according to people privy to the Huxi Bridge construction project, it was Liuzhou's ex-party boss Secretary Chen who approved the project. Secretary Chen acted as the chief of the city's communist party committee from the beginning of 1992 to the end of 1994. During his term of office in Liuzhou, Guangxi Province, he approved ten major projects and appointed his wife to supervise the construction of each of these projects. In other words, Secretary Chen and his wife could decide which construction companies would win the project contracts. As there were no safeguards to ensure the quality of the bridge, the steel bars that were supposed to reinforce the bridge were too brittle to support its weight permanently, and the cement used in building the bridge was equally substandard.

On January 4th 1999, a large bridge collapsed in a busy commercial district of Qijiang County (not far from Chongqing, Sichuan Province), killing forty people right on the spot. It was built in 1996 and was named The Rainbow Bridge. An investigation into the accident found out that the bridge had been built with substandard building materials and that in order to win the Rainbow Bridge project contract, the relevant contractor had bribed various officials with authority to approve building projects, including the secretary and deputy secretary of the communist party committee of the county, the magistrate and deputy magistrate of the county, and the director of the construction committee of the county.

The reader is likely to think that the practices employed by the business operators to establish "guanxi" (illicit ties) to the officials are clearly the signs of a corrupt society. Yes, they certainly are. But do the business operators have a choice? If they do not bribe the officials, they may soon be out of business. Ironically, in order to give whatever they do a good name, some operators call the practice of bribing officials "an innovative way of doing business in the new era of reform and openness". They are not ashamed of any shady transactions, because their livelihood depends on bureaucratic favors. Much as President Jiang Zemin may wish to sermonize on the evils of corruption, the question is: How can the business operators survive without resorting to corrupt practices under the circumstances?

According to sources close to China's construction industry, life is pretty tough for construction companies because of intense competition. While there are about ten million people looking for work at various construction sites around the country, the demand for their services is limited. So, there is a big surplus of labor, and those who seek to make a living in the construction sector are forced to adopt all sorts of unscrupulous practices to get business. For instance, peasants who come to the cities to seek jobs would bribe subcontractors, while subcontractors would bribe contractors, and finally, contractors would bribe state enterprise executives who have the authority to grant construction project contracts. All the expenditures thus incurred in bribing state enterprise executives and party officials would finally amount to a major proportion of the costs of the construction projects. By rough estimates, bribes offered to government and communist party officials may range from RMB 30,000 yuan to RMB 100,000 yuan [official exchange rate: US$1.00 = RMB 8.30 yuan]. In order to control costs, the contractors need to spend less on building materials. Thus, they tend to use cheap, substandard materials, thereby sacrificing the quality of the projects they build. No wonder, the number of accidents involving construction project collapses rose sharply in the 1990s.

More interestingly, corrupt behavior has also become commonplace among law enforcement personnel, to the extent that some local police substations are cooperating with minor offenders in order to make a quick buck. For instance, although it is illegal for ticket-touts to buy up a railway station's train tickets and then sell them to passengers at greatly inflated prices, some local police substations keep the ticket-touts in business, so that the police can get a piece of the action too. The law enforcement personnel of the substations know who are in the ticket-touting business. Yet there seems to be a tacit understanding between them and the ticket-touts, to the extent that a ridiculous phenomenon has emerged. Once in a while, the personnel of the substations will pick up the ticket-touts, but then, they will let the ticket-touts get off with only a fine. By rough estimates, the fines paid by the ticket-touts account for one third or one fourth of their profits. As the ticket-touts stay in business, charging the passengers greatly inflated prices for their train tickets, the police substations reap the benefits in the form of a steady income from the fines.

However, such ticket-tout transactions as mentioned above only involve small amounts of money, and the ridiculous "arrangement" between the police and the ticket-touts occurs at a grassroots level, which fact is insufficient to prove the seriousness of the corruption problem in China. However, based on media reports, corruption has already proliferated to much higher levels. For instance, toward the end of 1998, ex-minister of public security Tao Siju was suspended and investigated for corruption, and deputy minister of public security Li Jizhou was taken into custody for questioning on charges of corruption. On April 2nd 1999, Beijing's public security bureau chief Zhang Liangji was removed from office and investigated for corruption.

According to a report dated April 8th 1999 from the Central Political and Legal Commission, as of the end of March 1999, one hundred eighty-nine (189) public security bureau chiefs and eight hundred thirty-five (835) public security bureau deputy chiefs had been removed from office. Of the 189 public security bureau chiefs mentioned above, fifty-seven (57) had been investigated for corruption. Of the 835 public security bureau deputy chiefs mentioned above, two hundred and fifteen (215) had been investigated for corruption. (As of the end of March 1999), one hundred and fifty (150) chief public prosecutors and three hundred and sixty-seven (367) deputy public prosecutors had been removed from office. Of the 150 chief public prosecutors mentioned above, forty-seven (47) had been investigated for corruption, and of the 367 deputy public prosecutors mentioned above, one hundred and thirty (130) had been investigated for corruption. What about the judges? Well, (as of the end of March 1999), two hundred and twenty-two (222) judges and four hundred and thirty-three (433) deputy judges had been replaced. Of the 222 judges mentioned above, seventy-five (75) had been investigated for corruption, and of the 433 deputy judges mentioned above, one hundred and seventeen (117) had been investigated for corruption.

How many bad cops, bad public prosecutors and bad judges are there in all of China? God knows! Anyway, it looks like a mess. It does not strike me as a place where an honest businessman can run his operations successfully, because to play strictly by the book (i.e. the written law) may not work, whereas to bribe the officials for bureaucratic favors could get him in trouble if the law catches up with him.

On the other hand, an unscrupulous businessman bold enough to break the law when the occasion occurs may be able to make tons of money. In some places, those with "guanxi" (illicit ties) to local authorities engage in illegal business operations with impunity. They include: smuggling, selling pirated music compact disks and video compact disks (CD's and VCD's) in violation of intellectual property rights, manufacturing fake products etc. Although they do not enjoy the protection of law, they enjoy the friendship of the local committees of the

Communist Party, who know how to play the law. For instance, a local party committee could hold a meeting to approve a certain business-man's illegal business operations on the pretext of "trying to win bene-fits for the local organizations" controlled by the committee, because the businessman would share the profits with "the local organizations". With this approval, the businessman could run his illegal operations under the protection of the local party committee. In case higher authorities get wind of the illegal business operations being protected by the local party committee, none of its individual members could be held responsible, because the approval was granted by the committee as a whole, not by any of its individual members. Besides, "the local organ-izations" do need an income to maintain their slush funds, which they use to cover "special expenditures" not recorded in the books, such as gifts, dinner parties and bribes. That is because they ("the local organi-zations") need to deal with other officials to get things done, and in doing so, they always incur such "special expenditures". Otherwise, they cannot get anything done.

Corruption has also become one of the key factors causing the state-owned enterprises to suffer heavy losses. It is alleged that many state-owned enterprises have "satellite business operations" controlled by the relatives and friends of the executive officers of the state-owned enter-prises. Because of the special relationships between the executive offi-cers and their relatives and friends, the state-owned enterprises tend to give extremely preferential treatment to the "satellite business opera-tions" to ensure their profitability. The preferential treatment could include the offering of low-interest loans and low product prices to the "satellite business operations". As a result, the state-owned enterprises keep losing money, even as the privately controlled "satellite business operations" prosper. Some economists see this phenomenon as a process of "invisible privatization".

Apparently for ideological reasons, many officials of the Communist Party have strong objections to a formal privatization of the state-owned enterprises, because Marxism calls for nationalization, not privatization. They refuse to face the economic realities emerging in the country, clinging to the creeds, tenets, doctrines and dogmas of an extinct economic philosophy written centuries ago by a bookworm called Karl Marx. They refuse to acknowledge that the state's ownership of the enterprises plays into the hands of corrupt corporate executives, because the state is unable to prevent them from stealing its assets. Nothing could be more ridiculous than these party officials' misplaced faith in Marxism. Or, should we suspect that they may have an ax to grind for themselves in the name of Marxism? It would make far more sense if a formal privatization of the state-owned enterprises were carried out, since that would help the state raise funds without giving corrupt corporate executives a chance to feather their own nests.

According to media reports, some Western financial institutions have lent large sums of money to certain state-owned companies like Guangdong International Trust and Investment Company (GITIC) on the assumption that the Chinese government would guarantee repayment. Such assumptions must be very naive. Companies like GITIC were established, because the Chinese government wanted to use them to lure overseas investments in expensive infrastructure projects whose profitability has yet to be proven. To guarantee loan repayment was neither the purpose nor the priority in establishing them. Once money is lent to such state-owned companies, Western lenders have no control whatsoever over how the money will be spent and where the money will go. Given the country's strong culture of bribery and corruption, no one can guarantee that money thus lent by Western financial institutions will not be siphoned off by corrupt corporate executives (who, as a rule, are appointed by the Communist Party) into their private overseas accounts. Since there appear to be numerous ways for corrupt communist party officials to make money disappear into thin air, neither the central government nor the government of any province can afford to guarantee loan repayment. Western lenders should beware that they lend at their own risk and that to lend money without security or collateral has never been a wise banking policy.

Since the 1980s, many of the China-backed companies in Hong Kong have gotten into trouble, either because they have defaulted on loans, or because they have lost their capital, or because corrupt corporate executives have misappropriated corporate funds. The root cause of the problem is that the Chinese government does not have an effective mechanism to supervise its overseas business organizations, resulting in a situation where the China-backed companies' capital and asset accounts are in a state of chaos. Apparently, corrupt corporate executives have taken advantage of this chaos to falsify their companies' accounts. Some of them have gone so far as to use the funds of the China-backed companies they control as start money to establish their own private companies! According to statistics gathered by the end of November 1998, of the thirty-eight (38) China-backed business groups in Hong Kong, twenty-one (21) had lost money and contracted debts in the 1997-1998 period. Twenty-five (25) of the China-backed companies in Hong Kong had serious financial problems with an aggregate debt of more than HK$227 billion (US$29.30 billion) outstanding.

Of course, the Chinese government can instruct the country's state-run banks to lend more money to the loss-making China-backed companies in Hong Kong as well as to the state-owned enterprises in the mainland, but the entire state-owned sector (including both the China-backed companies in Hong Kong and the state-owned enterprises in China) could become a black hole that sucks in capital without producing much return on equity. Clearly, local Chinese depositors and overseas lenders are the state-owned sector's sources of capital. Besides, the Chinese government keeps issuing bonds to cover its budget deficits and to pay the interest on its previously issued bonds. It could also print more paper money to support the state-owned sector. But how long can this last? Will the local Chinese depositors and the Western lenders who have provided the capital to the state-owned sector be able to get back their principal in the end? Honestly, I am not sure. I only know that Russia defaulted in 1998. Can anyone rule out the possibility that the same situation that happened in Russia could happen in China as well, given the perennial ailments of China's state-owned sector such as low productivity and corruption?

While it is true that the forces of the marketplace in China are growing, the marketplace itself is manipulated by the authorities. This is because party officials play a disproportionately important role. Their influence penetrates every sector of the market, resulting in a so-called "double-track system", under which, abnormal market phenomena have emerged. For instance, a consumer product may be sold to two different consumers at two different prices. Likewise, a supplier may sell a raw material to two different companies at two different prices. Two different business operators may find that they have bought the same kind of equipment but at two different prices. A bank may sell a foreign currency to two different customers at two widely different prices. Bank loans of the same maturity may carry different interest rates with different borrowers. Different rent rates may be charged to different land users. Even shares and stocks could be sold to two different investors at the same time but at two different prices. All such phenomena have been caused by officials who have the power to determine prices. Thus, the influence of power distorts prices to the extent it prevents them from reflecting market reality. It also destroys the fairness of the marketplace.

Since no business transactions can be executed without party officials' approval for the relevant building projects, import and foreign exchange quotas, special business licenses, tax breaks, or project contracts, the power in their hands to grant such approval has become a valuable resource. In fact, it is more valuable than all the other resources required in business like land, capital, technology and labor, because without their approval, the access to the other resources is blocked. Thus, the approval of the officials is the prerequisite for any successful deployment of resources. No wonder business operators are willing to pay a price for the officials' approval. It is alleged that an unknown number of communist party officials are willing to grant their approval for a consideration. This exchange of power for money plays an important role in the development of the Chinese marketplace.

A few economists even claim that this exchange of power for money is an effective lubricant or catalyst in the operation of the Chinese economy and that without this lubricant or catalyst, the country's Soviet-style planned economy can never be transformed. In other words, they believe that corruption among communist party officials is an inevitable consequence of China's political structure, but since such corruption facilitates the necessary transactions in business, it may have certain positive effects during the initial stages of the country's economic transformation. Put in another way, they believe that corruption in China is "good" and "justifiable" and that greed will eventually change the communist system. So, like they say on Wall Street, greed is good!

In the 1980s, some of the sons and daughters of China's ranking communist party officials arrived in Hong Kong and became business people with Hong Kong resident status. Due to their special connections in China, they not only had various business opportunities but also enjoyed such incentives as tax breaks and foreign exchange conversion permits only available to Hong Kong business people. Rumor had it that the original capital (i.e. the start money) they used to commence their businesses had been provided by China's state-run organizations. Now, according to media reports, China is suffering from a serious flight of capital. By rough estimates, every day, an average of HK$100 million (US$12.9 million) is somehow transferred into various Hong Kong accounts. The question is: Who has the power to effect such transfers?

In July of 1998, President Jiang Zemin declared that the country's military personnel must stop their involvement in business activities and that all military-controlled businesses should be handed over to designated civilian authorities. Yet soon afterwards, investigators discovered that much of the assets of the military's business operations had been stolen and that their account books had been destroyed or altered. For instance, as of March 1997, the five hundred and seventy (570) businesses run by the Nanjing Military Region Command had a total of RMB 14.17 billion yuan (about US$1.70 billion) in assets. By November 1998 when the businesses were handed over, their total assets had fallen to only RMB 5.58 billion yuan (about US$672 million). As of January 1997, the fifty (50) businesses run by the Jinan Air Force Command had a total of RMB 2.88 billion (about US$346 million) in assets. By November 1998 when the businesses were handed over to the government of Shandong Province, their total assets had fallen to only RMB 720 million yuan (about US$86.74 million). Such hefty amounts of missing assets cannot but raise suspicions about corruption in the military.

10

Lawlessness—It's Not Really a Very Stable Situation

In autumn of 1994, I crossed the Hong Kong-China border into the best-known special economic zone in China, Shenzhen, apparently a booming town by any standards, to see an old friend of mine from my Shanghai days, George. 1994 was a good year for the Chinese economy. At the time, the country's paramount leader Deng Xiaoping was still alive though very weak. Earlier in 1992, he had made a tour of southern Chinese cities including Shenzhen, expressing his determination to push forward his economic reforms. No longer afraid of being called a "capitalist-roader" in his late years and annoyed by those who kept second-guessing his policies and insisted on labeling his reforms as "capitalist" in nature, he said "no more argument". He wanted his market-oriented economic reforms to be carried out anyway. So, major coastal cities like Shenzhen benefited big time, as overseas investors were convinced that capitalist business practices would take root in China and that the coastal cities were where they should invest their money. I noticed that laughing people were drinking Coca Cola and eating sandwiches in crowded McDonald's restaurants. Apparently, that was only one side of the story, as my friend George told me that a lot of people were critical of the government.

"Why?" I asked. "As far as I can see, people here are quite free. If you don't get involved in political activities, the government won't bother you. If you have money to spend, life could be quite comfortable here."

"True, but people complain. At heart they like socialism, believe it or not. They are not up to the new economic environment," replied George, to my surprise.

"Like socialism?" I wondered aloud, remembering the long years I spent in Shanghai during the Mao era when people secretly complained about socialism because it allowed them no economic freedom at all."

"In the old days under Mao when everybody was poor, people saw no contrast of wealth and poverty. They sought comfort in the fact that they were not alone in poverty. It was equality in poverty," George explained to me. "Today, things are different. Those with ability or opportunity have become quite well-off, while those without are left way behind. This sharp contrast between the haves and the have-nots now stares the poor in the face, causing them to complain about the market economy and reminisce about the old days under socialism."

"The rich are in the minority. It's the same everywhere. It's impossible for everybody to become rich. But, anyway, things are much better now than before," I said, aware that somehow I had become an apologist for the Chinese government as I focused on the benefits of Mr. Deng Xiaoping's economic reforms.

It was afternoon. George and I walked into a large public park where we found a bench to sit down. I remember we had a long conversation, during which I talked about my translation work in Hong Kong. I told him that even Hong Kong's translators like myself had benefited from Mr. Deng's economic reforms.

"Overseas investors have formed joint ventures with Chinese companies due to the economic reforms," I explained. "Each joint venture requires at least two documents in both English and Chinese. One is the joint venture contract. The other is a set of articles of association. That means a lot of work for translators. I sell my translation services to translation companies or directly to law firms involved in joint venture negotiations. That's how I make a living. That's what market capitalism is all about—you've got to have something to sell in order to make money."

For a moment, George was silent, but I thought he agreed that market capitalism was a tough reality one had to live with: Those with a good product to sell get ahead while those without get nowhere. He was teaching English in a private school in Shenzhen run by an entrepreneur from Shanghai. His income was too small to allow him a comfortable lifestyle, but he knew that was what his teaching services were worth in the marketplace. "No one can become a millionaire by selling translation or teaching services," I added. "But at least, we are allowed to sell what we have. Besides, we can build on whatever we might achieve."

In the evening, we had a simple meal in a small hotel restaurant. My plan was to cross the border back to Hong Kong before the customs check-point closed. Since there was plenty of time, we decided to have a walk after the meal along the main street. But soon I started to wonder whether we had made the right decision. First, the crowded main street did not seem to be a very safe route. Shortly after we set off, a group of street urchins came up, begging for money. I gave them a few coins only to make things worse, because this small act of charity on my part caught the attention of other beggars. A woman carrying a baby in her arms stopped us. Although I told her that I had no more coins to give, she refused to get out of my way. So, I gave her a ten-Hong-Kong-dollar note to make her disappear, before we could escape to the next section of the street, though not without a few more small urchins behind us. I remember that George had to stop to give them some small notes before they got lost.

However, that was not the end of our adventure. Having left the beggars-and-urchins' section of the street, I became aware that we were now in what some people would call "more interesting territory"—the prostitutes' section of the street. Approaching with a smile and touching my jacket sleeve, a nice-looking young woman asked quietly if I would like to have a good time with her. I said I had to hurry back home, then I quipped, "What about next time?" She smiled, as George and I walked on. Only a few steps later, another woman came near to my astonishment. This one was not as pretty and young. Realizing that it was unwise to linger in the main street of this booming town in the evening, we hurried off toward the border check-point.

During the entire course of our stroll, I did not see a single policeman show up in the street. In Shenzhen, the special economic zone, there was definitely a sense of freedom in the air—freedom from government intervention in people's lives, but for once, I said to myself that perhaps some government intervention was not that undesirable, because the absence of government authority on the main street had resulted in chaos. While living in Hong Kong under British rule, I never saw a prostitute soliciting business in the main street, nor was I ever pursued by street urchins. Undoubtedly, the Chinese government has a lot to learn from the British about the art of effective governance. Yet during my eleven years in Hong Kong, all the media reports were telling me that the Chinese government was far more concerned about the intentions of the British regarding the future of the territory, as if the British were about to leave some kind of a time bomb behind.

Since 1949 when Mao founded the People's Republic, the Chinese government has focused far more energies on the control of the country's major cities. Yet my experience in Shenzhen gave me the impression that the government might have difficulty maintaining effective control even in major cities like Shenzhen. So, what about the government's ability to maintain control in remote areas?

Economic liberalization has allowed the Chinese people far more freedom than they have ever enjoyed since 1949. In the meantime, the government's ability to maintain effective control may have been weakened. As a result, social unrest is most likely at the top of Beijing's list of concerns. Based on information disclosed by Chinese officials, China has ten unsafe railways, including the railway section cutting through the Hongliuhe Region between Xinjiang Province and Gansu Province, the railway section crossing from Gansu Province into Inner Mongolia, the railway section between Xining and Golmud, the Southern Xinjiang Railway, the railway section between Hunan Province and Guangxi Province, the railway section crossing from Sichuan Province into Shaanxi Province, the railway cutting through the Greater Khingan Range Region of Heilongjiang Province etc. The reason that these railways are unsafe is because armed bandits have attacked some trains traveling through the relevant regions.

The armed bandits active along the railway sections in Xinjiang Province, Qinghai Province, Gansu Province and Inner Mongolia during the 1990s were well organized and called themselves "The People's Railway Red Guard Brigade". The activities of this armed organization first got the attention of China's railway public security authorities in 1994. Perhaps, it had a membership of between one hundred and several hundred people, including jobless men, ex-soldiers and ex-policemen. As a rule, the bandits would target freight trains and military cargo trains. Each time they attacked, they would encourage the peasants living in the vicinity of the railway section to cart away the goods. "The People's Railway Red Guard Brigade" appeared to be privy to the train schedules and the contents of the carriages. So, the possibility that some railway officials might have tipped off the bandits could not be ruled out. In addition, some business organizations might have been involved in helping sell the stolen goods. According to China's public security authorities, in the 1990s, the value of the goods stolen from railway carriages plus the damage caused by the bandits to railway equipment amounted to more than RMB 2 billion yuan (about US$241 million) annually. Besides, the country's railway system could do with an extra ten thousand (10,000) armed policemen to ensure transport safety.

At eleven o'clock on the night of December 11th 1998, a military train heading from Tianjin toward Urumqi (Xinjiang Province) was moving on the railway section in the Hongliuhe area between Xinjiang Province and Gansu Province, when the traffic signals in front flashed to make it stop. As the guards stepped down the train to find out what was going on, a number of searchlights were turned on. In the glare, they saw about one hundred vehicles lurking in the dark on either side of the railway. At the same time, a mob of between four and five hundred people closed in upon the train, which consisted of forty-five freight cars carrying such goods as jeeps, motorcycles, small diesel engines, generators, household electrical appliances and so on.

Although the soldiers responsible for the security of the train immediately fired into the air to warn the mob against moving any nearer to the train, "The People's Railway Red Guard Brigade" took no notice. Instead, members of the gang fired back to provide cover for their comrades, who eventually took hold of the train and loaded the cargo therein on to their own vehicles. What's more, they set the train on fire before they fled. The heist lasted two hours, during which fifty-nine solders were either wounded or killed. Later, the Communist Party's Central Military Commission sent troops to launch a mopping-up operation in the area surrounding the crime scene, killing more than seventy bandits, some of whom were peasants.

According to a report by China's Central Public Security Administration Commission, dated December 24th 1998, on the status of security of railways, highways and waterways, armed criminal organizations have targeted state-run warehouses and military freight cars with the intention of destabilizing the political situation in the country. Since 1996, the number of armed robberies along China's transportation lines has been in an uptrend. The railway transport service witnessed forty-two (42) robberies in 1996, one hundred and fifty-nine (159) robberies in 1997 and seventy-one (71) robberies in 1998 (not including December). The waterway transport service witnessed one hundred and five (105) robberies in 1996, one hundred and twenty-seven (127) robberies in 1997 and one hundred and forty-two (142) robberies in 1998 (not including December). The highway transport service witnessed five hundred and twenty (520) robberies in 1996, six hundred and twelve (612) robberies in 1997 and six hundred and twenty-five (625) robberies in 1998 (not including December).

The government's failure to maintain effective control in certain rural areas may have induced lawlessness among people who, under normal conditions, would not break the law. That means that lawlessness is no longer limited to gangsters. Ordinary people with no criminal records could become lawless too when the occasion arises. In autumn of 1998, an incident involving local peasants occurred in Hunan Province, interrupting the railway construction project designed to link Zhuzhou (Hunan Province) to Liupanshui (Guizhou Province). The government agency responsible for the project found itself unable to cope with the demands of the local peasants who wanted far more compensation for relocation than government regulations would allow. When the government agency rejected their demands, the peasants started to use force to deter the project from proceeding. As it turned out, the local peasants had the backing of local officials working for the county and township authorities.

The incident described above may reflect a weakening of the central government's authority, since it clearly indicates that the local officials involved in instigating the peasants believed that they could get away with lawlessness. Such behavior by local officials has certainly set a bad example to ordinary people, leading them to think that they could get away with lawlessness too.

More disturbing to the public is the fact that lawless conduct is rampant among the country's law enforcement personnel. An early 1998 prison incident where several inmates beat up a prison guard may provide a glimpse of the problem. The story unfolds as follows:

It was a day when the inmates of the Hengzhou Prison (administered by the municipal authorities) in Hengyang, Hunan Province, were expecting visits from their family members. As Inmate Huang and

Inmate Qi walked out their prison cells, moving down the corridor toward the meeting room, they saw Prison Guard Chen sitting inside. "Looks like we're going to have a good time," Qi said to Huang. He meant to say that they could get some heroin from the guard. Both Qi and Huang were drug addicts, and Prison Guard Chen a part-time drug dealer.

As soon as they entered the meeting room, they asked Chen for heroin. Chen told them he had what they wanted but demanded cash in exchange for the goods. So, the transaction was completed in a few minutes' time. Qi and Huang got two small packets of white powder from Chen. Later, they invited another inmate, Liu, to "the party". The three of them snuck into a toilet, where they opened the small packets. To their surprise, the white powder in the packets was not heroin at all. It was dust scraped off from a wall! Realizing that they had been duped by Chen, the three addicts became very mad. Huang immediately went off to seek an explanation from Chen. Qi and Liu followed him. When they found Chen, they were told that there was no supply of heroin until two or three o'clock in the afternoon. Huang demanded a refund. Chen refused. "Do you want to revolt against the authorities?" he said, trying to remind the prison inmates that he, Prison Guard Chen, represented "the prison authorities". Taking no notice of what Chen had to say, Huang started to search him to see if he carried any cash. Liu helped out with the search. But they failed to find any cash on the prison guard. Outraged by his deceit, they beat him up.

This incident triggered an investigation into the prison drug addiction problem, and the evidence turned up by the investigators points to a big dark side to China's prison system. It transpired that of the one thousand and seven hundred (1,700) inmates in the Hengzhou Prison, one hundred and twenty-four (124) were drug addicts, each of whom had access to supplies of narcotics. Prison Guard Chen was not the only part-time drug dealer at the Hengzhou Prison. Other prison guards were in business too. In May of 1998, four prison guards at the prison (including Chen) were arrested, three of whom were drug addicts themselves. In Hengyang, Hunan Province, there is another prison, the Yannan Prison. Administered by the provincial authorities, the Yannan Prison is larger and holds more inmates than the Hengzhou Prison. To the investigators' surprise, there were far more inmates possessing narcotics in the Yannan Prison than in the Hengzhou Prison. They discovered that outside drug dealers on bicycles had been allowed in to deliver their goods and that even taxi cabs carrying drug dealers had entered the prison compound after midnight. There is no doubt that without the connivance of corrupt prison officers, no narcotics business could have been transacted on such a scale under the nose of the prison authorities.

Also, it is alleged that some grassroots Chinese law enforcement personnel use the authority in their hands to advance their own financial interests. The following anecdote, which I hope the reader will find intriguing, might shed some light:

In Xiquanzhen (which means West Fountain Town in Chinese), Fengyang, Anhui Province, there was an interesting joint operated by a business entrepreneur. Known as Fengxi Restaurant, it was a booming business. The reason behind its success was because customers could get more than just food. Prostitutes were soliciting at the restaurant. On the other hand, the police substation at Xiquanzhen often dispatched its law enforcement personnel to the restaurant to catch the clients of the prostitutes. Between 1995 and the end of 1997, the Xiquanzhen Police Substation made more than thirty raids on the restaurant and arrested more than fifty prostitute clients. Yet they never arrested any prostitutes.

To the police substation, the "got-you" operation was a lucrative business. Each prostitute client had to pay a fine of RMB 5,000 yuan (about US$600) if he was to be released. The personnel of the substation were working hard in order to make as much money as possible. Fengxi Restaurant was not the only joint they had raided. They targeted other places in Xiquanzhen as well. If a man arrested by them denied having patronized a prostitute, they would torture him until he admitted having patronized a prostitute. That way, they would have a legitimate reason to fine him. Innocent men were picked up and tortured too. The chief of the Police Substation knew what was going on, but he had only praises and words of encouragement for his men.

One evening, a bank security vehicle pulled up outside Fengxi Restaurant. It belonged to the Agriculture Bank of Huainan Municipality. Inside it, there were three employees of the bank, all of whom were men, including the deputy director of one of the bank's branch offices. A few prostitutes accosted them. Scarcely had the men responded to the solicitation, when a police car jumped out of the dark and turned round toward them. Realizing it was a set-up, the men sped off. But with the police car close behind, the bank security vehicle soon skidded into a large heap of sand. While one of the three men managed to escape arrest by hiding behind the heap of sand, the other two, including the bank branch deputy director, had no luck. They were arrested and taken to the Xiquanzhen Police Substation, where there were another five men who had earlier been taken into custody. So, on a single night, the substation personnel had picked up seven men on charges of patronizing prostitutes. As the prisoners all denied the charges, the substation personnel tortured them one by one. Under duress, five of the seven admitted the charges before daybreak. The other two refused to admit wrongdoing and so were tortured throughout the night. They were the two employees of the Agriculture Bank. After passing out under torture, the deputy director of the Agriculture Bank branch was sent to the People's Hospital of Huainan Municipality, where he died despite two brain operations performed by the hospital surgeons. His colleague survived, but a hospital examination found that he had suffered serious internal brain damage from the torture.

In late 1997, two police officers at the Xiquanzhen Police Substation were arrested for involvement in the torturing of the two bank employees. Later, the man who tortured the bank branch deputy director to death was sentenced to five years' imprisonment, while the other culprit was sentenced to one year's imprisonment. Dismissing the punishment as too light to fit the crime, the victims' families appealed the court ruling. Finally, the People's Court of Chuzhou Municipality increased the penalty for the murderer to ten years' imprisonment. The chief of the Xiquanzhen Police Substation who had encouraged his men to arrest suspected prostitute clients (including innocents) and connived at the torture was prosecuted.

Lawless conduct by corrupt officials plus tough economic conditions experienced by large numbers of ordinary Chinese citizens makes a perfect recipe for social unrest. Apparently, the senior members of the ruling party are aware of the potential risks the government may have to face going forward. In February of 1999, former Politburo member Qiao Shi, who stepped down as chairman of the Standing Committee of the National People's Congress in spring of 1998, expressed his concern about potential social unrest. He said, "I am worried that major disturbances and unrest might shock society. Such potential crises could be serious, whereas the factors likely to cause unrest are in evidence. For instance, corruption among party officials, massive layoffs, unemployment, excessive taxes and levies on peasants in the rural areas, infringement of ordinary citizens' interests by party and government authorities and so on could all spark major disturbances and unrest. If these issues are not properly addressed and resolved and if they are exacerbated by extraneous infiltration and instigation, a severe nationwide disturbance involving several regions could occur. It could evolve into violent political unrest on a large scale, in which case, a civil war would break out, splitting the country." Mr. Qiao Shi, who is widely seen as a party moderate by Western media, added that many people both inside and outside the ruling party were now concerned about China's future.

The question is whether unrest is already under way. Many of the country's loss-making state-owned factories began to lay off workers in the mid-1990s, because they could no longer pay wages. As a result, the number of jobless people has risen sharply since then. In June of 1999, the Ministry of Public Security issued an internal circular indicating that in May 1999 (alone), seven hundred and fifty-eight (758) bombing incidents had taken place in mainland China, causing twenty-five hundred and twenty (2,520) casualties. The internal circular pointed out that most of these crimes had been committed by jobless people. In addition, labor unrest has become a way of life. Although the government hopes that the communist party-controlled trade unions in the state-owned enterprises will help maintain social and political stability, the trade unions' performance has been disappointing at best. This is because local party and government authorities have relaxed their controls on the trade unions and the trade unions have relaxed their controls on the workers. Besides, laid-off workers may wonder why they should allow the state enterprises' trade unions to control them any more, now that they are no longer employed. Under these circumstances, some trade unions have evolved into so-called "opposition groups".

In December of 1998, China's communist party-controlled national labor organization, the All-China Confederation of Trade Unions, issued a document entitled "Trade Unions At All Levels Must Unequivocally Safeguard Social and Political Stability and Support Economic Reform". Since economic reform calls for an improvement in productivity and a return to profitability, inevitably leading the state-owned enterprises to cut labor costs, to request the trade unions to "support economic reform" sounds like a tall order. No wonder the document criticized some trade union officials for instigating state enterprise employees to demand that the Communist Party and the government allow them to form "independent and free" trade unions. But independent and free of what? Of communist control? Not without a sense of alarm, the document went on to warn that such a demand was tantamount to "opposition to the leadership of the Communist

Party" with the potential to turn the trade unions into political organizations. The document mentioned that some trade unions had been involved in instigating state enterprise employees to strike, to stage street demonstrations, or even to raid party and government offices. Apparently, the Communist Party does not want to see any independent labor organization similar to Poland's "Solidarity" emerging in China.

As ordinary Chinese citizens struggle for their financial survival by all possible means and laid-off workers protest the loss of their livelihood, to maintain law and order has become a tough job for the government, because criminals tend to be bolder than usual when they realize the government's ability to control has weakened. By rough estimates, the number of criminal cases rose by more than 20% per annum throughout the 1990s. According to official statistics, in 1998, a total of thirty-six thousand five hundred and twenty-seven (36,527) cases of murder or attempted murder took place in China. While this may not sound like a huge number in percentage terms, given China's vast population, the seriousness of the crime problem forces itself upon the public's awareness if a man well-known or related to somebody well-known to the public is murdered. That is exactly what happened on the evening of February 22nd 1999.

Mr. Zou Jingmeng, son of China's famous 1930s writer Zou Taofen and younger brother of former vice premier and current vice chairman of the National People's Congress Zou Jiahua, retired from his post as director of the Chinese Meteorological Bureau in 1997. He became an honorary director of the bureau and continued to act as chairman or director with five trading and holding companies based in Beijing, Tianjin, Shenzhen and Guangzhou. At about 7:40 p.m. on February 22nd 1999, Mr. Zou Jingmeng came out of a shopping mall with a young woman somewhere in the vicinity of the Chinese Meteorological Bureau in Beijing's Haidian District. Walking toward the parking lot in front of the Yanshan Hotel, they were about to step into his Mercedes, when three big men jumped out of a nearby mauve saloon and shoved Mr. Zou and his female companion into the Mercedes. "You've got power, influence and money and so this world belongs to you. But today I'll let you go to another world!" one of the thugs shouted, stabbing a dagger into Zou's chest. Mr. Zou died right on the spot. Without hurting the young woman, the three men fled in their mauve saloon, which the police found deserted in front of a restaurant the following morning.

Even in the military, there is also an urgent need to maintain law and order. In July of 1998, the Chinese government decided that the military should terminate its business activities and hand over the assets of all military-controlled enterprises to the civilian authorities designated by the government. Yet between mid-December of 1998 and early February of 1999, seventy-five violent clashes took place, resulting in bloodshed, because various groups in the military fought each other in order to control the assets. More than two hundred people were killed or wounded in these conflicts.

Toward the end of 1998, the personnel of the Guangdong Military Command clashed with the personnel of the South Sea Fleet over the assets of a joint venture between the two military groups. The joint venture owned three guesthouses and one holiday inn in Zhenjiang, Maoming and Zhuhai. From early November to early December of 1998, instead of handing over the assets, worth RMB 3.50 million yuan (about US$0.42 million), to the designated civilian authorities, the representatives of the joint venture partners had been haggling about how to divide the assets. As the two sides failed to reach a compromise settlement, a violent conflict ensued at a banquet thrown by the Zhuhai Garrison on December 17th 1998, injuring seventeen (17) people. Director Xiao of the Political Department of the Zhenjiang Naval Base, a unit under the jurisdiction of the South Sea Fleet, was hit on the head by a wine bottle. Later when he was hospitalized, doctors found that the blow had caused irreparable damage to his brains. He never recovered consciousness. In early January of 1999, he died in hospital.

In January of 1999, the personnel of the Military Command of Anhui Province clashed with the personnel of the headquarters of the provincial Armed Police over the assets of a joint venture between the Military Command of Anhui Province, the Military Garrison of Hefei Municipality and the provincial Armed Police headquarters. The joint venture had engaged in real estate business. As the deadline for handing over the assets to the designated civilian authorities approached, the Military Command of Anhui Province sold all the properties under its control for RMB 40 million yuan or so (about US$4.82 million) but told its joint venture partners that the proceeds of the sale amounted to only RMB 10 million yuan (about US$1.20 million). Suspecting fraud, the Military Garrison of Hefei Municipality sent its representatives to the Military Command of Anhui Province to demand a fair share of the proceeds. They were detained by the Military Command. When the Military Garrison dispatched its troops to the Military Command to demand the release of its representatives and its share of the proceeds, a fight between the two military groups broke out. On January 5th 1999, believing that the Armed Police of Anhui Province were behind the Military Garrison, the Military Command of Anhui Province sent its personnel to the headquarters of the Armed Police of Anhui Province to catch "the man who stirred up the trouble". This triggered a shoot-out involving the personnel of all the three joint venture partners. More than thirty (30) people were wounded, including five family members of military personnel.

Also in January of 1999, the personnel of the Military Command of Lanzhou (the capital of Gansu Province) clashed with the personnel of the Military Command of Gansu Province. The two military groups had interests in a business joint venture which, according to the instructions of the central government, had to be wound up. Negotiations over how to divide the assets of the business had been going on for some time without success. When it became clear that the dispute could not be settled amicably, the personnel of the Ordnance Department of the

Lanzhou Military Command, armed with machine cannons, broke into the Logistics Department of the Military Command of Gansu Province and seized more than thirty brand-new Japanese-made saloons, worth more than RMB 11 million yuan (about US$1.32 million), as "compensation". This provoked a quick reaction from the other party to the joint venture, the Military Command of Gansu Province, which dispatched troops in several trucks to the No. 075 Warehouse of the Lanzhou Military Command to seize the steel and equipment imported by the joint venture. Trying to stop the soldiers of the Military Command of Gansu Province from taking away the goods, several vehicles from the Lanzhou Military Command crashed into the provincial Military Command's trucks on the high way. A shoot-out broke out, killing twelve and wounding more than seventy.

In Guizhou Province, the personnel of the Military Command of Guizhou Province clashed with the personnel of the Military Garrison of Zunyi Municipality for two days, January 24th and 25th 1999, after the two military groups failed to reach an agreement on how to divide the assets of their joint venture. These assets were worth only RMB 2.60 million yuan (about US$0.31 million). During the clash, fifteen vehicles belonging to the two military groups were burned, and eight soldiers were killed and more than ninety wounded. About fifty of the wounded were sent to the Guiyang Military Hospital or the Chengdu Military Hospital for treatment because they had suffered severe injuries.

In Jinxi, Liaoning Province, the Military Garrison of Jinxi Region, which had a joint venture in electronics and chemical fertilizers with the artillery troops stationed in the region, was cheating its joint venture partner. Having sold RMB 50 million yuan (about US$6 million) worth of products, it kept the proceeds for itself, hoping the artillery troops would never find out about the transaction. But the artillery troops found out. Asked for an explanation, the Military Garrison said the money had been handed over to the designated civilian authorities. It was a lie. When the lie was nailed, the Military Garrison promised to pay one fifth of the proceeds to the artillery troops by the end of 1998. It never did. Its promise was intended to be a delaying tactic. So, on January 28th 1999, the artillery troops dispatched more than ten truckloads of soldiers to surround the Military Garrison building. The stalemate lasted for seventy hours till the commanders of both military groups arrived on the scene to call off the siege. Fortunately, no one was hurt.

In early February of 1999, the soldiers of the Military Garrison of Dongchuan Region, Yunnan Province, clashed with the personnel of the Air Force over the assets of a joint venture between the two groups. When the Military Garrison dispatched its troops to the Air Force base to protest, the personnel of the Air Force used military vehicles to drive the protestors out of the base, triggering a violent conflict, at the peak of which, about three thousand people were involved, including soldiers, employees of the joint venture and family members of military personnel.

One source of instability which may have escaped the focus of media attention is China's vast countryside, where arable land has contracted substantially in recent years because of the country's numerous building projects, even as grievances among its huge rural peasant population surge. Arable land which used to account for 13% of mainland China's territory now accounts for only 9% of its land. Take Beijing's suburban Haiding District as an example. The large fields of vegetables that used to be there across the district have all disappeared. Now, in their place, you can only see high-rises. This means that a certain number of Chinese peasants have lost their land to concrete structures. Once this happens to them, they have no choice but to crowd into the cities to find work. If they cannot find work there, they may resort to criminal means in order to survive. In the Pearl River Delta region of China's Guangdong Province, many peasants have been demanding compensation from local officials for land seized by the authorities. In 1998 when the government took over large pieces of land in Hubei Province for the Three Gorges Dam project, peasants there were so upset by the meager compensation offered to them that they complained like mad.

For those fortunate enough to continue plowing their own land, life isn't much easier, because of the ridiculously numerous taxes and levies imposed on them. When the Communist Party founded the People's Republic in 1949, it did not tax peasants. Sounds good, but that was a long time ago. Now, the list of taxes and levies burdening Chinese peasants is much longer than the one imposed by the Nationalist government of Generalissimo Chiang Kai-shek before the 1949 revolution. Look at the following taxes and levies and you will see what kind of a heavy tax burden Chinese peasants are bearing: (1) special produce tax; (2) water resources levy; (3) water conservancy financing levy; (4) broadcast enterprise levy; (5) live pig insurance premium; (6) bicycle tax; (7) township overall planning levy; (8) legal knowledge popularization fee; (9) joint security levy; (10) communist party construction levy; (11) public bathroom ticket fee; (12) militia training levy; and (13) excess child levy.

The last item—"excess child levy"—is a penalty to those who dare breach China's so-called one-couple-one-child birth control policy. Young Chinese peasants fear this "levy" more than any other taxes and levies. In 1993, somewhere in the outskirts of Anhui Province's Ma'anshan Municipality, a Chinese scholar saw a large billboard flashing a line of bold Chinese characters which put young peasants on notice: "Have one child too many and you're sure to be stony broke!" What an arrogant way for "the People's Government" to speak to the public!

As to Item No. 10 (the so-called "communist party construction levy"), there is nothing more ridiculous in the world than this one. A peasant household has to pay a "communist party construction levy", even though there is no communist party member in the family. Where does the money go? The "communist party construction levies" collected from the peasants tend to end up in a rural slush fund controlled by village cadres, who use the money for their own pleasure. The fact of the matter is that many village communist party branch secretaries and village chiefs in the rural areas have become China's new landlord class which oppresses and exploits peasants without the slightest compunction. Based on the findings of one investigation, the percentage of rural cadres (i.e. party officers) in breach of laws and regulations rose sharply in the 1990s—from 29% at the end of the 1980s to 55% in the mid-1990s.

In many cases, a peasant family's income could come close to zero despite a full year's hard work due to the heavy taxes and levies imposed on them. For instance, in some small villages of Jiangsu Province, a five-person family could make only RMB 1,000 yuan or so (about US$120) per year, but after payment of various taxes and levies, there would be as little as RMB 400 yuan or so (about US$48) left to tide the family over. In Hubei Province, one five-person family contracted (with rural communist party officers) to plow a plot of 12.40 mu (1 mu = 0.0667 hectares). After a full year of hard work, they discovered that their net income was only RMB 451 yuan, because they had to pay a long list of taxes and levies totaling RMB 1,629 yuan.

Chinese peasants are hardworking people well-known for their ability to endure life's hardships and social injustice. Normally, they do not openly express their grievances under the oppression of rural cadres. However, if bureaucratic oppression exceeds the limit of their endurance, tragedy could occur. In recent years, there have been quite a few incidences involving peasants killing rural cadres who sought to collect taxes and levies. In some cases, peasants unable to pay taxes and levies have committed suicide or have been beaten to death by rural cadres. In one small village of Anhui Province, rural cadres imposed an RMB 30 yuan levy on peasants with an overdue penalty of another RMB 30 yuan, despite the fact that the villagers were enduring severe hardships due to a flood which had earlier deluged the village. When a 26-year-old peasant failed to pay the levy, the cadres of the village started to reap the wheat in his field. The young peasant said that if they reaped the wheat, his family would starve to death. "Have mercy on us," he pleaded. But taking no notice of his plea, the cadres proceeded with the reaping. That really was the last straw. The young peasant went into his house and came out with a pack of dynamite. The next instant he had detonated the explosive, killing himself.

The Communist Party has repeatedly stressed that stability is its top priority. This means it intends to firmly control the situation in order to maintain its one-party dictatorship. Its obsession with "stability" (which is synonymous with control in its political glossary) has turned it into a paranoid, neurotic creature that sees destabilizing factors everywhere. Yet, strange to say, despite the ferocity of the communist state apparatus, many Chinese citizens remain fearless. Sometimes, they even catch the authorities with their pants down and take the ruling party's breath away. For instance, on April 25th 1999, more than ten thousand people surrounded "Zhongnanhai" (an area in Beijing where the leaders of the Communist Party live and work). They were members of a meditation group called "Falungong". There was no violence. These meditation practitioners just sat around "Zhongnanhai", protesting unfair treatment from the authorities. This alarmed the Communist Party.

First and foremost, the police had received no prior information about the meditation group's plan to protest. Second, the investigations launched by the authorities after the April 25th incident found that many communist party members had participated in the meditation group's activities. So, in order to "nip destabilizing factors in the bud" (in the words of President Jiang Zemin), the authorities made hundreds of arrests and outlawed "Falungong". In a reference to the large number of communist party members involved in "Falungong" activities, President Jiang said at a meeting held in summer of 1999, "In recent years, the Communist Party's internal crisis of faith hasn't been alleviated. On the contrary, this crisis of faith has turned into a political gap in our organization. If we don't issue warnings today, the gap will expand. In case some major incident breaks out, it could plunge the political situation into chaos, resulting in a civil war."

Well, China is a vast country with a huge population where numerous groups with vested interests (including those not approved by the authorities) vie with each other for influence. Apparently, the central government has a tough time ensuring that its authority is respected by all the provinces and all the vested interests so that stability can be maintained. The truth is that the weaknesses and shortcomings of the old system transplanted from the former Soviet Union are now catching up, challenging the Chinese leadership as if to say, "Either you find a way to overcome the deficiencies of the Soviet model, or you face instability." This leads to the subject of whether political reform is necessary for the sake of long-term stability.

In fact, calls for political reform can be heard every now and then. The question is: What kind of political reform? Cosmetic or real? As a pragmatist, my conclusion is simple: As long as the ruling party keeps its brand name "communist", political reform in China (if any) will have to be cosmetic at best. The Communist Party's Marxist-Leninist ruling philosophy of "proletarian dictatorship"is sure to put an end to any real political reform before it even begins. In other words, instability is likely to continue as long as the old system lives. There is no way to "nip destabilizing factors in the bud" if "the bud" grows out of the system.

Even if—and it's a big "if"—President Jiang Zemin took sides with the liberals on the issue of political reform, how to implement it would certainly pose a serious challenge to him. So far, there is no sign that he would make such a move. The liberals are weak. The conservative left wing is strong. The hardliners in the military are unlikely to endorse real political reform. Without the support of the military, President Jiang could hardly implement any political reform with success. I'd rather assume that should he go ahead with real democratic political reform without the consent of the military, he would jeopardize his own safety as well as the safety of his family. What happened to Mr.

Gorbachev of the former Soviet Union in 1991 could happen to Mr. Jiang Zemin too, should he dare defy the hardliners. That is why he has no choice but to maintain his middle-of-the-road image, mediating between the liberal reformers and the conservative hardliners.

While the Communist Party is doing everything possible to maintain its monopoly of political power in the name of "stability", Chinese political dissidents criticize it for refusing to allow pluralist democratization to flourish in the country. They believe that the lack of meaningful political reform in China is a strong indication that the ruling party has vested interests in the status quo. Clearly, it is in the best interest of the Chinese people as well as in the best interest of corporate America with its high exposure in China, if long-term stability there can be ensured. The question is: Can the Chinese government maintain stability without meaningful political reform? It may become difficult going forward. Eastern Europe's late twentieth-century history has already shown that stability could not be maintained under one-party rule over the long term.

The former Soviet Union lasted for seventy-four years—probably one of the longest records for dictatorships in modern history. Eventually, it collapsed, not because the Soviet Communist Party did not want to maintain "stability", not because Mr. Gorbachev relaxed state controls on people's lives, but because the Soviet Communists were unable to control the situation anyway on both the economic level and the political level. Sooner or later, there comes a time when the status quo simply cannot be preserved. How much longer can the Chinese Communists maintain "stability"? What implications will a fluid situation have for the tens of billions of dollars invested in China by America's multinational corporations, if the Party becomes incompetent someday? Occasionally, one may hear emerging markets investment strategists discuss "the China play", but I would like to know what risk control measures they have in mind in case chaos erupts in China.

11

Territorial Issues: Tibet, Xinjiang, Taiwan, Hong Kong, Macau

As of this moment, there is no evidence that China conceives territorial ambitions against any of the countries it shares borders with. It is a country undergoing enormous changes where the leadership has its work cut out for it to restructure the economy without damaging its authority. Chinese leaders face difficult options in tackling the numerous problems confronting the loss-making state-owned enterprises—the inefficient dinosaurs of the public sector. Under the circumstances, China simply does not have the resources to sustain a protracted invasion of any other country. It has plenty of natural resources but is badly in need of foreign capital to prop up its failing state-owned industries. Unlike Japan which depends on imports to meet its needs for raw materials, China does not have a record of fighting wars in order to win access to resources. But the possibility that communist China might seek expansion for ideological reasons in the future cannot be excluded, since Marxism is such a potent ideology that it could turn some people into irrational fanatics without their own awareness. As long as the ruling party upholds Marxism as its official philosophy, the future of the country is unpredictable. Some day, communist China might acquire the necessary capabilities to become really aggressive, but that would take some time. Historically speaking, communist China sent its troops to the Korean Peninsula to fight U.S. forces in the early 1950s and later gave substantial amounts of assistance to the Vietnamese Communists throughout the Vietnam War in the 1960s and 1970s.

Within the scope of what the Chinese government considers to be its territory, there are a few trouble spots including Tibet and the north-western province of Xinjiang which is inhabited by a large Muslim population. While Beijing is concerned about the unrest in the two regions and determined to maintain its control there, it shows no sign of interest in making a move into the oil-rich Near East (not far from Xinjing) by force. Such a move would certainly incur serious consequences for itself. The 1979 Soviet invasion of Afghanistan which had the Soviet Red Army entrapped in the Islamic country's mountainous terrains till 1985 was a disaster for the Soviet empire, since the war drained it of its resources. By the time the Red Army withdrew from the Afghan mountains, the Soviet Union had become a severely wounded country no long capable of fighting the Cold War against the West. There is no reason to believe that Chinese leaders—a group of well-educated technocrats with long memories—would have the insanity to order the People's Liberation Army to march on the Near East. Rather, they have a lot to worry about in their own turf, Xinjiang Province, where armed Muslim nationalists seeking independence for the region launched a number of attacks on military and police personnel in the late 1990s.

For instance, at about 7:10 p.m., on March 17th 1999, a vehicle carrying more than forty armed policemen was bombed, fifty kilometers west of Urumqi, the capital city of Xinjiang Province. Thirty of the policemen in the vehicle were killed and more than ten wounded. The wounded were sent to the General Hospital of Xinjinag Military Command, with the more seriously wounded transferred later to the Air Force General Hospital of Lanzhou Military Command. On March 26th 1999, when meeting with the victims' families, the Xinjiang

Autonomous Region's party boss, Wang Lequan, said that the armed police's vehicle had been attacked by hostile separatist forces. According to official sources, terrorist activities by Muslim separatist groups escalated from assassinations of officers on duty and patrol officers to attacks on outposts in remote areas, convoys and military camps. Weapons used by the terrorists included automatic rifles, assault rifles, hand grenades and explosives. According to sources close to the authorities, in 1998, more than seventy well-organized armed attacks on military and police personnel took place in Xinjiang Province, killing and wounding more than three hundred and eighty people. During the first quarter of 1999, Xinjiang's Muslim separatists launched a total of twenty-seven armed attacks on military and security personnel, killing and wounding more than one hundred people and damaging more than ten facilities. Obviously, Xinjiang Province is the worst trouble spot for the Chinese government.

On the Tibet issue, Beijing's position is completely different from some of the widely held views in the West. Whereas many Westerners believe that Tibet used to be an independent country before its annexation by communist China, the Chinese government asserts that "historically" Tibet has always been Chinese territory. Generalissimo Chiang Kai-shek's pre-revolution Nationalist government in Nanking also claimed that Tibet was part of China (The Republic of China) but did not exercise effective control over Tibet and its internal affairs. In 1950, the Communists sent troops to Tibet, establishing their effective control of the region and its internal affairs. Beijing appointed a communist party committee to manage the affairs of what is now known as "The Tibet Autonomous Region". In the meantime, Beijing implemented large-scale population relocations from China's majority ethnic group "Han" to strengthen Chinese rule in Tibet.

To use the Communist Party's favorite parlance, "historically" Tibet had never experienced such excessive control by the central government until 1950. "Historically" Tibetan monks (lamas) had never had to flee their own homeland until after 1950. That is why so many people in the West are sympathetic toward Tibetan religious leader Dalai Lama, a non-violent figure who fled Tibet in 1959 and has since lived in exile in India. In early January, 2000, the third-highest ranking spiritual leader of Tibet, the 14-year-old 17th Karmapa Lama, also fled Tibet. He arrived in India with blistered feet and scraped hands after a week-long trek over the Himalayas in the depths of winter.

It is noteworthy that although communism has proved itself ineffective in stimulating economic productivity, it is highly effective in establishing control. The problem is that Beijing's excessive control of Tibet's religious affairs is hardly welcome to the lamas. More than half a century ago when Generalissimo Chiang Kai-shek's Nationalist government in Nanking claimed sovereignty over Tibet, Tibetan monks neither protested nor fled their homeland. Now, the Communists maintain the same claim of sovereignty over Tibet. Yet it appears that the monks are now praying that Beijing will leave them alone someday. Will the Communists ever start soul-searching and ask themselves why they can't even convince a 14-year-old Tibetan boy to stay?

Since the founding of the People's Republic in 1949, Beijing has always maintained that Taiwan is an inalienable part of China. Any problem? Under normal circumstances, that should not be a problem. The people of Taiwan are Chinese who speak the same language and have the same cultural traditions and customs as the people in the Chinese mainland. But if Tibetan monks wish the Communists would leave them alone, why should the Taiwanese accept Beijing's control? Besides, although the United States and communist China agree that there is only one China and that Taiwan is part of China, Western media often refers to the island as a de facto independent nation with a democratically elected government. Few people in the West (except for pro-communist activists) would like to see the free people in Taiwan fall under the control and jurisdiction of the communist dictatorship in Beijing. That is where the problem lies. While Beijing calls on Taiwan to negotiate a "peaceful reunification" with the mainland, the Taiwanese see Beijing's call as a Communist trap to ensnare them, because they know that the term "peaceful reunification", in essence, means surrender on Beijing's terms and conditions. Opinion polls show that while only 15% of Taiwan people want formal independence, an even smaller percentage want "reunification" with the mainland. The absolute majority of Taiwan people reject "the beloved socialist motherland" controlled by the Communists. Who to blame?

In 1949, after losing the civil war with the Communists, Generalissimo Chiang Kai-shek and his Nationalist government fled the Chinese mainland and relocated in Taiwan, a large island across the Taiwan Strait from China's Fujian Province. Ever since then, the Taiwanese authorities have operated under the same name (and the same flag of "blue sky, white sun and red ground") as the Nationalist government in Nanking used before 1949: The Republic of China. When the Korean War broke out in 1950, the Seventh Fleet of the U.S. Navy cruised to the Taiwan Strait to provide protection for the Nationalist government, which at that time continued to enjoy U.S. diplomatic recognition. Until his death in 1975, Generalissimo Chiang Kai-shek considered the Beijing government to be a bunch of "Communist bandits", wishing that someday he could fight his way back to the mainland to recover his lost grounds. Despite his many mistakes in life (or crimes as the Communists would maintain), a certain number of Chinese (especially in Taiwan) continue to give the Generalissimo credit for his efforts to resist Japan's invasion and occupation of China during the 1930s and 1940s as well as for his anti-communist stance.

However, looking at history with the wisdom of hindsight, Generalissimo Chiang Kai-shek might have committed his worst mistake in the spring of 1927 when he ordered a severe crackdown on the Communists, forcing them to launch an armed struggle which eventually toppled his regime. In the 1920s, led by a group of intellectuals like

Mr. Chen Du-xiu and Mr. Li Da-zhao, the Communist Party was weak and basically non-violent. Even if the Communists had a few guns, they were not strong enough to pose a material threat to the Nationalist government in Nanking. If the Generalissimo had allowed the intellectuals of the Communist Party to have a voice in the parliament, a far more peaceful evolution of modern Chinese history might have resulted in the emergence of a far more democratic China. Yet, instead, he chose violence, the consequence of which was the rise of Mao Zedong, an expert at using violence to achieve political goals who told his followers, "Political power grows out of the barrel of a gun." After twenty-two years of armed struggle, Mao replaced the Generalissimo's dictatorship with a "people's democracy", which turned out to be a nightmare during the Cultural Revolution period (1966-1976) not only to liberal intellectuals but also to the senior officials of the Communist Party like state president Liu Shaoqi and Mr. Deng Xiaoping and the generals of the People's Liberation Army like Marshal Peng Dehuai and Marshal He Long.

In 1979, the Carter administration switched America's diplomatic recognition from Taiwan to Beijing. So, Washington now deals with the Communist government of The People's Republic of China as the sole representative of China. However, the United States continues to be committed to Taiwan's security under the Taiwan Relations Act. Put in another way, despite of her formal diplomatic ties with Beijing, America treats Taiwan as an alley and would regard any Communist invasion of the island as an act of aggression. In the meantime, Beijing refers to Taiwan as Chinese territory and acts as if it had effective jurisdiction over the island. Such a state of affairs certainly causes confusion to anyone who has not watched the evolution of Sino-U.S. relations closely since the early 1970s.

During his historic visit to China in February 1972, President Nixon signed an important document with China's late Premier Zhou Enlai— the Shanghai Joint Communique, which laid the groundwork for

America's diplomatic recognition of Beijing. Although it set out both sides' positions on the Taiwan issue without compromising either side, the document read like a study of the art of ambiguity to non-experts. The truth is that the ambiguous wording was designed to allow each side to interpret the Communique according to its own needs. In the document, the United States agreed that there was only one China, since both Taiwan and the mainland said there was only one China. (At the time, Generalissimo Chiang Kai-shek was still alive, and the United States continued to recognize his Nationalist government in Taiwan as "the sole legitimate representative of China". Generalissimo Chiang claimed that the Chinese mainland was the territory of his country— The Republic of China.) The same document also indicated that the United States would like to see a peaceful reunification of China. It was a hint that U.S. diplomatic recognition for Beijing would be conditional on peace across the Taiwan Strait. In reality, though, America's commitment to Taiwan's security would be tested.

During Taiwan's presidential election in March 1996, the People's Liberation Army (PLA) fired missiles into the Taiwan Strait as a warning against Taiwan president Lee Teng-hui's efforts to enhance Taiwan's international status. Did the Communists intend to invade Taiwan? Was the missile test a deliberate attempt by Beijing to test America's determination to protect Taiwan? Did the aircraft carriers dispatched to the Taiwan Strait by Washington prevent an invasion of the island? It is anybody's guess. But at the time, stock prices in Taiwan fell sharply, and (some) well-off Taiwanese speeded up their preparations for departure for some safe haven like Canada.

In recent years, media reports alleged that to the detriment of America's national security interests, two U.S. corporations (Loral and Hughes) had exported rocket technology with military applications to China under the auspices of the Clinton administration. If the allegation is credible and if the Communists have indeed acquired ICBM capabilities to accurately hit U.S. west-coast cities like Los Angeles, thanks to the rocket technology transfer, no one can rule out the possibility that Chinese rockets could hit Taipei, Taiwan, with more accuracy. Across the Taiwan Strait from Taiwan, in China's Fujian Province, the People's Liberation Army has installed 200 M-11 and M-9 missiles with ranges of 185 miles and 375 miles, respectively. It is known that in 1993, the ranges of Chinese missiles were only 30 to 50 miles. Apparently, the PLA has been upgrading its military technology at an alarming pace—perhaps with the help of the United States.

Also, according to media reports, hundreds of thousands (if not millions) of dollars worth of donations originated from China were funneled into Bill Clinton's 1996 presidential campaign coffers. Since the story broke, various questions about China's intentions have emerged. One of the questions is: What did the Communists want from Bill Clinton in exchange for the donations? Maybe, we need not look far for the answer. Beijing has repeated many times that it wants "reunification of the motherland" either through peace talks or by military force. This statement by Beijing is a clear indication of its intention—to take over Taiwan by all means. There is nothing that the Communists want more badly than the isolation and ultimate control of the island. In order to achieve this goal, they want the United States to transfer state-of-the-art technology to help upgrade their military capabilities to invade Taiwan. (They also want to purchase air-borne early warning systems from Israel.) In the meantime, they want the United States to suspend arms (and military technology) sales to Taiwan, so that the military balance across the Taiwan Strait will tilt further in Beijing's favor. In short, they want the United States to breach her commitment to Taiwan's security under the Taiwan Relations Act, because, that way, the island will sooner or later become ripe for a communist takeover.

The question "What do they want in return (for the donations)?" sounds silly, because the Communists' intention toward Taiwan has never been a secret since the 1949 revolution. "WE MUST LIBERATE TAIWAN!" is a slogan from the Communist Party's propaganda machine—known to every Chinese citizen on the mainland, young and old. It does not take a genius to figure out what the Communists want. They want to "liberate Taiwan". Thus, they would certainly like to receive some help from any U.S. politician (including Bill Clinton) in achieving their goal. Will Clinton oblige? At least, it seems that the Communists believe there is a chance. Otherwise, why did Johnny Chong and Charlie Trie (two Chinese men close to both the Clintons and the Communists) donate large sums of money (originated from China's intelligence establishment) to the Democratic Party's 1996 campaign coffers to ensure Clinton's re-election? No wonder critics say that Bill Clinton's China policy is not "constructive engagement" as claimed by himself, but appeasement. Judging from the escalation of Beijing's saber-rattling against Taiwan, which has strangely coincided with Clinton's "constructive engagement", it is difficult to conclude that the critics are wrong. Anyhow, we did not hear such loud saber-rattling from Beijing during the Reagan years and the Bush years. So, what caused Beijing to escalate its saber-rattling? What will Bill Clinton do in the event of a communist invasion of Taiwan? Nobody knows, thanks to his "policy of ambiguity", which may have led Beijing to doubt America's determination to protect Taiwan. One would ask: If you are determined to protect your alley, why not say so?

On July 9th 1999, while meeting a German reporter, Taiwan's president Lee Teng-hui said, "Since the constitution (of the Republic of China—Taiwan's official name) was amended in 1991, the relationship between the two sides of the Taiwan Strait has been framed as a state-to-state relationship, at least as a special state-to-state relationship." To Western media which often refers to the island as a de facto independent nation, President Lee Teng-hui's statement was nothing but a reflection of the political reality across the Taiwan Strait.

For instance, any American who wants to visit Beijing has to apply to a Chinese consulate for an entry visa. Only when he has gotten a Chinese visa stamp on his passport, can he set foot on Chinese soil. Whether he likes China's communist system or not is irrelevant. What is relevant is he must recognize the authority of the government of The People's Republic of China in order to enter the Chinese mainland. If he doesn't, he can stay at home or go somewhere else. If he doesn't, he should not apply to a Chinese consulate for an entry visa in the first place.

Likewise, any American who wants to visit Taiwan has to apply to a Republic-of-China representative office for an entry visa. Only when he has gotten a Republic-of-China visa stamp on his passport, can he enter Taiwan. He must recognize the authority of the Republic-of-China government in order to enter Taiwan. If he doesn't, he should not apply to any Republic-of-China representative office for an entry visa in the first place. Instead, he should apply to a People's-Republic-of-China consulate for a permit to enter Taiwan, and the PRC consulate should grant him a permit to enter Taiwan accordingly. Only it wouldn't work, because the existence of a separate political entity (The Republic of China) exercising effective jurisdiction over Taiwan is a reality, although it is a reality Beijing wants to change by all means.

Beijing said if President Lee Teng-hui insisted on his "state-to-state" theory, the People's Liberation Army would take military action. In February of 2000 when Taiwan's presidential race got into full swing, Beijing published its White Paper on the Taiwan Issue, which specified that if Taiwan indefinitely rejected peaceful re-unification with the mainland, Beijing would use military force. [On March 18th 2000, two candidates from the pro-independence Democratic Progressive Party, Mr. Chen Shui-bian (for president) and Ms. Annette Lu (for vice president), won Taiwan's presidential election.]

The message from Beijing is loud and clear: Taiwan must recognize Beijing as a central government with jurisdiction over Taiwan—in other words, accept Beijing's control—or face war. Beijing's intention toward Taiwan is also clear: Military action is in store unless Taiwan surrenders on Beijing's terms. Time is running out for Taiwan. Beijing's war preparations against Taiwan are accelerating. They are for real.

Anyone who thinks Beijing will not dare use military force against Taiwan (because of U.S. commitment to Taiwan's security under the Taiwan Relations Act) must be kidding himself. Remember what happened in June of 1989? At the time, Beijing's student demonstrators refused to leave Tiananmen Square even after the government had declared martial law. They thought the Communist regime would not dare use military force against them because Western media attention was focused on the Square. They were wrong. The People's Liberation Army opened fire on them.

Beijing's saber-rattling against Taiwan is an indication that the military balance across the Taiwan Strait has tilted very far in Beijing's favor—a senile, little man would not knock at your door and threaten you with his fists. In recent years, a lopsided arms race launched by the Communists has turned China into a major military power. Beijing is definitely not a senile, little man. Rather, it is tough and big. And if a tough, big guy living across the way rattles his saber in his yard, saying he will use it against you someday, you'd better believe him. If you still think he will not dare use his saber against you because the police are watching, you must be kidding yourself. At times, even the police are too busy to take care of you.

Still there are people who think all this saber-rattling is nothing but rhetoric, because in their opinion, Beijing does not have the necessary capabilities to invade Taiwan. True the Communists have not yet acquired all the necessary capabilities. Yet this does not mean they will never acquire all the necessary capabilities to achieve their goal. They have money, and there are few things in this world that money cannot buy. Even if the saber-rattling is rhetoric, it serves a purpose too. It is a trial balloon designed to test America's public opinion and America's determination to protect Taiwan. If opinion surveys show that most Americans do not want America to intervene in the event of war across the Taiwan Strait, thereby holding the Clinton-Gore Administration back, the chances of war would be higher rather than lower, especially if

Al Gore wins the 2000 presidential election, ensuring a continuation of the Clinton-Gore Administration's policy of "constructive engagement" (or policy of appeasement as critics have pointed out) toward China. So, my prediction is that a Gore victory in 2000 (i.e. an extension of the Clinton-Gore Administration) is likely to guarantee another four years of saber-rattling by Beijing with a 50-50 chance of some kind of military conflict breaking out across the Taiwan Strait.

To be sure, the Communists will closely watch Washington's and Taipei's responses to their saber-rattling, since the responses will help them spot their opponents' weaknesses. On the other hand, Beijing's saber-rattling is also designed to mask its own weaknesses. For instance, no matter how loud the saber-rattling may be, Beijing does not have the resources to fight a protracted war (at least as of this moment). Anyway, this is a dangerous poker game—a high-stake gamble—where each player holds a card face down, trying to figure out whether the other guy is bluffing.

Does Beijing have the right to launch a military attack on Taiwan? According to itself, it does, whereas for humanitarian and business reasons, many people (perhaps most people) in the West believe Beijing should not launch an attack on Taiwan. To them, whether Beijing has the right to use military force against Taiwan is a secondary issue. Until his death in 1975, Generalissimo Chiang Kai-shek maintained that his Nationalist government in Taiwan had the right to recover the Chinese mainland lost to "the Communist bandits" during the civil war. But he did not have the capabilities to achieve his goal, so his right to recover the mainland, true or not, became irrelevant.

Today, although Beijing has acquired certain capabilities to launch an attack on Taiwan, experts doubt that it has all the necessary capabilities to effectively invade and occupy the island. Resistance from Taiwan's military would be fierce, and losses of human lives on both sides severe and tragic. Anyone in his sound mind would think such military action to be morally wrong. But remember the Beijing regime is a Communist dictatorship without proper checks and balances to ensure rational conduct. It could become an irrational beast if the occasion arises. Its political moral principles are completely different from those observed by the international community. In its eyes, whatever contributes to its control is "absolutely right" regardless of the cost. So, with Beijing, to extend its control to Taiwan is a "holy cause to re-unify the mother-land", not an act of aggression against a free people unwilling to accept Communist rule. It would never agree that Taiwan's twenty-three (23) million residents should have the right to choose their own government and decide whether Taiwan should become an independent nation. (Likewise, it would never agree that the people of the Chinese mainland should have the right to choose their own government and decide whether China should scrap communism altogether.) If the military balance across the Taiwan Strait continues to deteriorate against Taiwan, the temptation to use military force against the island will become stronger by the day to the hardliners. At a certain point, if President Jiang Zemin (a moderate probably with every incentive to maintain peace for the sake of the Chinese economy) is unable to keep the hardliners in check, anything is possible.

However, based on certain media reports, it seems that the People's Liberation Army (the PLA) has its own problems. For instance, in early July of 1999, General Yu Yongbo, director of the General Political Department of the PLA, made a speech about the serious problems facing the military. He mentioned quite a few issues: (1) The senior officers of the military were basically lazy, lax and weak, and things were deteriorat-ing. (2) "Political thought work" (i.e. political brainwashing) conducted by the military authorities had little effect on rank and file spirits (i.e. morale). (3) The military establishment was permeated with organiza-tional laxity, disciplinary laxity, and behavioral licentiousness. (4) Corruption among the brass had affected the political, spiritual quality of the military. (5) Bureaucratic behavior and feudalistic notions among the brass had resulted in tensions and conflicts between different military groups, between senior officers and junior officers, and between the brass and the rank and file. (6) The number of soldiers disobeying orders, violating discipline, deserting or going AWOL (absent without leave) had increased. (7) The number of violent incidents involving soldiers had increased. (8) The number of soldiers using narcotics, gambling, and committing crimes on holidays had risen. (9) With lax discipline, the quality of education and training at the military academies had deteriorated. (10) Tensions and conflicts had emerged between the military and the local governments, because the military and the civilian authorities had failed to properly handle the relations between them. The question is: Can such an army effectively invade and occupy Taiwan, with or without the necessary capabilities?

In the meantime, it is most intriguing to note that some well-intentioned people have offered their advice to Taiwan: "Please don't provoke Beijing." Of course, Taiwan should not provoke Beijing. But the problem is that these "advisers" seem to believe that "provocation" is the cause of Beijing's saber-rattling, whereas the truth is that the saber-rattling is nothing but a reflection of Beijing's intention toward Taiwan—a reflection of the fact that the military balance across the Taiwan Strait has seriously deteriorated against Taiwan. It has nothing to do with "provocation". The "advisers" seem to say, "Don't provoke the tough guy, because if you do, you'll get in trouble." The fact of the matter is that both Taiwan and the United States are already in trouble. Taiwan has been in trouble for more than half a century, not because of "provocation", but because of Beijing's efforts to control Taiwan. If Beijing has the necessary capabilities to effectively invade and occupy Taiwan (and believes it will succeed), it will do so anyway, with or without "provocation". If the United States declares that she will stop arms sales to Taiwan and will not intervene in the event of war across the Taiwan Strait, then you can bet your last dollar that sooner or later, the People's Liberation Army will attack Taiwan, with or without "provocation". If I don't like you and want to beat you, you bet I'll see "provocation" in whatever you do or say. If you are weak and your enemy wants to attack you, it is easy for him to find an excuse to do so. The Communists are experts in power politics. They are rattling their sabers to force Taiwan to surrender. The cause of the saber-rattling is not "provocation", but the deteriorating military balance across the Taiwan Strait. If Taiwan were militarily stronger than Beijing, we would be hearing peace overtures rather than saber-rattling from Beijing.

Again, this is a dangerous, high-stake poker game. If Beijing does not stop rattling its saber, at some point, either Beijing or Washington will come to call the other side's bluff. As a rule, the guy with the deeper pocket (i.e. with more strength) stands a better chance to win—if the game is winnable. Judging from its arms purchases from Russia, its efforts to acquire sophisticated air-borne early warning systems from Israel and its success in upgrading the People's Liberation Army's missile technology, Beijing certainly knows how to play this poker game.

But how many party members and ordinary Chinese citizens want the People's Liberation Army (the PLA) to attack Taiwan? Not many, I guess. After more than twenty years of peace, economic reform and openness, many party officials and their relatives have become the wealthiest "proletarians" that ever walked on the planet. Why should they want a dangerous military poker game? Still, it seems that some hardliners in the military do want to up the ante. A book entitled "Unrestricted War" by two air force officers (Colonel Qiao Liang and Colonel Wang Xiang-sui) was published in 1999, suggesting that China launch a terrorist war against the United States in the event of U.S. military intervention to shield Taiwan from the PLA's invasion. Since the Chinese publishing industry is controlled by the authorities, the views expressed in the book should be regarded as a reflection of the thinking of the Communist Party's hardliners.

The authors of "Unrestricted War" hold that in case U. S. military forces intervene to protect Taiwan, China should push the war against the United States "beyond the limit". What limit? The book says that in order to take over Taiwan, China should not be restricted by the rules of war and the limitations stipulated in international treaties. Instead, the book says, China should use all possible means (including non-military means) to cause serious damage to the United States in every aspect, so as to achieve China's war goals. According to the authors of the book, China should use the following means to harm the United States: urban terrorism; financial terrorism; urban guerrilla warfare; computer hacker attacks; environmental destruction; narcotics distribution etc. Sounds like Colonel Qiao Liang and Colonel Wang Xiang-sui got their professional training in 1930s Nazi Germany. If they ever rose to the Politburo of the Communist Party and participated in China's foreign policy decision-making process, moderates like President Jiang Zemin and Premier Zhu Rongji should feel very worried, because the colonels would screw up U.S.-China relations big time. Their tendency to go "beyond the limit" borders upon madness.

Do the Communists intend to attack America with nuclear weapons? No, at least not now, because it would not make any sense. The United States is the largest market for Chinese products, absorbing more than 33% of China's exports. Only a fool would attack the largest market for his goods. President Jiang Zemin is no fool. Like the late paramount leader Deng Xiaoping, President Jiang knows better relations with the United States will help the Chinese economy. He knows American consumers keep many Chinese factories operating with a profit and many Chinese workers on payrolls. So, for America to enhance trade ties with China is one of the best ways to maintain world peace. Corporate America needs profit. China needs profit too. That is a common ground from which both sides will benefit. Hopefully, China's entry into the World Trade Organization (the WTO) will keep it focused on money-making rather than saber-rattling, though no one can guarantee that Beijing will honor the rules of the WTO—it could interpret WTO rules according to its own needs. [According to a report by Hong Kong political analyst Willy W. Lam (dated November 17th 1999), opposition to

Beijing's WTO entry was strong among the central government's various ministries and most regional administrations. After the U.S.-China WTO talks were resumed in September of 1999, a number of senior officials asked advisers to concoct open and hidden trade barriers that would dilute terms specified in the final deal.]

The problem is nobody (except President Jiang Zemin himself) knows whether President Jiang Zemin is strong enough to keep the hardliners in check, if a showdown between the United States and China on the Taiwan issue ever occurs. When Mr. Deng Xiaoping was alive, the generals of the People's Liberation Army (the PLA) demonstrated absolute respect and obedience to him because of his high prestige and his contributions to the country's economic reforms. The generals never tried to force his hand. Now, President Jiang may not be in as strong a position as Mr. Deng was. He appears to be a mediator between the hardliners and the reformers. How much control does he have over the military? The hardliners may pressurize him to take action by accusing him of being "soft" on Taiwan. The moderates (and the liberals) are well-educated people who weigh the pros and the cons all the time. They will certainly consider the consequences of any military action against Taiwan. Whereas, eager to show how "patriotic" they are, the hardliners may not be as rational. That's where the rub is.

In case the People' Liberation Army fired missiles on Taiwan and started an invasion of the island, would the United States intervene? Supposing the United States involved herself in a direct conflict with China over Taiwan, would the Communists fire nuclear warheads on such U.S. cities as New York and Los Angeles? According to NBC News, China has about twenty nuclear missiles capable of reaching the United States. Although Beijing says China would never become the first to use nuclear weapons against another nation, should the United States trust a Communist regime that promised not to use force against its own people but then called out tanks to crack down on peaceful demonstrators in June of 1989? All these questions are hypothetical and may remain moot as long as peace lasts. But the stories about U.S. companies selling state-of-the-art rocket technology to China, about money originated from China's military intelligence establishment finding its way into the Democratic Party's 1996 campaign coffers to ensure Bill Clinton's re-election and about Chinese spies stealing nuclear secrets from America's laboratories have naturally prompted worries about Beijing's intentions.

Needless to say, Beijing poses a material threat to Taiwan (where a pluralist political system has evolved since 1987 when the then president Chiang Jing Guo decided to lift restrictions on political party activities and media reports). According to an analysis by Dr. Chen Tijie of Radio Free Asia of Beijing's reaction to the proposed Theater Missile Defense program (an effort to enhance Taiwan's security), a crisis across the Taiwan Strait more serious than the PLA's March 1996 missile test might be approaching, because the PLA has made full preparations to invade Taiwan. The question is when.

According to a May 20th 2000 speech by Politburo member Qian Qishen (with responsibility for Taiwan affairs), Beijing has a timetable for "re-unification" (i.e. for extending its control to the island): (1) If the new Taiwan authorities accept Beijing's terms of "peaceful re-unification" (i.e. accept Beijing's control), Beijing will give Taiwan till 2011 (to surrender). (2) If the new Taiwan authorities refuse to accept Beijing's terms of "peaceful re-unification", then, between 2003 and 2008 at the latest, Beijing will announce by what means and at what time the Taiwan issue will be resolved. (3) If Taiwan declares independence, Beijing will take military action "to liberate Taiwan". Sources believe this timetable was formulated in April of 2000 and that the military was dissatisfied with it. The generals of the PLA would like to take early military action.

[It is my guess that the PLA might take some kind of military action against Taiwan in the next four years (2000-2004), especially if Al Gore wins the 2000 presidential election and then betrays an appearance of willingness to sacrifice Taiwan. On the other hand, if Republican presidential hopeful George W. Bush (governor of Texas) wins the election, bringing back a stable China policy with no ambiguity on the Taiwan issue, he might stand a better (rather than poorer) chance to improve U.S.-China relations (and trade ties). Ambiguity gives rise to uncertainty, which in turn encourages adventurism in the adversary's camp, and as a rule, (adversary) adventurism destabilizes bilateral relations. I figure that may be one of the reasons why some Wall Street analysts seem to be looking for Governor Bush to become the next president of the United States, predicting that Wall Street sentiment would be more positive for a Bush victory. Here are a couple of examples: In a Prudential Securities Inc. (research department) article dated June 14th 2000, Analyst Mark L. Melcher wrote: "In short, the Republican candidate (George W. Bush) appears to have arrogated the label 'New Progressive'....For instance, it seems clear, at least to me, that the GOP under 'W' (i.e. George W. Bush) is becoming what can only be described as the nation's 'New Progressive' party." He went on to conclude: "The new progressive Republicans are, I would guess, almost certain to carry the day." In another Prudential research report also dated June 14th 2000, Analyst Charles A. Gabriel, Jr. wrote: "Bush has led Vice President Al Gore in all but 5 of 173 head-to-head presidential match-ups conducted by pollsters since the beginning of 1999." Though he mentioned four scenarios of the 2000 presidential race, his emphasis was clearly on the first: "The first scenario—that Bush wins the presidency and the Republicans hang on narrowly to majority control in Congress—I give odds of slightly more than a tossup." Anyway, Wall Street does not like uncertainty. Nor does it want what it considers to be a left-wing socialist administration (with strong backing from the AFL-CIO) to continue for another four years.]

Basically speaking, Taiwan was a police state until 1988 when President Chiang Jing Guo died. His father, Generalissimo Chiang Kai-shek, who died in 1975, remained a dictator throughout his life—first in the Chinese mainland, then in Taiwan. It was when Mr. Lee Teng-hui of the Nationalist Party, a U.S.-educated agricultural expert, became Taiwan's president in 1988 that full-scale democratization was implemented on the island. Mr. Lee was re-elected in March 1996 despite Beijing's military threat designed to scare off Taiwan's voters. In March 2000, Mr. Chen Shui-bian of the pro-independence Democratic Progressive Party (a poor peasant's son and a Taiwan-educated lawyer who speaks no English) won Taiwan's presidential election. On May 20th 2000, President Lee Teng-hui handed over the presidency to Mr. Chen Shui-bian. The transition of power took place with neither violence nor bloodshed. The late Communist Party chairman Mao Zedong's 20th century dictum—"Political power grows out of the barrel of a gun"—does not apply in 21st century Taiwan, where political power grows out of the ballot box of a peaceful election.

The relations between the mainland and Taiwan (referred to as cross-Strait relations by the media these days) have been quite complicated. Officially, a state of war still exists across the Taiwan Strait, since the two sides have signed no agreement to declare an end to the civil war (between the Communists and the Nationalists) which broke out shortly after Japan surrendered in 1945 and resulted in the relocation in Taiwan of Generalissimo Chiang Kai-shek's Nationalist government. Now the Communists in the mainland claim sovereignty over Taiwan and threaten to use military force if the residents of the island refuse to surrender. Obviously, America's commitment to Taiwan's security under the Taiwan Relations Act is a major barrier to Beijing's attempt to control Taiwan by force, since any military action against Taiwan by the PLA would trigger U.S. involvement with unpredictable consequences. Presumably, U.S. multinational corporations would have to suspend their investments in the mainland, and Chinese products would be barred from U.S. soil, which in turn would exacerbate the already serious joblessness in the mainland and bring Beijing's economic modernization program to a halt.

On the other hand, the two sides of the Taiwan Strait have made several attempts to improve so-called cross-Strait relations—with Beijing eager to coax Taiwan into accepting its terms of "peaceful re-unification" and Taiwan eager to show its commitment to improving relations with Beijing. (Apparently in great fear of Beijing, Taiwan has been doing everything possible to please Beijing, rather than to "provoke" Beijing. But that won't work. Beijing wants nothing short of Taiwan's surrender.) On the economic front, Beijing has been successful in luring Taiwanese investments through its offers of preferential treatment to Taiwan businessmen willing to set up plants in the mainland. This has become a cause for concern to the Taiwan authorities, because an excessive flight of capital from Taiwan to the mainland is likely to induce an undesirable reliance on the mainland among Taiwan's industries, which Beijing could use to blackmail the island. Without question, attaching great importance to U.S.-Taiwan relations, the people of Taiwan are closely watching any development in the exchanges between Washington and Beijing which may have even the slightest implications for U.S. policy toward Taiwan. They know any appearance of likelihood that the United States might weaken her commitment to Taiwan's security (despite The Taiwan Relations Act) will inevitably encourage Beijing to exert more pressure on the island.

Although there are no direct transport, trade and postal links between the two sides, the Taiwan authorities allow the island's residents to travel to the mainland via Hong Kong. Cross-Strait trade is conducted also through Hong Kong. In addition, if you post a letter in Taiwan for somebody living in the mainland, he will receive it, because in Hong Kong, there is a transit station handling mail from Taiwan to the mainland and vice versa. So, for many years, Hong Kong, the former British crown colony, has played a role in promoting cross-Strait relations.

On July 1st 1997, Hong Kong was handed back to China by Great Britain in accordance with the 1984 Sino-British Joint Declaration. Macau, an enclave which was lost to the Portuguese during the Ming

Dynasty and whose economy depends heavily on the casino industry, was handed back to China in late 1999. However, it was alleged that the gambling city had been under de facto Chinese control from the late 1960s. This allegation gained credit when the media reported the story of James Peng, a Chinese-Australian businessman. It goes: Mr. Peng left China after his business partner, a Shenzhen-based Chinese state-owned textile company, incurred losses. One day in 1993, arriving from Australia, he checked into a Macau hotel. Soon he was kidnaped and transported to Shenzhen, where he was formally arrested on charges of fraud and embezzlement filed by his Chinese business partner. In 1995, James Peng was sentenced to sixteen years' imprisonment. His Australian passport could not protect him. The fact that Peng's abduction was carried out in Macau right under the nose of the Portuguese authorities fueled suspicions that Beijing might have extended its jurisdiction to Macau long before the 1999 official handover date. Who alerted the Chinese authorities when James Peng arrived in Macau? Secret Communist agents? How did the kidnappers manage to spirit Peng out of Macau without the knowledge of the Portuguese authorities there?

Described by many as the Pearl of the East, Hong Kong is a great success story built on the basis of the British common law system, which, during the one hundred and fifty-five years (1842-1997) of British rule, served as a prerequisite for the colony's prosperity and stability. Under British rule, Hong Kong's business community thrived, while its financial-banking system evolved into one of the most sophisticated in Asia by Western standards. Over the years, the people of Hong Kong have been served by an extremely well-educated and efficient civil service whose members are all fluent in both English and Chinese—this fact in itself reflects the success of the educational system transplanted in Hong Kong by the British.

Basically a Chinese community, Hong Kong has emerged as an affluent international city, where east meets west, where Chinese speak and read in English, watch CNN and Hollywood and work side by side with Brits and Americans in various business organizations, where huge office towers reach up to the sky like those in New York City, where English bars which entertain customers with pop or jazz music sport "Happy-Hour-2-4-1" notices. (Happy Hour 2-4-1 means you can get two cups of beer for the price of one during happy hour, usually from 4 p.m. to 7 p.m.) It is a great modernized city with strong British characteristics. No wonder Hong Kong has been a major tourist destination in the Far East well-known for its many attractions. So, one would ask why it had to be returned to China merely because the 1842 treaty between Great Britain and China's Qing Dynasty expired. The answer is simple: There was never a military option for Britain. A look at Hong Kong's map would tell you there was no way for the British to defend the colony. Former British prime minister Margaret Thatcher got the best deal possible for the people of Hong Kong. At least, Hong Kong capitalism would continue for a while.

During my eleven years in Hong Kong, the city's crime rate was low, thanks to a highly efficient and well-educated police force organized by Her Majesty's Government there. And because of Hong Kong's strict gun control regulations, nothing like the Jonesboro school shooting (March 1998, Arkansas, U.S.A.) or the Columbine High School shooting (April 20, 1999, Littleton, Colorado, U.S.A.) ever happened there. In the two decades prior to the end of British rule, the Government also developed an anti-corruption force called the ICAC (Independent Commission Against Corruption), which proved to be an effective deterrent to graft and illegal transactions (such as insider trading).

In various conversations, I discovered that both Brits and local Chinese were proud of Hong Kong. Once I found myself sitting next to an Englishman in a Causeway Bay hotel bar who told me that Hong Kong was a jewel Beijing would not spoil. "They are not stupid," he said. "This place is like New York. It's a jewel. Why should they spoil it?" On another occasion, in a crowded Kowloon McDonald's restaurant, a tourist from the U.K. sat down at my table, marveling at the skyline of the city. "But what will become of it after '97?" he added with a sad look. I was under the impression that the British were proud of Hong Kong because they felt British rule had turned it into a great city, while local Chinese were proud of Hong Kong because they had participated in creating a booming economy and also because there was solid proof that they were smart, hard-working and quick to learn whatever was necessary to make Hong Kong successful.

True that the British trained local Chinese to be Hong Kong's efficient civil servants. But no matter how great the common law system proves to be, the British could not have transplanted it in Hong Kong with such amazing success, if local Chinese had not been so smart. I don't believe these facts are lost upon Chinese leaders, though they have yet to admit that Hong Kong's success is based on the British common law system. Apparently, China's late paramount leader Deng Xiaoping knew the reasons for Hong Kong's prosperity when he decided to give the free port another fifty years of capitalism. A few years before his death, he concluded that if not reformed, the Chinese economy would squeeze into a blind alley. His instructions: Chinese cities should be built after the Hong Kong model. "Let's build tens of cities like Hong Kong," said the elderly statesman.

Since 1949, Hong Kong has been a great help to the Chinese economy. First of all, it is a lucrative market for the mainland. Though not as large as a province in size, Hong Kong's population exceeds that of many a small country in the world. Seven million people live in the city, consuming large quantities of food and other products on a daily basis, most of which come from the mainland. Hong Kong is surrounded by sea, and since sea water is not potable, fresh water has to be imported from the mainland. Hong Kong has its own currency, the Hong Kong dollar, a hard currency pegged to the U.S. dollar at HK$7.80. So all the purchases of food, consumer goods and fresh water from the mainland amount to a huge foreign exchange income for China. Secondly, most of the foreign investments in the mainland have come either from Hong Kong or via Hong Kong. Thirdly, Hong Kong is a transit port for Chinese products on their way to North America, Europe and other overseas markets. Fourthly, Beijing controls a number of Hong Kong-registered companies with considerable investments in the city's various industries ranging from the banking sector to publishing to grocery to department stores to real estate development.

Furthermore, in recent years, a number of Chinese state-owned enterprises made IPO's (initial public offerings) on Hong Kong's stock market, raising funds in hard currency to prop up the failing state-owned sector of the Chinese economy. Hong Kong's usefulness to the mainland could hardly be overstated. [Stocks connected to the state-owned enterprises in the mainland but listed in Hong Kong are known as "Red Chips" or "China Concept" stocks. In 1997, many "Red Chips" traded at price/earnings (P/E) multiples of 300 times as sucker investors bet their life's savings on "the China Concept", i.e. "the great long-term potential of the China market". Later when it became clear that "the China Concept" had more to do with brokerage analyst hype than with corporate fundamentals, the "Red Chips" fell like a stone, bringing their P/E ratios down to below 10 times earnings.]

Based on my long years of observation on the Communist Party's propensities, no matter how useful Hong Kong has been to the Chinese economy, to exercise full control over the territory remains Beijing's top priority. The fact that more than half a century of Communist control (and state intervention) in the mainland has resulted in an irrational and inflexible structure prone to vicious cycles of stagnation and chaos is unlikely to deter the Communists from achieving their ultimate goal—full and complete control of Hong Kong. As the British must have learned, to try to persuade Beijing to leave Hong Kong alone so that Hong Kong could contribute more to the Chinese economy would be a waste of time. Does Beijing want Hong Kong to remain prosperous? Sure, it does. It says it will do everything possible to help maintain

Hong Kong's prosperity and stability. The question is: What does "stability" mean from Beijing's point of view? Most probably, "stability" means control in the Communist glossary. So, firstly, Beijing wants control. Secondly, Beijing wants Hong Kong to prosper as well. Why not? The risk is Beijing may want to have the cake and eat it too.

During the last few years of British rule, Hong Kong Governor Chris Patten, an expert in Chinese affairs, helped establish a democracy in the territory with a directly elected legislature. That was the last thing Beijing wanted to see happening in Hong Kong. After Chris Patten's plan for direct Legislative Council elections was announced in the early 1990s, Beijing signaled its strong objections. In the meantime, Beijing turned up its pressure on the British to scrap the plan altogether. Then Beijing expressed its hopes that Chris Patten would "become a friend of the Chinese people" by shelving his plan. The Governor certainly knew what that meant. In order "to become a friend of the Chinese people", he would have to do what Beijing wanted him to. In the end, he was content not "to become a friend of the Chinese people" and decided to proceed with Hong Kong's direct elections.

Soon Chinese officials began to call Chris Patten names, some of which sounded preposterous. For instance, the head of China's Hong Kong and Macau Affairs Office, Mr. Lu Ping (usually an urbane gentleman who graduated from pre-revolution Shanghai's most prestigious university St. John's and commands an excellent knowledge of the English language), said if Chris Patten implemented his plan, he would become "a sinner of the millennium". But he did not explain why a directly elected legislature in Hong Kong would be such a dangerous idea. The truth is in his capacity as Beijing's point man with orders to stop Hong Kong's direct elections, Mr. Lu Ping had no choice but to condemn the Patten plan. To do so, he had to use whatever hyperboles came to his lips first in response to media reporters' questions. It seems "sinner of the millennium" happened to be one of them.

Although aware Beijing would not allow the directly elected legislature to continue after 1997, Governor Patten carried his democracy promise through. He said he had built a house (of democracy). What if somebody wanted to tear it down? The Governor shrugged his shoulders. He stood by his principles and performed his duties, regardless of whether he would become "a friend of the Chinese people" or "a sinner of the millennium". His job was not to please Beijing by doing what Beijing wanted him to. No one could blame him for not giving Hong Kong people what they wanted. At least for a few years prior to the July 1st 1997 handover, Hong Kong people had a taste of democracy. If democracy was taken away from them, they would know who did it. They would certainly be able to tell the difference between a directly elected democracy and a manipulated rubber stamp. That is why Beijing hated the Patten plan in the first place.

On July 1st 1997 when the People Liberation Army marched into Hong Kong, ending one hundred and fifty-five years (1842-1997) of British rule, Hong Kong's directly elected Legislative Council was replaced by a Beijing-appointed rubber stamp. From that moment onward, Hong Kong people would have to live under Communist control, since Hong Kong's history as part of the Free World came to a conclusion with the rise of China's red flag in the territory. I stayed in Hong Kong till July 16th 1997 when I boarded a Canadian Airline DC-10 for Vancouver. While I was there, most Hong Kong people did not seem to be worried. Nothing much changed after the July 1st 1997 handover, at least on the surface. Hong Kong's new chief executive Mr. C.H. Tung (appointed by Beijing) decided to allow the entire British-trained civil service (including the popular Chief Secretary Anson Chan) to remain in office. Hong Kong's stock market continued to soar with the Hang Seng index surpassing the 16000 mark in summer of 1997. After all, Hong Kong is a great commercial city whose residents are basically business-oriented. Politics aside, as long as there is money to be made, funds flow in.

Beneath the surface, however, fundamental changes began after July 1st 1997. First, it would be naive to think Hong Kong's British-trained civil service would enjoy Beijing's unreserved trust. I'd rather presume that the performances of individual civil servants are closely watched by Beijing's agents in Hong Kong. What they say and do would serve as a measure of their loyalty to Beijing. Those considered disloyal or disobedient are likely to be replaced gradually by those trusted by Beijing. Sooner or later, those who feel uncomfortable serving under the new master will quit. Hong Kong's senior civil servants are all very wealthy. Why should they stay if they feel uncomfortable? Somewhere down the road, Hong Kong's British-trained civil servants will be out of the scene. By then, the changes in Hong Kong will have become more visible. Senior civil servants like Chief Secretary Anson Chan and Financial Secretary Donald Tsang are tantamount to a symbol of Hong Kong's free lifestyles. If they are gone, Hong Kong residents may begin to wonder whether they still live in a free society.

In spring of 1999, Chief Executive C.H. Tung announced that Chief Secretary Anson Chan would continue in office after she reached 60, the age at which Hong Kong civil servants usually retire. Political analysts believed that the decision to keep Ms. Anson Chan in office after her retirement age must have come from Beijing, indicating Chinese leaders were concerned about Hong Kong's stability. Shortly after the handover, Hong Kong's fortunes started to slide downhill amid Asia's financial crisis, while its unemployment numbers rose. Ms. Anson Chan's continuation in office was definitely good news for Hong Kong people, but she could not continue forever. Well known for his willingness to toe the Beijing line, Mr. C.H. Tung could hardly replace Ms. Anson Chan as a symbol of Hong Kong's freedom. Rather, he acts like a cautious representative from Beijing determined to carry out the Party's intentions, that is, to help the Communists exert their control over the territory. Anyone who expects Mr. Tung to defend individual rights in Hong Kong must be under a delusion. Eager to show how "patriotic" (i.e. how loyal to Beijing) he was, he says that while Americans set great store by individual rights, Hong Kong people should ask themselves how to contribute to the motherland. Sounds like a collectivistic view that Hong Kong should forget about individual rights.

To illustrate Mr. C.H. Tung's role in Hong Kong, here is a case in point. Hong Kong's Basic Law provides that Hong Kong permanent residents' mainland-born children shall have the right of abode in Hong Kong. In early 1999, Hong Kong's Court of Final Appeal ruled that mainland-born children of Hong Kong parentage who had entered Hong Kong by illegal means could stay in the territory because of their right of abode and should not be repatriated. But in May of 1999, citing the difficulties the community would face in coping with the influx of such mainland-born children, Mr. Tung's administration turned to the National People's Congress (China's rubber stamp parliament) for a re-interpretation of the Basic Law. As a result, the Court of Final Appeal ate humble pie, overturning its own ruling, and the government was happy that the Court of Final Appeal had "corrected its mistakes". Thus, although its name "Court of Final Appeal" lives on, the Court of Final Appeal in Hong Kong is no longer final in the true sense of the term, since the final word comes from Beijing.

The question is: How can Hong Kong remain a free society, if its laws are interpreted by a rubber stamp parliament controlled by the Communist Party? The Chinese constitution provides for all sorts of freedoms and rights: freedom of speech, freedom of assembly, political rights, you name it. But under the interpretation (i.e. control) of the National People's Congress (the NPC), all those freedoms and rights stipulated in the constitution come to zilch. Most Chinese citizens never even dream of exercising their "stipulated rights", because they know so-called rights only exist on paper. They just shut up and put up like enslaved creatures. Only a small minority (known as political dissidents) dare exercise their "stipulated constitutional rights", but, as a rule, they end up in jail—the price for their bravery.

Shortly after the July 1st 1997 handover, Hong Kong's provisional legislative council (a rubber stamp set up by Beijing) passed a law making it a crime to desecrate China's red national flag. In January of 1998, two Hong Kong men (Ng Kung-siu, 25, and Lee Kin-yun, 19) were arrested at a peaceful demonstration, after waving a national flag which bore the Chinese character for "shame" and had the large star inked out. They were convicted of desecrating the national flag by a district court. But the Court of Appeal overturned their convictions on the grounds that the National Flag and National Emblem Ordinance passed by the provisional legislative council was in contravention of Hong Kong's mini-constitution (the Basic Law) and the United Nations International Covenant on Civil and Political Rights which provides for free expression. Hong Kong's pro-Beijing political figures called for the National People's Congress (the NPC) to "re-interpret" the law, and Mr. Tung's administration challenged the Court of Appeal ruling at the Court of Final Appeal. Knowing Beijing would intervene if the government's challenge failed, the Court of Final Appeal overturned the Court of Appeal ruling. The government was satisfied that "The Court of Final Appeal" had learned how to behaved itself this time. Is Hong Kong's common law system still alive? The answer is no. With a Beijing-controlled Tung administration, a Beijing-manipulated Legislative Council and a Beijing-interpreted law system, Hong Kong is 100% under Communist control in my opinion. Still, I guess Beijing is not yet satisfied. Overkill may be in the offing.

It is clear any re-interpretation of Hong Kong's Basic Law by the NPC is a re-interpretation by the Communist Party. The problem is as a Marxist-Leninist political organization, the Communist Party has to interpret the Basic Law from the viewpoint of Marxism-Leninism, not from the perspective of the common law system created by the British and perfected over the centuries. To put it bluntly, a re-interpretation of the Basic Law by the NPC (i.e. by the Communist Party) amounts to an end to Hong Kong's rule of law as defined under the common law system. Take the United Nations International Covenant on Civil and Political Rights (which Beijing signed in 1998) as an example. Any person in his sound mind would think that the Covenant provides for free expression and the right to organize political groups including opposition political parties. Not the Communists. They have a penchant for unilaterally interpreting international treaties to serve their own needs. By their Marxist-Leninist "interpretation", the United Nations International Covenant on Civil and Political Rights does not provide for the existence of opposition political parties on Chinese soil, so toward the end of 1998, Beijing arrested dozens of Chinese citizens attempting to organize the Chinese Democratic Party.

In Hong Kong, Mr. C.H. Tung's administration has a plan to reform the civil service. Some analysts suspect the government might use the reform program to purge the British-trained civil service which is unlikely to win Beijing's trust. They believe during the course of the program, Hong Kong's British-trained civil servants will have to vacate a number of key positions to enable Beijing's agents to infiltrate the civil service with more ease. In summer of 1999 (i.e. two years after the handover), a retired civil servant (who used to serve with Her Majesty's Government in Hong Kong) told a reporter that he was still in contact with some of his former colleagues but they had changed so much in personality since the '97 handover that he felt they were not the same people he had known. What caused the change? The environment, I guess. Since July 1st 1997, Hong Kong's environment has changed, both politically and economically. Civil servants who used to serve with Her Majesty's Government began to feel the pinch of pressure after the handover. To Western observers, the pressure may not be visible, but it is there. Like other Chinese citizens, Hong Kong's civil servants now have to learn to "behave themselves" under Communist rule. If they are not careful—for instance, if what they say displeases their new master—they could lose their livelihood. That perception in itself is pressure enough.

In summer of 1998, while visiting Hong Kong in celebration of the first anniversary of the handover, President Jiang Zemin said to local residents: "Gradually, you'll get accustomed (to it)." Though he did not specify exactly what Hong Kong residents would gradually get accustomed to, I guess he was referring to Beijing's control over the territory. His understanding of Hong Kong residents' concern about Communist control should be appreciated. He knew local residents were not accustomed to Communist rule and came very close to admitting it. Given his artistic versatility and his often improvisational style (as a political star), I guess President Jiang himself may have had a difficult time getting "accustomed to it" during the leftist Mao era. I can hardly believe that Premier Zhu Rongji was "accustomed to it" when he fell victim to the late Communist Party chairman Mao's crackdown on liberal intellectuals in 1957. For decades (1949-1986) I myself lived under communism. Though not "accustomed to it", I put up with it. I am glad I got out when I did. The absolute majority of Chinese (and now the absolute majority of Hong Kong residents) have no choice but to "get accustomed to it".

In 1997, a Swedish friend of mine sent me a letter, asking whether Hong Kong's academic freedom could be preserved. In my reply, I wrote basically speaking, nothing could remain free under communism. I said: "Dear Professor, if 'academic freedom' means freedom to discuss nephrology (or kidney transplant) [which he taught in a Swedish university], then you can have all the freedom you want to discuss your subject with anybody not only in Hong Kong but also in the entire Chinese mainland." The thing is that the term "academic" shall include politically sensitive issues such as Beijing's human rights abuses, the June 4th 1989 Tiananmen Square massacre, the Tibet issue and the Taiwan independence movement. When it comes to these topics, "academic freedom" is most likely to become a casualty under communism.

One example shall be sufficient to illustrate the point. Toward the end of March 2000, Hong Kong's Cable TV broadcasted its interview with Taiwan's vice president elect, Ms. Annette Lu, whose comments [basically to the effect that Taiwan's twenty-three (23) million residents shall have the right to decide whether the island should become an independent nation] disturbed Beijing so much that it authorized its Liaison Office in Hong Kong to issue a warning to the territory's media. On April 12th 2000, Liaison Office spokesman Wang Feng-chao told Hong Kong media not to broadcast or report pro-independence comments. Academic freedom in Hong Kong? Hong Kong media is not even allowed to report Taiwan pro-independence politicians' comments. How can Hong Kong's political sciences academics feel free to hold any intellectual discussion on whether Taiwan residents should have the right to declare independence? To use Beijing's parlance, freedom is "not absolute" (because, in its eyes, only control is absolute). Freedom of the press is "not absolute". Freedom of expression is "not absolute", either. By simple deduction, academic freedom in Hong Kong can hardly be absolute. That means Beijing is poised to impose restrictions on any freedom if the occasion arises. Put in another way, under Communist rule, Hong Kong' various freedoms (be they academic or otherwise) are controlled. The question is: Can we call "controlled freedom" freedom? Definitely not by Western standards. But in Hong Kong, "controlled freedom" is better than no freedom at all.

When the Communist Party was founded in summer of 1921, China was under the control of the Northern Warlords who would definitely not tolerate the Communist movement. Later, the Communist Party entered into an alliance with Dr. Sun Yat-sen's Nationalist Party against the Northern Warlords. But the cooperation between the two parties did not last long. When Dr. Sun Yat-sen (founder of the Republic of China) died in 1925, his successor Generalissimo Chiang Kai-shek became the leader of the Nationalist Party and led the alliance's war against the Northern Warlords to victory. Then, fearful that the Communists should threaten his regime, the Generalissimo triggered a bloody crackdown on the Communist-led Worker Pickets in Shanghai on April 12th 1927, pushing the Communist movement underground. Soon, one of the leaders of the Communist Party, Mao Zedong, organized an armed rebellion in the rural areas of Hunan Province. Later, he led his peasant army to the Jinggang Mountains in Jiangxi Province, where he met with Marshal Zhu De, who had been a brigade commander with the Nationalist army before he revolted against the Nationalist government in Nanking and led his troops to the Jinggang Mountains region. Together, they established a military revolutionary base for the Communist movement in the Jinggang Mountains in August of 1927.

So, from the very beginning, the Communist Party was organized as a secret society and had to operate underground for decades until its victory in 1949. Given the history and nature of the Party, it would be naive to think that the Communists have not expanded its secret operations to Hong Kong. I would be surprised if anyone tells me that there is no secret network of Communist agents in Hong Kong. Presumably, while Westerners feel they are very free in Hong Kong despite the handover, local Chinese with strong political views may not feel the same, because they know the legal protection they used to enjoy under British rule of law is gone forever. They know their activities are watched by Communist agents who have long infiltrated Hong Kong's various campuses and organizations. They know if they are openly critical of Beijing's policy toward Hong Kong, they could very well make Beijing's blacklist.

Mr. Martin Lee, chairman of Hong Kong's Democratic Party, who has been critical of Beijing since the 1980s, says Beijing's policy toward Hong Kong can be summarized in a single word "control". Though aware that his name is on Beijing's blacklist, he refuses to shut up. The question is: How many Hong Kong residents want to run the risk of offending Beijing like Martin Lee? The fact that Hong Kong is now under Communist control is intimidating enough to shut up most Hong Kong Chinese citizens. One of the basic lessons I learned from decades of living under communism is that it does not pay to criticize the Communist authorities—they are presumed right on all issues and at all times until proven wrong by harsh reality. Even after being proven wrong by reality, they tend not to admit their mistake. Criticism won't work with the Communists. They like praises and flatteries. They like to hear academics advocating Beijing's policies. So, if a mainland Chinese or Hong Kong academic repeats Beijing's views on every issue like a parrot to demonstrate his "patriotism", I wouldn't be surprised at all. But is that "academic freedom"?

Because of Hong Kong's geographical closeness to the mainland, local residents must have learned quite a lot about how Beijing's tentacles operate in the territory. During my final days in the former British crown colony, I tried to sound out a few local residents on their perspectives about Communist rule. Their usual response was: "I am not interested in politics." It was their way of saying, "Please don't discuss politics, because I don't want to get in trouble," or "With Hong Kong already under Communist control, it is no use talking about it, like it or not." Can Hong Kong's "academic freedom" be preserved under the circumstances? I doubt it.

One thing that convinced me that changes in Hong Kong would come sooner rather than later was the fact that the political views published in Hong Kong's major newspapers suddenly switched from anti-Beijing to pro-Beijing with the approach of the July 1st 1997 handover. At the time, I was preparing to get out of the territory as quickly as I could. So, I had to regularly visit my property agent, Michael Wong, to find out when I could sign a contract to sell my home in Hong Kong. One day, I saw a copy of Oriental Daily (one of Hong Kong's major Chinese-language newspapers) lying on his desk. I knew for decades Oriental Daily had printed articles quite critical of the Communist authorities in Beijing. But browsing through the editorial page, I became aware that all the articles there bore strong pro-Beijing tones and were critical of Martin Lee's Democratic Party.

Did I pick up the wrong newspaper? I turned the pages back to find the masthead. It was Oriental Daily. No mistake. I asked Michael how come Oriental Daily had changed its tune so suddenly, though there were still a few weeks to go before the handover. Michael told me that Oriental Daily's ownership had changed. Somebody with ties to Beijing had bought a major interest in the newspaper. Michael's words reminded me that other people had told me similar stories, basically to the effect that organizations connected to Beijing had been on a buying spree to acquire controlling stakes in Hong Kong's newspapers and magazines.

"Hong Kong is finished," I blurted out. Michael disagreed, saying Hong Kong's prosperity would continue despite Beijing's influences. He told me he was fully invested in the so-called Red Chips (Hong Kong-registered companies with connections to China's state-owned enterprises). When I learned that he had more than HK$1 million (US$129,000) margin debt in his portfolio, I said: "That's very risky." I went on to explain, "Anything red smells fishy to me. Red is the color of fire and blood. It's a warning, a signal of danger and disaster. I'd rather avoid. If red flags are up at the beach, sharks are lurking nearby." Again, Michael disagreed. Hong Kong's stock market was soaring. He was happy to hold his Red Chips because the newspapers told him that the Red Chips' state-owned parent companies were about to "inject assets at low valuations". Despite an impulse to ask why the state-owned enterprises should want to "inject assets at low valuations" into the Red Chips, I refrained. I didn't want to pour cold water on his high expectations.

Three months after my arrival in Canada, a financial crisis which had started in Thailand in July of 1997 spread to other parts of Asia. In Hong Kong, as property prices plummeted, the local Hang Seng stock index fell from 16000 to below 10000. As financial institutions dumped the Red Chips, tens of thousands of Hong Kong housewives and other sucker investors who held the Red Chips saw their investments go down the drain. They couldn't figure out why. They had never bothered to examine the Red Chips' earnings performances. It was amazing that despite numerous media reports about the heavy losses suffered by China's state-owned enterprises, so many suckers had audaciously put their life's savings in the Red Chips without asking: "How can the loss-making state-owned enterprises become success stories with 'great long-term potential' by merely registering in Hong Kong as Red Chip companies?" One day, an investor called me from Hong Kong, saying her Red Chip warrants had all become worthless wallpaper. Suppressing a laugh, I mumbled, "Didn't I warn you when I was in Hong Kong?"

In summer of 1998, the Hang Seng stock index fell below the 7000 mark, triggering an intervention by the new Hong Kong government, which bought up nearly 9% of the shares in the Hang Seng Index component companies, thereby becoming Hong Kong's largest shareholder. Although the government of the Hong Kong Special Administrative Region (the official name of the new government after the handover) made every effort to rescue the local economy, Hong Kong plunged into a deep recession after Beijing's red national flag rose in the territory. It did not bring good luck.

Yet, at least on the surface, the immediate cause of the recession was the financial crisis in the region known as "the Asian contagion", which was characterized by deflation, overcapacity and lack of demand. For the first half of 1998, the number of tourists visiting Hong Kong was down 21% from the first half of 1997, while total revenues for the tourist industry fell by 35.6%. Retail sales numbers were down. Hotel occupancy rates were down. Hong Kong's third quarter 1998 GDP was down 7% from the same period in 1997. The only thing up was unemployment. By the end of 1998, even Hong Kong's richest man, property tycoon Li Kai-shing, found it necessary to express his concern about the situation. He said Hong Kong's political environment had changed so much that he had to shelve a HK$10 billion (US$1.29 billion) local investment plan. The question is: Had Beijing allowed British rule to continue, might the British have handled Hong Kong's economic adversities with less pain? Nobody can tell. But as we know, Hong Kong has a market economy, which needs psychological support. In the past, British rule of law provided Hong Kong's market and market economy with both protection and psychological support. Will Communist control provide Hong Kong's market and market economy with as much protection and psychological support?

Most Hong Kong residents are far more interested in making money than in Communist politics. They don't care whether or not the Communists are trying to acquire controlling stakes in Hong Kong's newspapers to ensure their pro-Beijing editorial positions, as long as the Red Chips offer them a chance to become rich. The harsh reality is when Hong Kong's press is controlled by Beijing, the credibility of the information provided by it will be open to question. If the local papers say that the so-called Red Chips have "great long-term potential", should Hong Kong investors take it at face value?

One afternoon in July 1997, a few days after the handover, walking by a boutique in Hong Kong's busy shopping district Causeway Bay, I noticed the few red national flags which had decorated its show windows on July 1st, the day of the handover, were gone. "Obviously, the red flags didn't help business," I thought, moving on to The Excelcior Hotel's Dickens' Bar, where I picked up a copy of South China Morning Post, Hong Kong's number one English newspaper. For decades, its editorials had never been known to be pro-Beijing. So, when I noticed that instead of condemning Beijing for dismantling Hong Kong's democratically elected Legislative Council, its editorial of the day was criticizing ex-governor Chris Patten for executing his direct election plan, I thought the paper's ownership must have changed. According to the editorial, Chris Patten should not have introduced a directly elected legislature in Hong Kong, because he knew Beijing would tear it down. However, the author did not tell the reader what made him think Chris Patten should have participated in Beijing's scheme for a rubber stamp in Hong Kong. Nor did he explain why Her Majesty's Government should have put a seal of approval on it against the will of Hong Kong's residents.

After all, Chris Patten is a smart politician who remains a jolly good fellow in many Hong Kong residents' eyes to this day. In October of 1998, returning to Hong Kong for a visit, he had to spend long hours in bookstores autographing numerous copies of his book <<East and West>> for large crowds of Hong Kong residents who cheered him like a hero. Nothing could have demonstrated more clearly that he did the right thing when he implemented his direct election program in Hong Kong. Governor Patten gave the people of Hong Kong what they wanted—an opportunity to express their will in direct elections. Many Hong Kong residents will remember him as a great friend. An opinion survey conducted in 1998 among Hong Kong's Chinese residents by the Sociological Research Center of Hong Kong University found that 66.6% of those polled believed Great Britain deserves much credit for Hong Kong's success, that 43.5% thought Chris Patten's performance as Hong Kong governor was better than that of Beijing-appointed chief executive C.H. Tung, and that 45.2% believed Hong Kong would have been better off if British rule had been allowed to continue.

No matter how Hong Kong residents feel about Communist rule, Beijing's efforts to control Hong Kong's press and media industries are likely to continue. In 1998, Mr. Feng Xiaoping, a man with close ties to the Chinese authorities, bought Hong Kong's Asia TV. In the same year, Mr. Shao Zhong, also known for his ties to Beijing, bought a Hong Kong publishing house. Then in late autumn of 1998, one of Hong Kong's major Chinese-language newspapers (T T Daily) was sold to a company controlled by Mr. Zhang Yonglin, who used to be managing director of Yue Hai Investment Corporation, a Beijing-controlled business organization in Hong Kong. The fact that the three transactions mentioned above were consummated within a short period of time after the handover is an indication of the urgency Beijing must have felt for controlling Hong Kong's press, publishing and media industries.

Traditionally, to control people's thinking has always been a top priority with the Communist Party. In order to achieve this goal, the Party must control the newspapers, the magazines, the TV stations and the publishing houses which operate in its jurisdictions. There is no doubt that today Hong Kong is part of China, that is, one of the Party's jurisdictions. As such, its media must come under absolute Communist control. It is only a matter of time. The people of Hong Kong have no choice but to "get accustomed to it".

True there are still a few publications in Hong Kong which continue to express views critical of the Communist regime in Beijing. Hong Kong's best-known (Chinese-language) political magazine <<Cheng Ming>> is one of them. Yet, according to its editor-in-chief, Mr. Wen Hui, since the July 1st 1997 handover, the magazine has been under enormous pressure to fold up. Believing Hong Kong's legislature, judiciary and executive branch are all under Beijing's control, he says secret Communist agents have already infiltrated Hong Kong's media organizations. The Communist Party, he says, has an underground network operating in Hong Kong. In his opinion, under these circumstances, Hong Kong's freedom of the press and freedom of speech has already been "compressed". In May of 1998, the owner of the publishing house responsible for the release of the magazine <<Cheng Ming>> disappeared. The publishing house owed <<Cheng Ming>> more than HK$1.50 million (about US$200,000). This unfortunate incident brought the magazine to the brink of bankruptcy. According to Mr. Wen Hui, it was the third time <<Cheng Ming>> was forced into such an embarrassing situation. What's more, shortly after the disappearance of the owner of the publishing house, a correspondent working for Hong Kong's largest Chinese-language newspaper "The Oriental Daily" discovered that the absconder and his family were hiding in China's Guangdong Province under the protection of the Chinese government.

12

Conclusion—Does History Repeat Itself in 60-Year Cycles?

There is an ancient Chinese fatalistic theory: "The fortunes of the land revolve in 60-year cycles." [A literal translation of this saying would be: "The winds and waters of the land revolve in 60-year cycles." In the Chinese language, the term "feng-shui" (winds and waters) means fortunes.] I first heard it as a teenager. I did not understand what it was about. Nor did I attach much importance to it. I thought it was just one of those old Chinese sayings. As mentioned in previous chapters, China has a 5000-year history of civilization and a mystic culture which has produced countless old sayings (and proverbs), some of which had their origins in the Spring-Autumn and Warring States period (770-221 B.C.) of ancient Chinese history. The ancestors of the Chinese handed the proverbs down through the generations. While it is impossible to evaluate the old sayings and proverbs from the perspective of modern science and technology, they reflect the experiences and observations of numerous past generations. When I was a student, one of my English-language tutors instructed me to read <<A Practical Guide to Colloquial Idiom>> by W.J. Ball, M.A. (That was a long time ago, but I still have the book in my bookcase.) I tried to memorize as many English proverbs from it as possible, because I was greatly impressed by the common sense they taught me. I said to myself the British must be a very smart people. In short, proverbs reflect wisdom, be they English or Chinese.

Later when I was in my early twenties, a friend of mine bought me a Chinese astrology book from a second-hand book store in Fuzhou Road (Shanghai)—Ancient Chinese Book Store. It was a thick treatise (a set of four volumes, to be exact) written in ancient Chinese by Shanghai's famous (pre-revolution) Astrologist Yuan Shu-shan—honestly, pretty heavy material for me to comprehend. But I read it through anyway to learn the basics of Chinese astrology. Unexpectedly, I came to discover the reason behind the Chinese proverb: "The fortunes of the land revolve in 60-year cycles."

There was a chapter discussing the Chinese Almanac, which, unlike the Solar Calendar (created on the basis of the sun's movement), was created thousands of years ago according to the moon's movement. So, it is also called the Lunar Calendar. The Chinese Zodiac is divided into 12 equal parts represented by 12 different animals: the rat; the ox; the tiger; the rabbit; the dragon; the snake; the horse; the goat; the monkey; the cock; the dog; and the pig. In Chinese astrology, these 12 animals are represented by 12 Chinese characters (known as "di-zhi"), whose pronunciations are: "zi" for the rat; "chou" for the ox; "yin" for the tiger; "mao" for the rabbit; "chen" for the dragon; "si" for the snake; "wu" for the forse; "wei" for the goat; "shen" for the monkey; "you" for the cock; "shu" for the dog; and "hai" for the pig. In addition to the 12 "di-zhi", the Chinese Almanac uses an extra 10 Chinese characters (known as "tian-gan") in denoting the years. The pronunciations of the 10 "tian-gan" are: "jia"; "yi"; "bing"; "ding"; "wu"; "ji"; "geng"; "xin"; "ren"; and "kui".

Each year is given two Chinese characters, one at the top, the other at the bottom. The one at the top has to be a "tian-gan" and the one at the bottom a "di-zhi". If you permute the 10 "tian-gan" and the 12 "di-zhi" while limiting the "tian-gan" to the top and the "di-zhi" to the bottom, you get 60 permutations, each of which represents a year in the Chinese

Almanac. For example, the Chinese call the 1911 revolution led by Dr. Sun Yat-sen to overthrow the Qing Dynasty "the Xin-Hai Revolution", because the Chinese Almanac denotes the year 1911 with the two Chinese characters "xin-hai". Sixty (60) years after the 1911 revolution, came the year 1971. The Chinese Almanac denotes the year 1971 with the same two Chinese characters "xin-hai". As you can see, to the Chinese, 1911 was a "xin-hai" year, 1971 was also a "xin-hai" year, and 2031 will be another "xin-hai" year.

According to Chinese astrology, the moon moves into the same position every 60 years. Hence, believe it or not, "The fortunes of the land revolve in 60-year cycles." In other words, based on this ancient Chinese fatalistic forecasting method, history repeats itself every 60 years, or certain similar historical events recur in 60-year cycles. I am not yet ready to dismiss it as completely groundless, because I think a mystic theory from a country with an extremely long history like China calls for an open mind.

In 1973, two friends of mine—actually, they were brothers—and I were sharing a conversation over tea in Shanghai's Fu-xing Park on a sunny afternoon. At the time, with Mao Zedong still alive, the Cultural Revolution was continuing. But there was a sense of relaxation in the air on the news that China's Number Two Capitalist Roader Deng Xiaoping was about to resume office after a 7-year disappearance from public view. One of them, the younger brother, asked me whether I knew the meaning of "hong-yang-jie". I said no. The two brothers told me to consult the huge ancient Chinese Kang-Xi Dictionary (compiled during the reign of Emperor Kang-Xi of the Qing Dynasty). "The first two years of the Cultural Revolution, 1966 and 1967, were a hong-yang-jie," they said mysteriously. So, the first thing I did on my return home was to look up the term "hong-yang-jie" in my Chinese dictionary, which was not the Emperor Kang-Xi Dictionary but which was pretty old too. I got it. Literally, "hong-yang-jie" means "red goat calamity". I read the interpretation of the term carefully. Although I failed to pack my Chinese dictionary before my departure from Shanghai in 1986, I remember its interpretation of "hong-yang-jie" as follows:

For 500 years during the Spring-Autumn and Warring States period (770-221 B.C.), war recurred every 60 years in two particular consecutive years, the year of "bing-wu" and the year of "ding-wei", in the Central Plains region (the middle and lower reaches of China's Yellow River—the cradle of Chinese culture). Since in Chinese astrology, the four characters "bing-wu" and "ding-wei" all signify fire (which is red in color) and the character "wei" represents the goat in the Chinese Zodiac, the ancestors of the Chinese decided that the two war-ridden years "bing-wu" and "ding-wei" were "a red goat calamity" which would recur in 60-year cycles. The Chinese Almanac shows that 1966 happened to be a "bing-wu" year and 1967 a "ding-wei" year. [Countless lives (including that of then state president Liu Shaoqi, known as China's Number One Capitalist Roader) were lost during the Cultural Revolution launched by the Communist Party's late chairman, Mao Zedong, in 1966. After Mao's death, the Cultural Revolution was labeled as "a 10-year calamity" by the Communist Party itself.] If the reader has a good knowledge of the Chinese language, he could consult some ancient Chinese dictionary and the Chinese Almanac to find the same information.

One day in 1998 while browsing in a public library in Surrey (British Columbia, Canada) I came across the following paragraph in a financial newsletter: "Mr. Nikolai Kondratier (a 1930s Russian scholar who would end up in one of Stalin's labor camps) identified a recurring pattern of crises, occurring twice a century. The average period of the Kondratier cycle is around 54 years. It was 60 years from 1929 (the year of the Wall Street stock market crash) to 1989 (when the Japanese stock market plunged). A global Kondratier crisis started in Japan in 1989."

In fact, as I remember, thanks to the Federal Reserve Board's repeated interest rate hikes in 1989, the U.S. economy was squeezed into a recession, which lasted throughout the early 1990s, costing President George Bush his re-election. Although the recession was not as severe as the

Great Depression following the 1929 crash, it was exactly 60 years from the early 1930s economic crisis to the early 1990s recession.

* * * * * * * * * *

I would like to compare other historical moments to see if similar events recurred in 60-year cycles in the past:

(1) A:—First, I want to re-mention the 1911 revolution led by Dr. Sun Yat-sen (known in China as "the Xin-Hai Revolution") which overthrew the Qing Dynasty. In autumn of that year, a large-scale uprising was launched by Dr. Sun Yat-sen's followers in Wuchang, Wubei Province. Within a month, the Qing Dynasty lost control of over two-thirds of the country. A republic (The Republic of China) was established in Nanking with Dr. Sun Yat-sen as the Provisional President. However, Dr. Sun Yat-sen did not control China's military forces, which continued to take orders from the leader of the so-called Northern Warlords, Yuan Shi-kai, who, while serving with the Qing Dynasty as Minister of Northern Provinces, had trained the Qing Dynasty's New Army, which was armed with weapons imported from the West. Yuan Shi-kai was born in 1859 in Henan, one of China's inner provinces.

B:—Sixty (60) years later, in autumn of 1971 (also a "xin-hai" year in the Chinese Almanac), an event of equal historical importance (known as "the Lin Biao Incident") occurred in China. According to the Communist Party, Marshal Lin Biao (Mao's heir apparent) died in a plane crash in Mongolia in September of 1971 while trying to escape to the Soviet Union after his plot to assassinate Mao Zedong failed. Although the detail of the incident remains shrouded in mystery to this day, it is clear that some kind of a coup de'tat took place in China in September (i.e. autumn) of 1971. Within a month, the moderate forces of the ruling party led by then Premier Zhou Enlai staged a strong comeback, which eventually resulted in the re-appearance of Capitalist Roader No. 2 Deng Xiaoping. However, Premier Zhou Enlai did not control China's military forces, which continued to take orders from the Communist Party's warlord, Chairman of the Central Military Commission Mao Zedong, who was born in 1893 in Hunan, one of China's inner provinces.

- - - - - - - - - -

(2) A:—In 1916, Warlord Yuan Shi-kai died. The country heaved a sigh of relief. Although the Northern Warlords who had served under Yuan Shi-kai seized political power, China was poised for change.

B:—In 1976, exactly 60 years after Warlord Yuan Shi-kai's death, the Communist Party's warlord, Mao Zedong, died. The country heaved a sigh of relief. Although Mao's appointee, Hua Guo-feng, and Mao's palace guard chief, Wang Dong-xing, took control of the government, China was poised for change. Later in 1978, after consolidating their positions, Mr. Deng Xiaoping and his followers began to introduce their economic liberalization programs.

- - - - - - - - - -

(3) A:—In spring of 1919, Beijing's young intellectuals (students and academics) took to the streets to protest against the Northern Warlords' government, calling for democracy. After 1919, many young Chinese traveled to the West to pursue their studies (including Zhou Enlai and Deng Xiaoping who would later become the leaders of the Communist Party). As Western ideas spread in China, enormous changes emerged in the areas of culture and education.

B:—Sixty (60) years later, in spring of 1979, Beijing's young people (including students and academics) launched what became known as "the Democracy Wall Movement". Thousands of young people took to the streets to protest against the conservative forces of the Communist Party, calling for democracy. (The leader of the movement, Mr. Wei Jing-sheng, posted his pro-democracy article on the Democracy Wall, for which he was arrested and jailed for 15 years. In 1997, the government exiled him to the United States.) After 1979, many young Chinese traveled to the West (e.g. the United States) to pursue their studies. As Western ideas spread in China, enormous changes emerged in the areas of culture and education.

- - - - - - - - - -

(4) A:—In the early 1920s, Dr. Sun Yat-sen's Nationalist Party formed a political alliance with the Communist Party in Guangdong Province against the Northern Warlords. As the troops of the alliance advanced from the south toward the north, the forces of change spread to the entire country. But the alliance collapsed in spring of 1927 when Dr. Sun Yat-sen's successor, Generalissimo Chiang Kai-shek, triggered a bloody crackdown on the Communists. [Dr. Sun died in 1925.] As the Nationalist government managed to restrict the Communist rebellion to its military base [first in the Jinggang Mountains region of Jiangxi Province (1927-1934), then in Yanan, Shaanxi Province], coastal cities like Shanghai continued to prosper until 1937 when Japanese troops invaded China. Japan's economy was in a slump. Its leaders thought they could find a solution through military expansion in Asia.

B:—In the early 1980s [i.e. sixty (60) years after the early 1920s], China's paramount leader Deng Xiaoping launched his bold economic reforms by allowing capitalistic special economic zones like Shenzhen to emerge in Guangdong Province. The influences of Guangdong Province's economic reforms spread from the south toward the north. In early 1987 [i.e. sixty (60) years after Generalissimo Chiang Kai-shek's crackdown on the Communists], the conservative forces of the Communist Party cracked down on the liberals, ousting the Party's liberal-minded secretary general Hu Yaobang. [Though there was no bloodshed in 1987, pent-up grievances against the conservative forces of the Communist Party began to accumulate among liberal intellectuals. Then in spring of 1989, Beijing's students and liberal intellectuals took to the streets, calling for democracy. On June 4th 1989 when the People's Liberation Army's tanks rumbled toward Tiananmen Square, hundreds of lives were lost.] However, as Mr. Deng Xiaoping was determined to implement his market-oriented reforms, coastal cities like Shanghai continued to prosper. In 1992, Mr. Deng toured southern China, calling for further capitalistic reforms. As a result, the 1990s turned out to be a great period of economic boom in China, just like the 1930s. But the Chinese economy suffered a setback in 1997-98 when "the Asian flu" which started in Thailand because of the devaluation of its currency turned into a full-blown financial crisis throughout Asia. [Strange to say, the weakness of the Japanese economy was the cause of the 1997-98 financial crisis in Asia, just as Japan's economic crisis was the root cause of its military invasion of China in 1937.]

- - - - - - - - - -

(5) A:—In the 1930s (and 1940s), the bureaucracy serving with Generalissimo Chiang Kai-shek's Nationalist Government was corrupt. This does not necessarily mean that the Generalissimo himself was corrupt. The problem was he could not eliminate corruption among the bureaucrats he relied upon to operate the state machine, as businesses with ties to the Nationalist bureaucracy enjoyed an unfair leverage over those without such ties. In the meantime, the country was a class society with a high level of economic freedom, the bureaucrats of the Nationalist Government and their families as well as business people with ties to the Nationalist bureaucracy being the upper class. To maintain stability (i.e. one-party rule), the Nationalist Government relied on secret agents (from the Military Statistics Commission and the Central Investigation and Statistics Bureau) to hunt down underground Communists and their sympathizers (China's 1930s-40s political dissidents), many of whom were students and young intellectuals (like

President Jiang Zemin and Premier Zhu Rongji in their youth) demanding democracy from what they saw as "the Nationalist reactionaries". Yet, the Nationalist Government told the Chinese people that its "mandatory rule" was necessary for the country before constitutional rule could be introduced.

[Generalissimo Chiang Kai-shek was born in 1888 in an upper-class family in Fenghua, Zhejiang, one of the coastal provinces near China's largest metropolis, Shanghai, where he started his political career. The Generalissimo had a great interest in having the support of the United States and remained a staunch alley to America throughout his life. By the way, the proper "pin-yin" (pronunciation) of the Generalissimo's surname in Mandarin (the official Chinese language) should be "Jiang", not "Chiang".]

B:—Sixty (60) years later in the 1990s, the bureaucracy serving with President Jiang Zemin's People's Government was reportedly as corrupt as Generalissimo Chiang Kai-shek's Nationalist bureaucracy. (It remains reportedly corrupt as of this moment.) This does not necessarily mean that President Jiang Zemin himself is corrupt. The problem is he and Premier Zhu Rongji are unable to eliminate corruption among the bureaucrats they rely upon to operate the state machine, as businesses with "guan-xi" (special ties) to the Communist bureaucracy enjoy an unfair leverage over those without such ties. In the meantime, despite its Marxist brand name, the country has again become a class society with considerable economic freedom, the bureaucrats of the People's Government and their families as well as businessmen with ties to the Communist bureaucracy being the upper class. The old elite of communism has become the new elite of capitalistic economic boom, primarily by appropriating the state resources they previously controlled. Whatever the label: "Nationalist", "Communist", "Marxist-Leninist", "Socialist", "Proletarian", "Revolutionary", "Patriotic", "Workers'", "Peasants'", or "People's", we (human beings) are all sinners, because we all need money in order to survive. So, God, help us, amen!

[Not pretty, is it? Yet, for all the negative press about bureaucratic corruption, China's current class society is still much better than Mao Zedong's egalitarian society, where everybody was poor because nobody was allowed to become rich.] To maintain stability (i.e. one-party rule), the People's Government relies on secret agents (from the State Security Ministry and the Public Security Bureau) to hunt down political dissidents (including students and liberal intellectuals) who demand democracy from the People's Government, even as it insists that its "People's Democracy" is much better than any Western-style pluralist democracy. (Believe it or not, that's exactly what they say!)

[President Jiang Zemin was born in an upper-class family—his grandfather was a well-known artist (painter)—in Yangzhou (a beautiful city famous for its cultural heritage and nice-looking women), Jiangsu, one of the coastal provinces, which, before the 1949 revolution, included China's largest metropolis, Shanghai, where he received his university education and later became a political star in the 1980s. As a moderate of the ruling party, President Jiang Zemin has an interest in establishing "a strategic partnership" with the United States and certainly needs America's cooperation in his effort to maintain stability in China. On the other hand, since U.S. multinational corporations now have a high exposure in China, Wall Street definitely has a vested interest in President Jiang Zemin's (and Premier Zhu Rongji's) ability to maintain stability in China. Hopefully, the two moderate politicians of the ruling party will further consolidate their positions in Chinese politics to make long-term stability possible. Some of the sons and daughters of the ruling party's senior officials (e.g. President Jiang Zemin's son, Dr. Jiang Mianheng, and the late paramount leader Deng Xiaoping's son, Dr. Deng Zhifang) received their higher education and training in the United States. Again, hopefully, this will become a positive factor to U.S.-China relations (and trade ties) in the future.]

- - - - - - - - - -

(6) A:—In 1940, as much of China was under Japanese occupation, Generalissimo Chiang Kai-shek had to direct the Nationalist resistence forces from his headquarters in Chongqing, Sichuan Province, whereas the Communist movement continued to grow at its revolutionary base in Yanan, (northern) Shaanxi Province, after Mao Zedong led his Chinese Workers' and Peasants' Red Army out of the Jinggang Mountains (Jiangxi Province) on a 12,500-km long march (1934-35). By August of 1945 when Japan surrendered, the Communist movement had become very strong in part because of the assistance provided by the Soviet Union. In 1947, a full-scale civil war broke out between the Nationalists and the Communists. Two years later in 1949, as the Communists took control of the Chinese mainland, Generalissimo Chiang Kai-shek's Nationalist Government was forced to relocate in Taiwan, a large island across the Taiwan Strait from China's Fujian Province. In brief, the 1940s was a period of enormous political change in China.

Also in 1940, benefiting from the sharp increases in demand for U.S. products brought about by the second World War which broke out in 1939, the U.S. economy continued to enjoy robust growth. In fact, the entire 1940s was a period of incredible prosperity for the United States which turned corporate America into a major pillar of the world economy.

B:—Right now [in 2000, sixty (60) years after 1940], as no foreign power occupies any part of China, President Jiang Zemin has far more luck than Generalissimo Chiang Kai-shek had in 1940. Besides, there is no rebel-controlled revolutionary base in China. Nor would it serve any practical purpose for any rebel group to establish a revolutionary base there, because they would certainly stand no chance of success. [History shows but for Japan's invasion of China and the Soviet Union's assistance to the Communist rebels, even Mao Zedong could not have succeeded.] However, no one can guarantee that the 2000s will not turn out to be a period of enormous political change in China like the 1940s. As a matter of fact, with public grievances against bureaucratic corruption palpable in the air, pressures for political change (known in China as "political reform") are building up. The ruling party may need to change with the changing times for the sake (and in the best interest) of itself, the country and the people.

This year (2000), benefiting from strong domestic consumer spending and a global economic recovery which started in 1999, the U.S. economy continues to enjoy robust growth. In fact, concerned about the prospect of strong growth fueling inflationary pressures, Federal Reserve Board chairman Alan Greenspan and his colleagues raised interest rates (the Fed Funds rate) six times between spring of 1999 and spring of 2000 to prevent economic overheating. This has caused fears of a possible recession on Wall Street. But if you believe in the 1930s Russian scholar Nikolai Kondratier's theory about global economic cycles or the ancient Chinese theory about a 60-year recurring pattern of events, you should not worry about a U.S. economic recession in the 2000s at all. Rather, you should be happy to own the stocks of America's strongest multinational corporations like General Electric (GE), Intel (INTC), Microsoft (MSFT), Pfizer (PFE), Merck (MRK), Johnson & Johnson (JNJ), Lucent (LU), even (America's best-known investor and stock-picker) Mr. Warren Buffet's favorite company, Coca Cola (KO) (which has a large operation in the world's most populous country China), since these growth-sector companies are likely to generate handsome profits in the years to come, if the 2000s turns out to be a period of great economic prosperity for America like the 1940s and especially if the pro-business Republicans control both the White House and Congress.

* * * * * * * * * *

In the final analysis, politics is business, big business. (At least to me, there is no difference at all between politics and business.) It is about money—about the control of public resources. Someday, the Communist

Party will find it difficult to keep doing business as a monopoly, because, dissatisfied with the poor quality of service (or even raw deal) from the monopoly, ordinary Chinese citizens—theoretically, the customers of the Communist Monopoly Franchise—are likely to demand that competition be allowed to induce better quality of service. Then, the Party will see the need to adopt a proactive approach by adjusting its business practices and business philosophies, even its brand name, trade mark, business logo etc., according to the changing conditions of the marketplace, so as to stay in business and profit from it. I guess the reason Mr. Deng Xiaoping chose two moderates (Jiang Zemin and Zhu Rongji) as party boss and premier (i.e. as CEO and General Manage) to run the business despite the strong influences of the conservatives (the major shareholders of the Communist Monopoly Franchise) was because he saw the need for change. (The late paramount leader knew quite a few things. Got to give him some credit, no matter how you feel about China's horrendous political system.)

After all, "Serve the people" is a business slogan initiated by none other than the first CEO (chief-executive-officer) of the Communist Monopoly, Mao Zedong, shortly after he announced to the world that the Chinese people had become "the master of the country" in 1949. Now, having had a taste of economic freedom (thanks to Mr. Deng Xiaoping's capitalistic economic reforms), "the master of the country" is poised to ask for more. Will the ruling party—theoretically, "the servant of the people"—deliver? Probably not, because we are not talking about an ordinary servant. In present-day China, "the master of the country" (the people) cannot fire "the servant of the people" (the ruling party) for poor service, because "the servant of the people" (the ruling party) is a monopoly political service provider who controls not only the political service market of the country, but also "the master of the country" (the people). For more than half a century, "the servant" (the ruling party) has repeatedly reminded "the master" (the people) that in this house called The People's Republic of China, "the master" must obey "the servant", not the other way round. Such a strange "master-servant" relationship is sure to rouse suspicions that either "the master" or "the servant" is a phoney.

Unfortunately, whereas the Nationalist Government in Nanking had the decency not to call its "mandatory rule" democracy, the Communist Party remains boxed by the myth of "People's Democracy" created by Mao Zedong, which is so perfectly manipulated by the Party that only the mentally retarded would accept it as true democracy, for which, fair (and peaceful) competition conducted with words and ideas (instead of guns and tanks) is a prerequisite, not monopoly. To call a spade a spade, the Communist revolutionaries' "People's Democracy" is nothing but a monopoly dictatorship as pretty or ugly (depending on how you look at the picture) as the Nationalist reactionaries' "mandatory rule" of 60 years ago. This is a simple truth the major shareholders of the Communist Monopoly Franchise (i.e. the conservatives of the Communist Party) have yet to come to terms with. Until then (i.e. until the major shareholders of the monopoly franchise become honest with themselves about the true nature of their business), the Party is not free (i.e. not free from crises), because only the truth can set it free. But, here, the question is: Does history repeat itself in 60-year cycles? Or do the fortunes of the land "revolve in 60-year cycles" as the ancestors of the Chinese suspected? It is up to you, the reader, to decide.

THE END

(Date of completion: June 20, 2000)

www.ingramcontent.com/pod-product-compliance
Lightning Source LLC
Chambersburg PA
CBHW061349280526
45784CB00001B/195